Scientific Repair and Rehabilitation of Books

Scientific Repair and Rehabilitation of Books

N.N. Sarkar

Draftman Mech., B.Sc. Chem. Hons., M.Sc. Chem., B. Lib. Sc.

Retired Chemist, Deputy Librarian (LIO)

Science and Technology,

National Library Kolkata.

Ess Ess Publications

New Delhi

Ess Ess Publications
4837/24, Ansari Road,
Darya Ganj,
New Delhi-110 002.

Tel.: 23260807, 41563444
Fax: 41563334
E-mail: info@essessreference.com
www.essessreference.com

Rs.825/-

First Published - 2009

ISBN: 978-81-7000-574-2

Published By Ess Ess Publications and printed at Salasar Imaging Systems

PRINTED IN INDIA

Contents

Foreword

The author is a renowned conservator, who has retired as Deputy Librarian, Science and Technology, from the National Library, Kolkata. He has deep knowledge — both academic and practical, in the field of Conservation and Preservation of Library documents. It is his second publication on modern technology and restoration besides commercial binding. Appropriate preservative materials, adhesives, papers, equipments, machineries and techniques are adopted with a view to upkeep the cultural heritage.

This publication is expected to be considered as a text book as well as a workshop manual, where large number of diagrams, illustrations are incorporated to make out the procedure of repair and rehabilitation, which will help craftsman, conservation trainee and library personnel. These techniques are confined to large depository libraries; like the National Library, Kolkata, the National Archives, New Delhi, the Asiatic Society, Kolkata, etc. This document will guide dissemination of restoration function to persons connected with other categories of libraries and archives and of course those who are interested in it, but are not aware of modern conservation techniques. Commercial Binders, Trainee menders, Trainee Restorer and Library personnel can learn modern techniques of repair and rehabilitation of antique, through this book, where easy English language and local terms of binding and mending are simultaneously used.

Unfortunately, Preservation and Conservation work is neglected in our library service. I feel that this volume will be quite helpful in overcoming the limitation of conservation and preservation of library service.

I consider it is an outstanding document, which will be appreciated by all the connected connected people and professionals in the field of conservation and preservation work.

22.05.2011

Prof. P. Roychowdhury
Former Head Department
of Library and Information Science
Jadavpur University
Kolkata

Preface

During my tenure as Deputy Librarian, Science & Technology Division, National Library, Calcutta, a book written under the title "Preservation of Document" on control of bio-chemical deterioration was published by the National Library on the eve of celebration of 50th Independence Day.

Till the said publication, I was wandering about omission of repair and rehabilitation, mainly in modern technology of binding. The menders and binders have never actually cared much about the durability of binding. They use inferior quality of preservative material and adhesives.

Deterioration is controlled by using acid-free material and adhesives. Different modern equipments and instruments are used for quick restoration.

Each method of repairing and binding is performed after an analyses pros and cons, according to brittleness of documents. Different methods of binding with its variations and common problems have been discussed in this book.

Adhesive is an essential constituent of the restoration material. Sewing process of laminated pages and new system for book sewing, with the machine, is the quicker process of binding. Acid free bond paper, Nepalese handmade paper and other handmade paper are used for preparation of end leaves and the guard.

Lens tissue paper is used for lamination of Leather, canvas, jaconet cloth, while, unbleached cloth is used for dressing. D. B. board and masonite board are used in place of straw board. Tone and Nylon thread is used in the binding work. Wheat paste with copper sulphate mixture has been replaced with tamarind seed paste and very little epoxy resin adhesive mixture, which acts as both insecticide and increase stickiness for binding. Gold lettering is done for ornamental getup of a document. Modern Technology is adapted with a view to rehabilitate the cultural heritage. Rehabilitation of vellum and palm leaf is discussed thoroughly. These are some of the issues addressed in the present title.

Repair and rehabilitation of a document in its original format is more durable and useful than the digitization of an antique one. More over Physical conservation is essential before digitization. Concept of modern library building is also discussed.

It is a text book as well as workshop manual, where large number of diagrams and illustrations are incorporated to help conservation trainees, binding trainees, library professionals and the craftsmen. Though this book is written in English, local terms of binding are used to make it each to understand for all readers.

20.05.2011

Narender Nath Sarkar

Author

Introduction

Shri N. N. Sarkar, the former Deputy Librarian of the National Library, Kolkata is a dedicated professional, who took his job as a mission of life. While acting as in-charge of the Science and Technology Division of the National Library, he introduced many modern methods in Preservation and Restoration of reading materials.

He has already written a book named, "Preservation of Documents," published by the National Library, Kolkata, wherein he has elaborately dealt with various methods for Preservation of reading materials.

The present publication "*Scientific Repair and Rehabilitation of Books*" which he has written after retirement from service, is an important document so far as binding is concerned. Preservation of book requires good binding. Unfortunately, the binding jobs are being neglected in most of the libraries. The task of binding is left with the outside contractors, who do the job in an un-scientific manner. The binders are not properly trained, and have even no proper education. As a result, the bound books done by them for the libraries by these contractors are below standard and get damaged easily. Even new books, with poor binding need rehabilitation.

Shri Sarkar has raised many a vital question regarding these problems and has also suggested remedies for the same. Many illustrations, charts and pictures, which he has provided in this book will help readers to understand the subject well.

This type of book is seldom published in India. It will serve as a text book for the Library Science students and as well as to those, who are in this trade for basic and up-to-date knowledge.

I wish it to receive wide recognition from the general readers also, who are normally aloof to this lesser known area of knowledge in Library Science.

Kolkata,
1st May 2011

Dr. D. N.Banerjee
(Former Director, National Library, Kolkata)

Acknowledgements

On the eve of bringing out this publication, it is my foremost duty to express, at the outset, my deep indebtedness and gratitude to the Dr. Dwarika Nath Banerjee, former Director of the National Library, who inspired me to write my previous publication, under the title 'Preservation of Documents'. He has been kind enough to write an 'Introduction' for the present publication, under the title, "Scientific Repair and Rehabilitation of Books".

I am also very grateful to Prof. Probir Roychowdhury Retired Ex-Head Department of Library & Information Science, Jadavpur University who has extended his support for my efforts and favoured me graciously by writing a foreword for this publication.

I would like to extend my deepest thanks to my colleagues like Dr. R. Ramachandan, Principal Library and Information Officer and Mr. H.P. Gedam, of the National Library, who inspired me to write on an uncovered area of Preservation and Conservation. They have helped me in making available the study material and a few relevent photographs.

Mrs. Malabika Ghosh (ALIO Chemist), Mr. N. Sardar (Superintendent) of the National Library, who have assisted the author in getting copies of various documents.

I am also grateful to Mr. S.K. Das, Conservation

Officer, who gave me a chance to conduct a few tests at the Asiatic Society, Kolkata and reviewed this manuscript also, and Mr. O.P. Agarwal, former Director, The National Research Laboratory for Conservation of Cultural Property, Lucknow, has been kind enough to review this manuscript.

It is difficult for me to fully express my gratitude to my beloved younger son P.P. Sarkar, who has drawn most difficult pictures and diagrams, while I was deeply engrossed with the preparation of this manuscript.

The author acknowledges his deepest gratitude to M/s. Ess Ess Publications further for their gracious acceptance to publish this work and for their sincere efforts in bringing out this publication on time.

N.N. Sarkar

1

Anatomy of the Book

The science of book-structure is as good as anatomy of book. The anatomy of book is made of many printed same size paper leaves/sheets, collated which is sewn with thread and dressed through different processes.

The preservation of book is performed through operational method of repair. The chief constituent of book is 'paper' which is fabricated with organic cellulose fibre with loading and sizing material contain relative humidity at constant temperature. All these factors are compared with bone muscle and temperature, respectively.

The selection of binding style, sewing and dressing depends upon the physical condition of the book which determined through the date of publication and on the other hand brittleness. The brittleness/fragile can also be determined physically through folding and stencils strength and chemical spot test.

Author deals with the rebinding and repair of old fragile antique/manuscript after chemical treatment. If it does not permit physical preservation and conservation then their indirect retrieval can be done through microfilm, microfiche, compact disc, etc. but

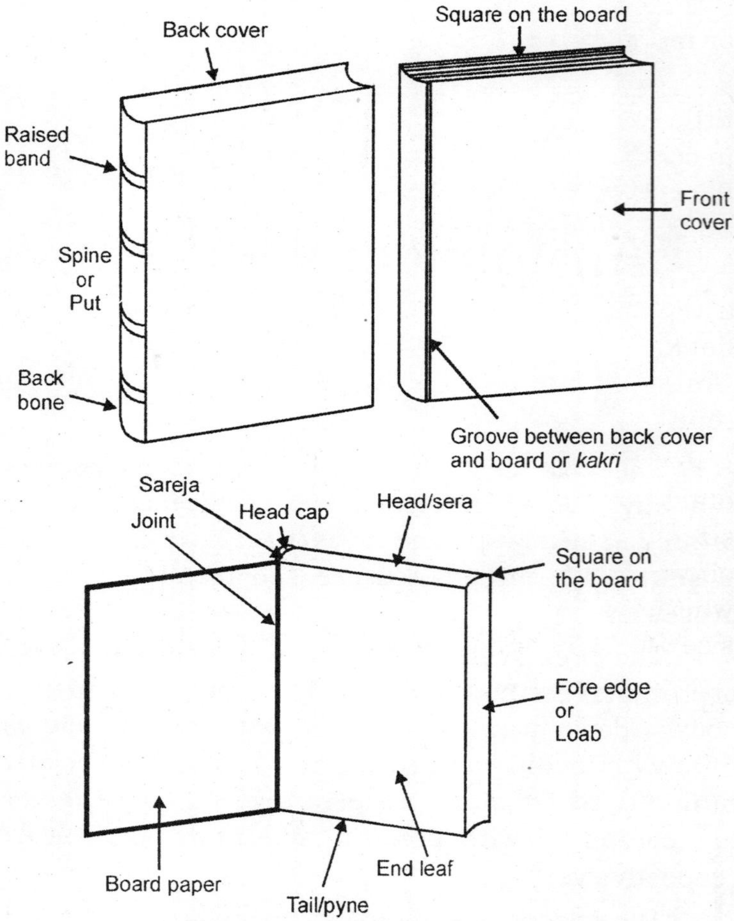

Fig. 1.1. Case or Bradel Binding (Juse)

it has no or minimal comparative interest for the reader as compares to its original format. The bio-deterioration and its remedy is discussed in "Preservation of Document".

In many books, the publication date appears on the title page or if not, there in the copywrite information on the verso of the title page or at end of the preface, verso is the left hand page of an open book or manuscript and recto is the right hand page.

Occasionally, one finds a puzzling date on the tittle page of an old volume. The following key is useful in converting these to more conventional dates: C, 100; I), or D, 500; (1) or M, 1,000; I)) 5,000; ((1)) 10,000; 1))) 50,000; (((1))) 100,000. Thus, (1), 1) (IXXXVIII-1688.

After the French Revolution and France became a republic, some books printed in the country were dated to indicate the age of the republic, for instance. "An XIII" = 1805, that being the thirteenth year of the republic, which began in 1792.

The book sizes customarily used by cataloguers and bibliographers originally referred not to the actual size of the book, but to the number of times the sheet on which it was printed had been folded. This applied when books were printed on a more or less standard size of paper. For many years, however, paper has been

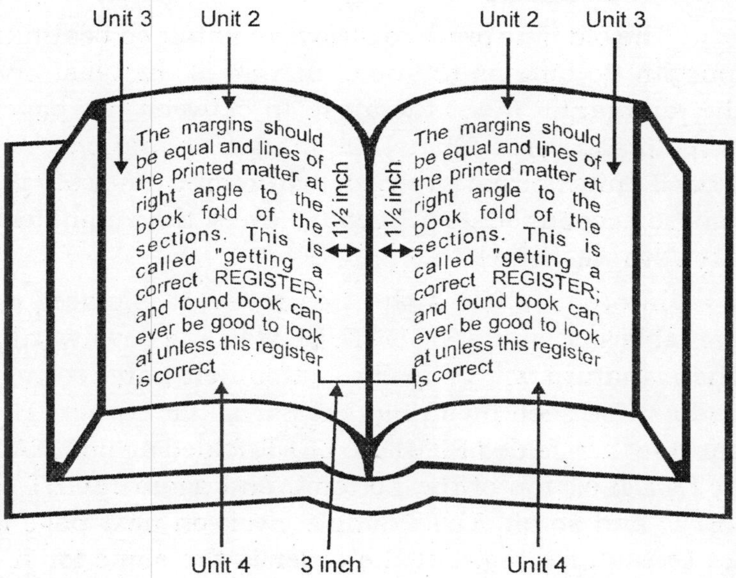

Fig. 1.2

made in a great variety of sizes, and these term have lost their true meaning. They are used to day primarily to indicate the approximate size of a book, regardless of the number of folds or the number of pages in a signature. It should be noted that most library Catalogue Cards Carry the size of books in centimeters.

FOLDING

The margins should be equal and lines of the printed matter at right angle to the book fold of the sections. This is called "getting a correct Register" and bound book can ever be good to look at unless this register is correct.

Many printers fulfil the beauty to minimise the paper cost. Binder will feel difficulty to sewing in case of less margine. At the time of second binding, binder will unable to open the book properly and readable in case of old book.

The old time printers always maintained beautiful margin. So long as the head margin is the least and the tail margin the is the most. In between two pages is recto and verso (Spine) the margin should be 1½ + 1½ = 3 units normal for which two of three times sewing can be accommodated. Because every time spine will cut down at ¼ inch.

In order to fold a sheet correctly, it is placed on the table so that the SIGNATURE is facing downwards. The signature will be in the bottom left-hand corner, and can be seen by lifting that particular corner. The sheet is then folded RIGHT to LEFT, folded again HEAD to TAIL (i.e., top of the bottom), and again RIGHT to LEFT, and so on. The example given on next page is an **Octavo** folding, but the order is the same for the other folding.

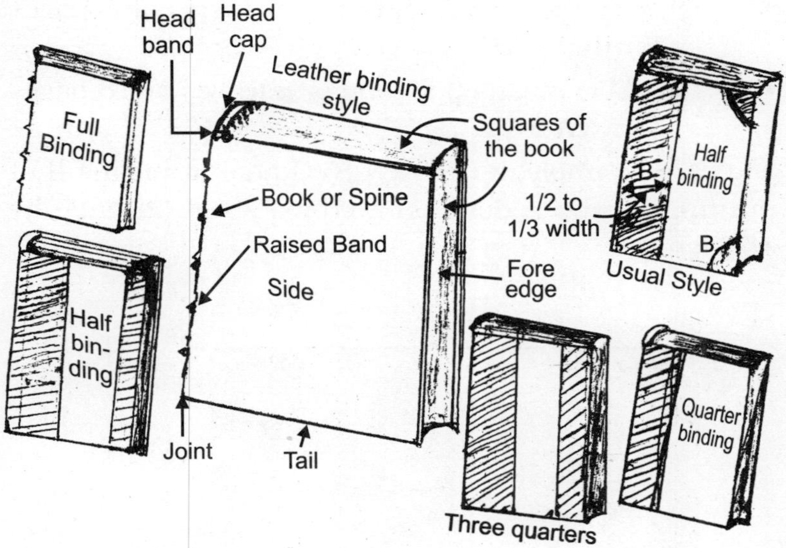

Fig. 1.3

It is useful to remember that the page containing the signature never moves from its original position— on the bench during the whole of the folding. As the sheets are folded they should be held up to the right in order to check the register of the printing. This operation is called **Shining'** them.

When a sheet has been folded it is then called **Section** or **Quire**, *Joase* (Bangali) and a book is built up from number of such sections. Books sizes depend upon the size of the sheet/leave used by the printer, and number of folding of each sheet. The names given to the sizes of books indicate two things. One is the size of the sheet before folding and the other the number of folding required to make the book section.

Octavo Folding of a Printed Sheet

- FOLIO means 1 folding or 2 leaves or 4 pages — Written FO

- QUARTO means 2 folding or 4 leaves or 8 pages — Written 4 TO
- OCTAVO means 3 folding or 8 leaves or 16 pages — Written 8 VO

For example, a CROWN 8VO book it means that printing has been done on a crown sheet (20 inch by 15 inch).

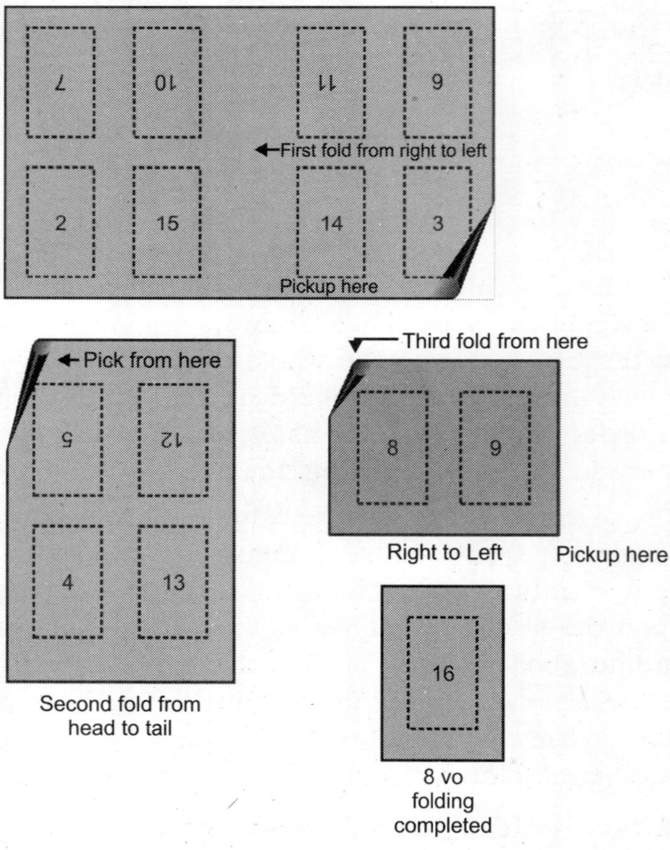

2
Binding Materials

REQUIREMENT

1. **Sewing materials**
   (a) Thread (Tone Thread)
   (b) Tape
   (c) Cord
2. **Lining**
   (a) Crash or super
   (b) Flannel
   (c) Headband
   (d) Paper
3. **Covering**
   (a) Paste and glue
   (b) Leather
   (c) Cloth
   (d) Chatai rexine
   (e) Canvas
   (f) D. B. Board
   (g) Masonite board

In the beginning of 20th century concept of conservation begin to grow up and it has become conservation of library resources as an industry. Every preservative material should be preliminary tested before preparation. Binding material has been changed to some extent simultaneously with the development of technology of conservation. A good craftsman should know the quality, durability, appropriateness and reaction of binding materials when handled. He must know what materials are available in the indigenous angle or what they could produce themselves. Hand-made materials of known quality are becoming increasingly scarce and hand binders are confronted with a wide choice of materials of unknown quality in almost every phase of their work. Author has experimented the adhesive for durability of binding, lamination which is applied in later on and black colouring leather, etc.

SEWING THREAD

An unbleached linen thread is advisible for hand sewing. It is very strong, smooth and slightly yellowish in colour section (juse). Sewing in machine is usually done with white tone cotton, but nylon also is used for the both hand and machine sewing. These are available in different grades. A thin book composed of thick sections requires heavy thread to produce a slight swell by the back of the book.

On the other hand, a thick book of thin sections must be sewn with thin thread so that there will not be excessive swell. Bibles and prayer books are printed on such a thin paper that even the finest linen thread would cause too much swell, so they are sewn with silk thread.

TAPE

The thread passes down the center of the folded

sections. They out and arround the sewing cords or tapes. The tape is an unbleached linen or cotton 3/8 to 1/2 inches wide which is light weight and strong closely woven and has practically no stretch.

CORDS

For use in raised bands, and ornamental decoration unbleached hemp or sunken cord which is most durable, and made in a variety of diameters. This type of raised band is almost obsolete. The cord, which is specially made from long fibre jute, must be very strong, soft flexible must fray easily. It is laced through holes in the boards and frayed into long fibres in order that the lacings will lie flat against board. These fibres must not be brittle, since they bend every time the cover is opened.

NEEDLES

One does not need to buy "binder's needles." A package contains 10 needles—with eyes large enough to take the sewing threads cost Rs. 15 only in China bazar, Kolkata.

LINING MATERIAL

Crash/Tajma (Unbleached cloth) Markinthan

Crash is an open-weave cloth resembling stiff chess cloth. It is glued directly on the spine of the book, the open weaves allow the glue to strike through the crash to obtain a good grip on the threads. A special grade of reinforced lining crash has heavier threads running across the cloth at small intervals.

Wollen Stuff/Flannel

That is fleeced only on one side, known as *canton flannel*, is used for back lining when greater strength is required as on rebind documents.

Khole/Special Paper

Thick paper (1 mm) which lines the back of books adds strength and makes it possible to open them in a gradual curve. This special paper are used mainly machine binding.

The weight of the paper which lines the back should be suited to the weight of the book, for a heavy book requires heavy lining which may be made of several thickness of paper glued together or ½ pound thick board may be used as khole lining.

Headband

Headbank is a small ornamental strip which is placed at the head and tail of the book. In local term it is cotton headband are woven in a two colour pattern or made by folding striped cotton cloth arround a piece of string. Silk head band are woven in two or more colours. They lend practically no strength to the binding. Detailed discription of head and tail band is discussed in the later chapter 17.

COVERING MATERIAL

Paste and glue are used to fasten the material together. Prepared paste and glue are available in the market which are used for commercial binding.

Leather

The more conventional and commonly tanned leather for book binding are listed below:

Cowhide is the most common for blank or account books as it is durable and easily worked.

Morocco is goatshin tanned leather available in a variety of colour. It is fairly thick and coarsely grained. The range in size from 7 to 9 square feet. It is soft, durable leather that is easily worked and has a distinctive pebbled grain.

Pigskin is the most durable of all leathers in undyed state because of the large amount of oil contains in it. Books bound in pigskin have been observed to be excellent condition even after hundred years. The skins are rather evenly grained and can be easily identified by the hair follicles that penetrate the entire skin when held up light can be seen through these penlike holes. Its use should be confined to its large volumes where it will require minimum paring. Because of the many little holes in the skin, paring weakens it greatly. The undyed skins are a deep buff in colour, and they range in size from 8 to 13 square feet.

Cloth

Binding cloths are available in different weights, finishes and colours (blue, red, marun, green, etc.) are available at Baithak Kana Road, Calcutta. Closely woven cloth made from either cotton or flase and sized to prevent adhesives from oozing through the threads. Canvas is coarsely woven, flexible cloth containing no filler. It is durable but soils readily.

Bukram is heavier filled cloth woven of heavier thread and it has clay or starch filler. It is durable and suitable for library binding. Waterproof bucram is impregnated with pyroxylin and is vermin proof which makes it very desirable binding materials.

From the conservation point of view, it is proved that non-acidic unbleached lawn (yellow) cloth more durable than ordinary white cloth. It is used for making hinge/tajma/lining spine of the documents. It is preparable in handwork to the loosely woven super or will used in edition binding. Nowadays many librarians are interested to get it done rexine binding in place of canvas cloth, etc. As rexine is less costlier than leather binding it has glosy, shining surface gold lettering can be done of the document nicely. In course of time, on account of weathering it becomes hard and crack. Instead of that it is used as durable. From the preservation point of view the rexine binding is not good but it looks beautiful.

Boards

D.B. Board and masonate board are used for preservation of book. Binders board most readily available large city in the India which is fabricated besides straw materials. They are many sizes, thickness and in gray or brown in colour. Principally for edition binding or black which is much stronger and harder and good for hand binding cheapboard and strawboard are light weight, soft, weak boards obtainable in various thickness for backings and cheap binding work. *Bhupal* board is suitable for book binding. Davey "green label" a dense blackboard is considered superior than all other pulpboard.

Some binders have found a satisfactory substitute for these boards in a made or laminated board consisting of several sheets of an all-rag, acid free mounting board, pulp board. It is a cream coloured, smooth finished board made from wood pulp. It makes a good work surface for a table top and is useful to press pages and to protect the side of a book while in a finishing press. A stock size is 33 × 44 inches. It is made in a variety of weight. Any type of inexpensive, undyed, lightweight board that has a smooth surface a reasonable substitute.

Chipboard: The kind that lundries use in folding ironed shirts, works well for many small job. Pulp board and the other boards should not be incorporated in a binding or protective case. They have virtually no strength and become quite acid in a short time.

Bristol Board: There are many types and

quantities of Bristol. The one recommended here has a smooth or plate finish and a hear neutral pH. A good average weight is a 220 M. It is used as the spine in case and Bradel bindings and is incorporated in other binding in a number of ways. It is also useful as a moisture barrier in some pressing jobs.

Mill Board

Thickness	Substance	Ash Content	PH
Less than 1.5mm	1500 GSM	Not more than	Not less
Less than 3.5 mm	3500 GSM	10%	Than 6.5
Less than 4.5 mm	4500 GSM		

FINISHING MATERIALS

Finishing materials are fillers, sizes, foils, inks and varnishers. Fillers such as gelatin and paste are used to fill the pores of leathers. Paste is the most common filler and it is washed over the leather in a very thin solution. Some very greasy leathers resist the gold finish to the extent that they must be washed with alcohol or other solvents to destroy the greasy film.

In order to make gold lettering to the leather when heat is applied, the leather is treated with size, sometimes known as *Glair.* There are two kinds of sizing or glair—albumin and shellac. Albumin sizing made of egg which is used before gold lettering, in the National Library, Kolkata.

Finishing Powder is frequently used which is a finely ground mixture of resins that melts when heat is applied and binds the gold to the covering material.

Imitation gold and colour foils are used in gold tooling. It is beaten into sheets approximately .01 mm thick which must be handled with special tools. It must be free from pinholes and defects. Imitation gold made of brass is used on cloth and paper bindings but not on leather because the oil in the leather will tarnish it in a short time. Even when it is used on cloth, it will tarnish gradually with age and handling. Coloured foils are available in variety of colours which has cloth and paper greater covering power than ink.

Ferrogallotanatic, blue, black containing not less than 0.4 gm iron in 100 cc of fluid ink is recommended for permanent records.

Nowadays ball pen ink is using for writing on the cover page which will not squeeze out when heavy pressure is exerted. Printing ink is carbon ink which does not damage the document.

Varnishes/Leather preservative mixture are used on leather binding book which has become crumble brittle and insect attacked a mixture prepared with the following formulae has been used in the National Library which is quite satisfactorily.

1.	Lanolin anhyodrous	800 gm
2.	Bees wax	15 gm
3.	Ceder wood oil	30 ml
4.	Benzene	350 ml

Benzene is slightly heated and the wax is dissolved in it. Cedar wood oil is added next and then lanolin, which should be previously softened by warming. The mixture should be thoroughly shaken before use.

Press board is used when strength and stiffness are required in a relatively thin sheet of board. It is made in two colours, red and gray, with a mottled surface that is smooth and highly polished. It is almost as hard as a sheet of fiber and is used for notebook or tabler covers.

3

Paper

1. **Composition**
   (a) Fibres
   (b) Filler
   (c) Loading
   (d) Sizing
2. **Category**
   (a) Nepalese hand-made paper
   (b) Wax paper
   (c) Lens tissue paper (Imported)
   (d) Tissue paper (Indian)
   (e) Hand-made paper
   (f) Cartridge paper
   (g) Craft paper,
   (h) Acid free paper, bond paper
3. **Weight and Size**
4. **Proper Use**
5. **Grain**

COMPOSITION

Mender/Binder is required to know the ingredient, source of paper pulp and manufacturing processes of paper. There are three kinds of cellulose in paper such as alfa, beta, gama and each cellulose consisting of number of glucose structure. The cellulose fibres matted together have formed the basic structure of paper.

Rag, cotton linen manila hemp, etc. which contain high alpha cellulose (95%), low copper number 0.5%, acidity pH is over 6 such as lens tissue paper (imported) and hand-made paper which are not been used in sizing, loading. But the search for cheaper fibres organic materials are wood, grases, esperto, jute and bamboo. The cellulose in wood and other allied materials is containing lignin, pectin, tanin, gum and resin. Reducing these impurities from the pulp, drastic chemical treatment with alkali is necessary. These alkaline treatments which make use of sodium hydroxide are sodium carbonate, sodium sulphate, magnesium and calcium bisulphates. Coupled with chlorine bleaching help reducing cellulose chain length, if proper controls are not applied further additions of loading and sizing material which determine the end use, viz. writing or printing ability of paper introduce some residual acidity which further degrades cellulose structure. These include Rosin-alam, starch, glue, cesein, sodium silicate, gelatin, etc. as sizes and China clay, kaolin, gypsum, barium sulphate as loading of filling materials.Coupled to these processes are finishing operation of calendering and coating which make use of a variety of diverse chemical substances such as casein, zine oxide, titanium oxide, etc. Chemical pulping processes requiring controlled operations further gave rise to mechanical pulping which gives a very quick and cheap paper but of a very poor quality because of impurities present in pulp.

In the first stage of paper making pulp is prepared

through different process. The ingredients (filler, loading, sizing) pulp fibre are mixed with water in heading engines and the mixture their passes over a belt of wire screen where it is deposited in a thin layer. The water drains from the paper as the belt moves along and the Jarring motion of the screen helps to compact the fibres. The paper passes under a dandy roll which imprints it with the desired water mark and then is pressed by passing under a felt covered roller, then from the wire belt to felt belts. The felt belts carry past heated drying drums and finally between calendering rollers that give machine finish is smoother because it is run through calender rolls. Super calendered is run through additional rolls and is smoother than machine finish. Coated or enameled receives a mineral coating such as clay and is then calendered.

WEIGHT AND SIZE

The weight of paper is measured by the weight of a given number of sheets of a basic size, referred to as basic size in the government printing office. For example, in commercial use substance 40 indicates that 500 sheets of a certain size weight 40 pounds.

Basic sizes of sheets differ, 25 × 38 inches being the basic size for book, 17 × 22 inches for writting paper, 20 × 26 inches for cover paper, etc.

Full escape size 12 × 8½ inches half demy

International Paper Sizes

- A_0 841 mm × 1189 cm, 33.11 in × 46.8 in
- A_1 594 mm × 841 mm, 23.39 in × 33.1 in
- A_2 420 mm × 594 mm, 16.54 in × 23.39 in
- A_3 297 mm × 420 mm, 11.69 in × 16.54 in
- A_4 210 mm × 297 mm, 8.27 in × 11.69 in

CATEGORY

Bond Paper: It is almost acid free paper, 9 kg weight is a good average weight for lining out boards, and patch work for old book lamination. A light weight bond about 3.545 kg is useful in making design patterns and rubbings.

Back-Lining Paper: It is very strong and flexible. Its use as back lining permits the book to open in a smooth curve rather than in a sharp break.

Kraft Paper: It is useful in the bindery for waste sheets and lining for marble-paper end sheets. It is strong, brown wrapping paper of great flexibility. Marble paper is now and then lined with craft paper to give it strength when it is to be used for end sheets for account book, since this lining does not show.

Photo Cartridge Paper: It is used for cover paper which are heavy thick and strong, available in many colours and finishes. Now and then the lighter weight are used for end sheets. Voluminous books are some time lined on the spine with heavy cover paper.

Ledger Paper: It is strong, smooth and wear resistant. It is specially suitable for rolling. Most account, addition books are made of ledger paper, since it is durable paper for ink writting.

Hand-Made Paper: It is acid, loading, sizing free, soft made by hand. Long fibered cotton, rag are used for manufacturing of this paper. Different colours of papers are produced which are used as end leave, lining backing. The stensile and folding strength is tested in the National Library which are observed 10 kg and 2000 nos respectively, thick and thin both are available in the Baithak Khana Road, Calcutta. The size weight of the hand-made paper is 28 inches by 20 inches size and weight 22 lbs, respectively.

Nepalise Hand-Made Paper: It is rare produce in the world. It has a cottage industries in Nepal which is produced by the buck of a tree. It grows lower region of Himalayan. The paper is fabricated as yellow in colour which contain high per cent of lignin tanin pectin. It is unbleached non-acidic paper. It is thick (0.3 mm to 0.8 mm) long fibre and rough surface paper. The National Library, Calcutta using the asorted sizes paper for map mounting, painting, illustration, miniature picture. R.D. cloth map mounting is replaced with the paper for short sizes map.

Lens Tissue Paper: It is the chief resource material among the laminations which is imported from London. It is acid and starch free, long fibered, transparent white tissue paper. It contains: (a) high per cent (88%) alfa, cellulose, (b) weight 9 to 10 gms/ square meter, (c) ash contain not more than .5%, (d) pH not less than 6, (e) free from oily and waxy. Constituents: A full prove method solvent lamination which is comprising with, tissue, cellulose acetate foil and acetone. Another method is that tissue lamination composed with tissue and sodium salt of carboxy methyl cellulose or methyl cellulose which is less durable than lens tissue with solvent lamination. Ordinary tissue paper is produced in India and China which is used for lamination of old document, due to less costlier and non availability imported lens tissue paper. It is short fibre strach has been used during manufacturing of this Indian and Chinese papers. They are comparatively less transparent than lens tissue paper. The solvent lamination cannot be done with these Indian and Chinese tissue. M/s Padamjee Mill in Pune is the only manufacturer in India.

Blotting Paper: It is white and soft. Unembossed blotting paper is useful in the preliminary drying of sheets that have been washed or soaked. It is very important to dry up the deacidified wet sheets of a document. It is also used to dry up the water damaged documents.

Wax Paper: Craft paper coated with thin wax at the both sides. It is used for tissue lamination. During deacidification brittle immerged page in alkaline solution can be easily removed without any damaged. It serves the endleaves, board and covering papers that are removed from books to be rebound. These are frequently useful in replacing missing corners in future jobs. Wax paper can easily be removed from the boards by soaking in a pan of lukewarm water for several hours. These should then be put under light weight to dry.

GRAIN

Durability of the binding depends upon the physical properties of the paper used in it. Paper has a very definite grains by its fibre. During the manufacting, the fibres are arranged in one direction. Just as a bundle of wood will withstand a greater full lengthwise that it will across its grain, however, paper has greater tensile strength with the grain than against it. The tear across the grain is very easy because of the resistance of the fibres to the tearing action.

It is much easier to fold paper with grain than against it. A thick cover paper will crack when it is folded across the grain and it bends easiest with the grain. Therefore, the pages of a book should be imposed to print on the sheet of paper so that the grain runs parallel to spine of the book. On account of this the pages are more flexible and thus the book opens more easily.

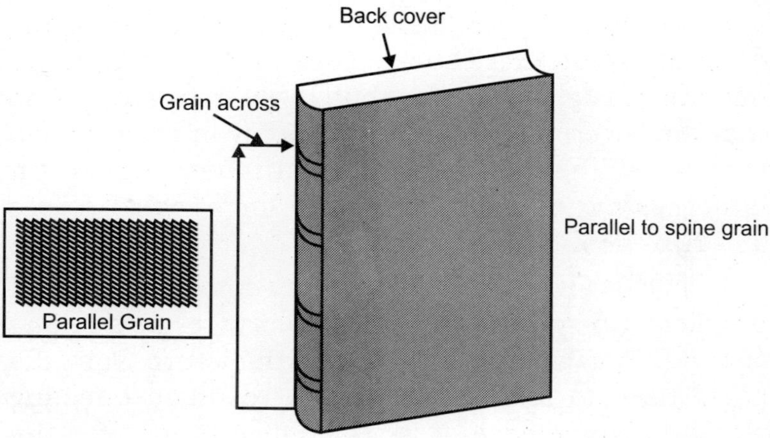

Fig. 3.1

Paper for pamphlet covers should be cut so that the grain is parallel to the spine, for two reasons.

The first is to allow the cover to bend with the pages of the book, without breaking in a zigzag crease. The appearance and durability of many a pamphlet has been destroyed the first time it was used on account of the cover creased down the center when the grain ran the wrong way. Cover paper can be bent to some extent with the grain without harm, but the same bend against the grain will break the fibres.

The second reason to have the grain run parallel to the spine is on account of expansion of whole paper when moist. The glue used to fasten the cover contains a certain amount of moisture which causes the cover paper to expand. All cellulosic matters such as wood swell or shinks across the grain. If the grain is parallel to the spine no harm is done, but if it runs across the spine, that part of the cover paper that is glued will attempt to expand lengthwise of the spine. The front and back of the cover do not expand, which results in the back strip of the cover buckling up and pulling loose from the spine. Spine the glue sets before the cover dries out, these buckled places remain. They are not only unsightly but they pull away from the glue so that the cover is held to the spine only in spots. When the grain of the cover paper does run the wrong way, it is necessary to watch the spines for buckled places and rub them before the dry up.

The grain of the end sheets should also run parallel with spine of the book, otherwise the swelling of the paper when it is absorbed moisture from the paste used to affix the cover will result in buckling along the spine edge. It is very difficulty to apply the cover of a book when the grain run crosswise of the end paper without having wrinkle appear in the board sheets in the finished product.

4

Adhesive

Source	*Basic*	*Adhesive*
Natural	Animal	Animal glue, Albumen, Beeswax
	Vegitable	Natural resins : Gam arabic, Processed Tamarind seed powder, Balsam Protiens (Sayabean) (Carbohydrate) (Starch, flour, Dextine)
Synthetic	Thermoplastic	Epoxy Resins : Fevicol Jebnjor Denrite Areldite
		Cellulosies : Methyl Cellulose, Carboxy methyl cellulose, Cellulose Nitrate, Cellulose Tri Acetates.
		Vinyl Polymers : Polymethyl metha carylate, Poly Vinyl Acetate, Poly Vinyl Alcohol

Adhesives are the composition of different ingredient which play a very important role in reinforcing, repairing, laminating and binding of old frazile cellulosic documents. In the last few decades, natural adhesives have undergone remarkable improvement and large variety of synthetic adhesives have appeared in the market which do not give so much acidic effect as harmful of copper sulphate used starch, flour paste.

Author's long experience in the National Library,

Kolkata, is that a few natural and synthetic adhesives have been examined and used. It observes feasibility and elucidate durability of the library resources.

ANIMAL GLUE

Animal glue is a versatile adhesive. This natural high polymer is an organic colloidal derived from collagen—principally a protein constituent of skins, connective tissue and bones. Its unique ability to deposit a tacky viscous film from a warm watery solution which on cooling a few degrees passes into a firm jelled state providing an immediate moderately strong initial bond. On gradually drying the glue gives permanent, strong bond between board and cloth, leather, paper, etc. The glue is comparatively low cost and quick operation are the most difficult features of the "glue".

Animal Glue are of Two Categories: Hide and bone are of cattle origin. Both are hydrolysis product of collagen found in the hide or connective tissue or bony structure. As a protein animal glue is essentially composed of polyamides of certain alpha, amino acids, these amino acids are present in animal glue not in free state but rather as residues which are joined together by elimination of water to form long polypeptide chains.

The animal glue is uniform product which has preserving capacity against bacterial or fungus infection. It is a dry hard from light amber to brown colour cake form available in the market. Its density is approximately 1.27 and moisture content of 8 to 10% in dry condition. Then hide glue is having neutral pH in watery solution in the range of 6.65 to 7.75. Bone glue is to some extent is acidic with pH value 5.85 to 6.35. The glue solutions are uniform continuous, noncrystallising, permanent, passes great strength and rebound..It is water soluble glue lacquer act as sizing material against oil, fat, waxes. Animal glue solution are consistant with frequently modified by plasticizers such as glycerine, sorbital, glycos, sugars, etc. To reduce the cost of adhesive they may be added with other adhesive such as starches, dextine, etc.

They are graded by their jelly and viscocity value. This adhesive is prepared for book binding by the direct addition of glue cake in hot water (80–90°C). The glue cake dissolves in hot water by moderate agitation. The another method is to pre-stock the cake in cold water for 1 to 2 hours and then transfer the water glue to melting tank with agitation. The solution is prepared at 30 to 40% concentration at 140°F which permit spreading and deposition of a thin continuous adhesive film at the joint. The adhesive can be used as book dressing, sizing and coating of paper, textile, etc. The glue provides a protective film on the surface of paper. To close the pores, eliminate feathering of ink, increase surface strength, resist picking of fibres during painting, increase bursting, folding and tearing strength.

FLEXIBLE GLUE

This is a hide glue to which glycerine or sorbitol terpineol has been added. The additive slows up the drying a bit and reduces the amount of pull to a minimum. It is useful in making large portfolio but it is not recommended as an all purpose adhesive. This glue remains flexible in its cold state. It is like straight hide glue, should be soaked in water, heated, and kept hot while in use.

NATURAL RESIN

Tamarind seed powder is used as versatile adhesive. Protein base starch, dextrin, flour, etc. are discarded, because these protein base adhesive are most delicious food of insect. These pastes are using as book dressing since long back, and natural resin like tamarind powder replaces as it does not attack insect. On the other hand, actually it has no food value. It is a alkaline base adhesive.

It has been observed that in library book binding even flour paste mixed with copper sulphate is very popular for use as adhesive for dressing of book.

During manufacturing of paper, aluminium sulphate is used as sizing material which oxidise gradually in presence of copper sulphate and acts as a catalyst. As a result, acidity is developed in paper. Starch glue is a necessary evil in so far as it imparts unnecessary bulk, develops acidity and a perpetual source of fungus attack. The practice may be done away with by application of low cost tamarind seed powder adhesive. Having varying viscosity and jelling properties, tamarind powder are readily adapted to any specific adhesive requirements. Salient features (criteria) in favour of ideal adhesive are observed from test result at the Asiatic Society, Kolkata with the help of conservation officer (Shri S. K. Das) through the modern digital pH meter. Folding and stensile tests, ageing test through electric oven, etc.

Fresh sample is prepared with 5 gm processed tamarind seed powder. The solution is prepared with distilled water and filtered. The filtered is examined pH (7.65 at 32.5°C) which is quite alkaline. It has low viscosity according to thickness of the paste. Tamarind seed paste is capable to wet the surface of the document and strong bond is formed with paper to paper, paper to board which takes at least 24 hours for curing at room temperature.

A case study about bio-deterioration has been done with only tamarind powder as a glue and dressed a blank book by binding cloth and board. This dressing is dried for 2 to 3 days and kept among the book in the shelve. Another book dressed with binding cloth, board and 10 : 1 proportionate tamarind powder and Jibanjor is used as adhesive. The book is dried properly and kept among the book in shelve and 3 months at an interval, observed upto one year but there is no insect and fungus outbreak. Two years have already been passed in the Town Hall Library there is no insect outbreak and fungus infestation. Epoxy resin adhesive (Jibanjor, Fevicol) is using in the laboratory about one decay or more hypothetically. Author has taken it under observation and he performs a few physiochemical text in Asiatic Society Laboratory with the help of Shri Sudhir Das (Conservation Officer). It appears an ideal adhesive which has both functioning, increase strength of the book binding but not too hard and act as insecticide, fungicide copper sulphate mixed with flour paste is used as insecticide and fungicide. It is replaced with Jebanjor, synthetic adhesive. Insects and fungus do not attack to synthetic adhesive.

It is proved that sulphate copper is acting as catalist to accelerate the acidity gathers in paper. For example, spine of the binding book is more acidic as a result, in course of time fungus grow up. If it is pull out the blank book it will come out from cover easily, where pH is less than 4, folding and stensile strength is zero. In this condition, insect will not attack as because it is highly acidic zone.

Formula

Tamarind seed powder	100 gm in weight
Water	800–1200cc as required
Jibanjor, favicol	5-10% in weight
Calcium hydroxide	10cc of 2% solution.

Preparation

100 gm of tamarind seed powder mixed with water (requisite quantity) taken in a such pan (*degehi*) and made into a paste taking care that no lumps or nodules are formed at the bottom. After addition of the requisite quantity of water with tamarind powder has been so mixed. The mixture is then cooked on fire or electric stove, till it starts forthing. During cooking paste is kept well stirred so that there may not be any charring of powder at the bottom due to over heating .5 gm Jibanjor is taken in a small beaker and add it 10 c.c. (.2%) Calcium Hydroxide Solution and gradually add to prepared glue and stirred well.

The above mentioned formation has been prepared after prolong experiments at the Asiatic Society Laboratory.

Case I Tamarind seed paste pH 7.55, carboxymethyl cellulose pH 6.85, Fevicol pH 4.91, Jebanjor pH 5.75, (epoxy resin) all are at temperature 32°C.

Case II Tamarind seed paste and Jebanjor mixture 10:2 proportionate. pH is 6.85, tamarind seed paste Jebanjor mixture 10 : 1 proportionate pH is 6.65.

Carboxymethyl cellulose and Jebanjor mixture 10 : 1 proportionate. pH is 7.60.

Case III Carboxy methyl cellulose and Jebanjor mixture 10 : 0.5 proportionate. pH is 7.05, all are at temperature 32.5°C.

It appears from the above test and observation that instead use of copper sulphate in glue for insecticide/fungicide 10 : 1 to 10 : .5 tamarind seed paste and Jebanjor is a versatile use in the field of book dressing. But in case of tissue lamination, carboxy methyl cellulose (C.M.C) and Jebanjor 10 : 0.5 or 0.4 is being used for both functions strengthening of lamination and transparency as well as developed as bond formation in between paper and tissue paper, is better of course releasing the air bubble in the lamination. Tamarind seed powder paste is mixed with different proportion of Jebanjor/Fevicol. For strengthening and curing at room temperature, on the other hand, synthetic adhesive does not attack insect or fungus. Fevicol is more acidic than Jebanjor samples from different quantity of both and have been tested as it is commercial product of synthetic adhesive. Therefore, slightly alkaline treatment that is 2%. Calcium hydroxide with Fevicol is needed as fungicide resistance to moisture and solvent. It is reversible process of lamination with warm water.

Epoxy Resin Adhesive Formula

Jebanjor, Fevicol and Denrite are commercial names. Their basic element is Epoxy Resin Adhesive at different components curing, filler, different temperature and time.

1. *General Purpose* — room temperature, cure, flexible adhesive with good impact resistance.

Part A	
Epoxy resin (37-128)	10 Parts
Asbestos shorts	20–30 Parts

Part B	
Polyamide curring agent	6–8 Parts

Mix part A with part B untill smooth pot life 1 to 2 hours, cure time 1 to 2 days. For increased flexibility and impart resistance, use 8 to 12 parts of part B.

2. *Fast Room Temperature* — Curing, general purpose adhesive.

Part A	
Epoxy resin (37–139)	100 Parts
Asbestos shoots	1 Part
Alumina T-60	1 Part
Part B	
Modified amine adduct	2.5 Part
Asbestos shorts	1 Part
Alumina T-60	1 Part

Mix part A with part B. Untill smooth pot life 7 to 15 min cure time is 30 min at 150°F.

Epoxy resin adhesives have the following advantages: Adhesion, Epoxies are one of the best adhesives for bondings a wide range of adhesive in both specific and mechanical adhesion. These adhere well to most metals, plastic, wood, paper, palm leaf, all cellulosic substances glass ceramics, etc. This is due to those wetting and penetrating ability, those low viscosity, and the presence of highly polar groups in the molecule. Wetting allows the adhesive, in a low viscosity liquid form to come into intimate contact with the adherend which allow the adhesive forces to become active (van der Waal's law of interaction between absorbent and absorbate). The fact that the epoxy molecule also contains a variety of functional groups, both polar and non-polar, is advantageous, because this provides good affinity between dissimilar substance, such as metal to plastics.

Cohesion: The internal strength of epoxies to resist cohesive failure is generally good, although this may be affected some what by the choice of fillers modifiers and bond line thickness.

100 Per cent solids: The epoxies cure without releasing moisture or other by product.

Low Shrinkage Factor: Epoxies cure with only a fraction of the shrinkage of other resinous system such as polysters. Consequently, shrinkage stresses are minimized, resulting in a stronger and more durable bond.

Low Heat and Pressure Cures, Low Creep Under Load: It is resistance to moisture and solvent. Unlike proteins, starch, dextrins, gums, and polyvinyl alcohol, the epoxies are insensitive to moisture. Its resistance to solvents is also outstanding and accounts for their rapid advance in the coatings field. There are effective barriers to heat and electric current. The properties of epoxy adhesive can be changed by: (a) selection of base resin and curing agent, (b) compoundings with fillers, (c) alloying the epoxy with other resin. Resistance to wide temperature range:

Celluloses

Carboxy methyl cellulose	3 to 4% in warm water, cellulose nitrate 8% in alcohol.
Methyl cellulose	3 to 5% (Analytical quality) in warm water.

Adhesive sodium salt of carboxy methyl cellulose

3 to 4% in water is prepared by cooking as tamarind seed paste. It is a very important synthetic adhesive in the field of tissue lamination after deacidifying the frazile manuscripts. It has been observed that lamination with lens tissue and good quality C.M.C., gives cent per cent transparency of the document. But lamination with indigenous tissue paper (Padamjee/ Chinese) with good quality C.M.C. needs Jebanjor, for strengthening adhesive in order to increase of transparency due to formation strong bonding between document and C.M.C. Of course pressure is needed during the curing time. pH of Jebanjor is 5.75 and combination emulsion of Jebanjore and C.M.C. .5 : 10 pH is 7.05 and this proportionate of emulsion gives very good result of transperency of frazile book lamination. C.M.C. and Jebanjor synthetic adhesive has both functioning non-penetration of air pollution and act as adhesive for tissue lamination. It is a reversible process of lamination Padamjee made in (India) and Chinese tissue are available in the market. It is used in loading and sizing, which is short fibre material in the manufacturing and is not the same as imported lens tissue paper. Lens tissue paper is valuable, unavailable in the market now and then.

Methyl Cellulose

Nowadays 3–4% methyl cellulose is used as an adhesive for tissue lamination instead of C.M.C. It is a costly affairs which is involved ₹ 2000 for 440 gm. But in case of mixture carboxy methyl cellulose and Jebanjor 10 : .5 proportionate is best for large scale tissue lamination as adhesive. The cost of carboxy methyl cellulose is ₹150 for 500 gm and Jebanjor is ₹ 90 for 500 gm more over it is required small quantity.

Polymethyl mathacrylate 1–2% emulsion in

tolune, on application on the document as reinforcing is required. Polymethyl methacrylate has been found much useful, reinforcement of document. It is required to carry out either by immersing the sheet in the emulsion for one minute or applying the solution by brush. The paper of which has become brittle from ageing and has become porous should be treated with 1–2% emulsion. After treatment the documents is dried under room temperature. Paper treated with emulsion appears an increased folding and stensile strength. The 4–5% emulsion acts as a good adhesive between paper and paper, paper and board, leather and board. Paper and resin, board and rexin is absorbed by all kinds of materials used in books. When two such surfaces are glued together, a film is formed which adheres strongly and closely to each other.

The following strength of emulsion is found suitable for sizing material of brittle manuscripts in respect of proportionate:

(a) 1–2% Polyvinyl Acetate in tolune.

(b) 1–3% Polyvinyl Alcohol in tolune.

(c) 2–6% Solution of Bedacryl in acetone.

Antique, old picture, illustration, miniature painting, etc. needs chemical treatment, simultaneously reinforcing with the above emulsion. Probably these documents have been used different acid/base dye inks, colour, etc. which are water soluble or not. Therefore, water soluble test at the corner of the document should be made. The reaction of solvent on the document is observed before impregnation. In order to fixation of ink verso side is required to brush out properly with the emulsion and wait for one hour or two. These recto side can be deacidified with alkali solution, carbon, shoot and printers ink need not require any fixation as because these are not water soluble. Care is taken at the time of deacidification and bleaching of water soluble inks. The dirty, stains, mildew foxing from the documents is cleaned with alcohol or any other organic solvent. 1 : 10 amonia gas fumigation is better for neutralize the acid in the case of big size illustrated document.

Pencilling note on the brittle mildew and acid gathered document needs special care. 1-2% solution of polyvinyl acetate cannot venish, more concentrate 4-5% polyvinyl acetate solution in volume is needed to vanish the pencil mark.

Documents which are in good condition, prolong use, it becomes wrinkle and multiple folds they are difficult to restore. Flattening it is a simple method. These can be completed carefully opening the papers and then interleaving it between damp blotters, and keep it light press, for 8 to 12 hours. If you keep several hours there is every possibility of fungus growth in the documents. Alternatively 0.3% thymol or 0.1% sodium orthophenyl in acetone solution can be used for damping the blotter. The document will be thoroughly sterilized during the interleaving blotter method.

QUESTIONS FOR DISCUSSION

1. What are natural and synthetic adhesives?
2. Why will you use processed tamarind paste on the other hand discard the starch, dextrin and flour?
3. As insecticide, why will you use jebanjor instead of copper sulphate?
4. Describe the preparation of tamarind paste and its formula.
5. Describe a few other adhesives and its proportionate use.

5
Equipments

With the advancement of new technology of repair and rehabilitation of the cultural heritage, variety of equipments has come up for smooth functioning of large conservation workshop. Detailed function of local and foreign equipments for binding and a few for both use of mending and binding are described.

It is to give an idea of what types of things one should look for. Also included are some suggestions for improving certain pieces of equipments. The equipment is divided into the following groups, *e.g.* heavy equipments, wooden equipments, gluing and pasting equipment, tools for pairing leather, and miscellaneous items. In general their use is discussed in this chapter, but in some cases, where a specific technique or operation represents its primary use, it is listed in the appropriate chapter alongwith technique. Rest of the equipments are discussed in the "Preservation of Documents".

The beginner should visit a handbook binding workshop and discuss possible equipments to be purchased with an experienced binder. If, however, the information must come from a manual, first read the mannual completely, then decide type or style of binding which depends upon the condition of the book in most appealing. Buy only the necessary equipment to produce it. As interset and experience increase, additions can be made. If the objective is a professional career, buy the most efficient obtainable equipment. Good equipment if treated with reasonable care, it has a long life. At least one good stout table or work surface 4 or 5 feet long and 2 feet 6 inches wide is required in an one person shop. Its surface should be smooth and not easily damaged. Height should be such that it is comfortable to work at either in standing or sitting position. If a person is, for example, 5 feet 5 inches tall a table will be 34 inches height and a stool or chair 26 inches in height that serve well. One glass top good stout table about 5 ft × 3 ft and 31 inches height will serve the purpose of lamination and one long table is required for dry deacidification, etc.

Alternatively wooden one inch thick plank about 27 inches length and 15 inches breath and 6 inches height by two wooden block at the bottom (grit) is called board, *Takhti* (local name). One can perform the binding work on the *takhti* by sitting in the mat.

HEAVY EQUIPMENT

This part covers cutting machine, sewing machine, board shears, guillotine, standing press, job backer, stamping press trimmer and pairing of leather machine. Of these pieces, the only 4 that are highly desirable—if not essential in a small home workshop are board shears, a standing press (better lamination) and trimmer, etc.

Cutting Machine (Fig. 5.1)

It is electically operated heavy blatted (3 ft long) valuable machine. In a single operation 5 to 6 books one inch thick can be trimmed one edge at a time. In order to make good of the finishing. Three edges; for

Fig. 5.1: Cutting Machine

edges head and tail are essential to trimming after sewing and end paper fixation.

Board Shear (Fig. 5.2)

It works on the principle of a pair of scissors. The blades or knives are ground with a rather board edge. One blade is attached to the board in a fixed position. The other blade is movable. Thus, providing the cutting action, many of these cutters are equipped with a pressure bar, which holds the material to be cut in position, preventing it from shifting when the blade stickes it. They are also equipped with two gauges, one on the board or table, the other, outside gauge, is on the right-hand side knife. Attached in a fixed position to the end of the board (where the operator stands) in a shop, which is usually marked off in inches and serves also as a ruler. The two gauges are parallel to the cutting edge, and the stop is at right angles to all three of these. Both gauges can be set and locked or tightened for repetitive cutting.

These cutters are made in a wide range of sizes, in floor and table models, and with the pressure bar controlled by a foot paddle or a hand lever. The two gauges are desirable features, and the pressure bar is almost essential in the accurate cutting of board.

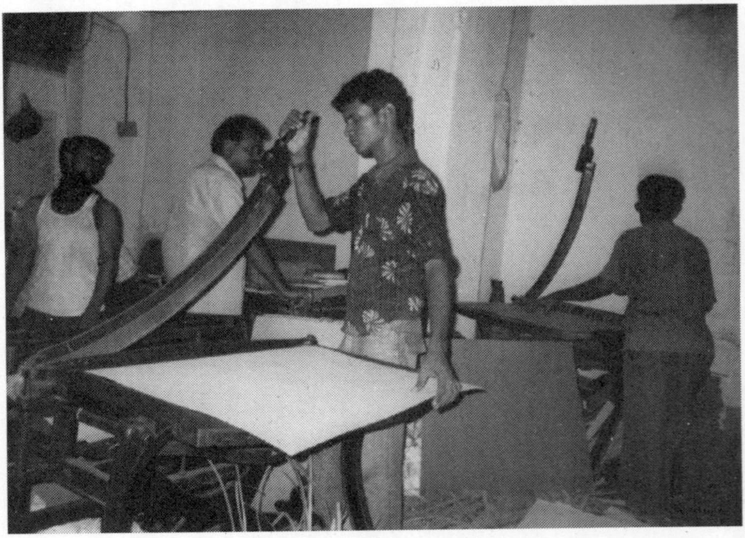

Fig. 5.2: Board Shears

Fig. 5.3: Standing Press

Standing Press (Fig. 5.3)

This press is made in a variety of styles and sizes. It is made of iron which sizes are 12 × 18 inches or 18 × 22 inches, etc. The movable plate or platen that is controlled by the threaded screw of an average and useful size. The movable platen should have some kind of guide rods or grooves to hold it steady in its up and down motions. It is very important equipment to the mender, for proper setting of tissue paper on the document during lamination which brings transparency of the document.

Fig. 5.4: Job Backer

Job Backer (Fig. 5.4)

It consists of a heavy metal vise. One jaw is fixed in a position, and the other is movable and controlled by a threaded screw with a wheel on the free end. The whole thing is mounted on a wooden stand. The work in it can be done, in a lying press. It is useful to a big binder shop. (Fig. 5.3, 5.4, 5.5)

Fig. 5.5: Stamping Press

Stamping Press (Fig. 5.5)

It is used primarily for *titling* and die stamping. It does in essence what can be done with a hand pallet and type or handle letters. A number of makes and models are available. Desirable features are accurate gauges, thermostatically controlled heat, ability to adjust the pressure, and capacity for stamping more than one line at a time.

Fig. 5.6: Paring Machine

Paring Machine (Fig. 5.6)

This is sometimes referred to as a skiving machine. It has been designed primarily to pare edges and small pieces of leather. It has a cylindrical or circular knife that removes at high speed and an emary feed roll that carries the leather into contact with knife, thus, splitting the leather. It is readily adjustable and can be set to thin a piece of leather evenly or produce a gradual thining or *bevelled* edge. It pares rapidly and evenly when properly adjusted and is a time-saver in a professional shop.

Fig. 5.7: Sewing Frame

WOODEN EQUIPMENTS

This average size sewing frame (Fig. 5.7) consists of flat board, 2 uprights and a crossbar (24 inches between uprights). Its construction has changed little over the centuries. The basic purpose of this frame is to hold the tapes or cordes on which a book is to the sewn in a fixed and upright position. The threaded posts permit the raising or lowering of the cross bar to which the tapes are attached, and the cut out area in the board keeps the tapes in a vertical position. A

Fig. 5.8: Home Binders Backing Press

satisfactory substitute can be easily fashioned by anyone reasonably handy with wood working tools, the threaded posts are not an essential feature.

The pieces of equipment discussed here are average or usual.

Lying Press (Fig. 5.9)

These presses are vises (18 inches difference between screws). These presses are used primarily for the backing of a book. These lying presses are also useful for simply holding of a book firmly in position when working on its spine or edges.

Finishing Press (Fig. 5.9)

This is a very useful press (14 inches difference between screws). It is little bit light and easy to handle, and its depth makes it particularly useful in the titling and tooling of a book spine. It is not heavily enough built, however, to be used in the backing of a book. Two pieces of one inch plywood, about 12 inches long and 7 inches wide, and 2 large clamps make a

Fig. 5.9: Wooden Equipments

reasonable substitute for this and the lying press. It is used as putuly wood for gold tooling on the book.

PRESSING EQUIPMENTS

Press Boards (Fig. 5.10)

These are rectangular pieces plywood 1/2 inch thick, with the ends routed out and a small piece of wood set in to prevent warping. Tempered Masonate 1/4 inch width of the both surfaces are smooth, accurately makes satisfactory pressboard. Several pair of boards in a range of sizes are desirable, such as 6 × 9, 8 × 11, 12 × 18 inches.

Brass Bound Boards (Fig. 5.10)

These are similar to press board with the addition of a protruding brass edge about 1/16 inch deep. They are made with all 4 edges bound in bars, which extent beyond the surface of the board.

On both sides, and they can be purchased with brass on only 1 edge, which meets most requirements.

Fig. 5.10: Pressing Equipments

One pair 8 × 11 inches will serve the needs of most small shops or 1 × 8 × 11 inches smooth surfaced teak wood will serve the purpose. It is a sharp edges rectangular hard wood block.

Gildring Boards (Fig. 5.10)

These are similar in shape to backing boards except that boards edge are straight or square. They are useful in the treatment of the edges of books, particularly the fore edge.

Zinc Sheets (Fig. 5.10)

Zinc sheet about 20–25 guage and 8×12 inches are handy when the signature of an entire book require pressing.

GLUING AND PASTING EQUIPMENTS

A Thermostatically controlled elcetric pot is the most satisfactory. It maintains constant temperature ranging between 140° and 150°F (60°–66°C). They are made in a different of sizes from 1-quarter capacity

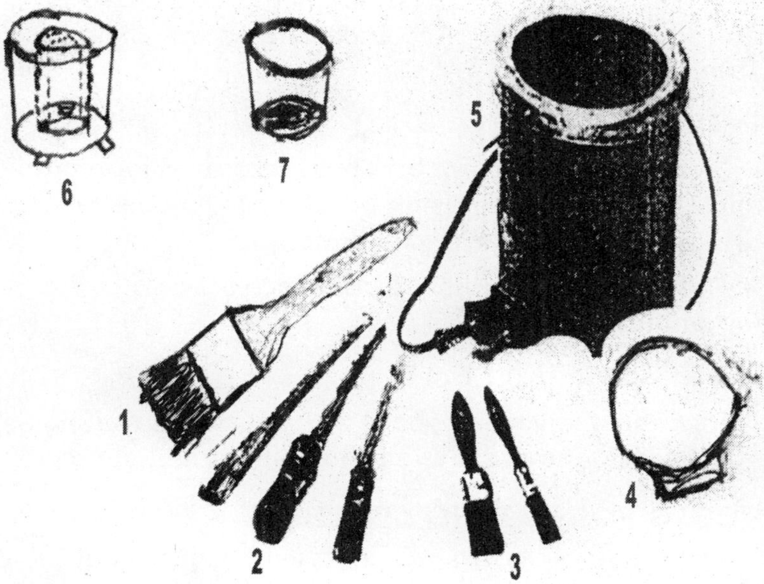

Fig. 5.11: Equipment for Pasting and Gluing. (1) Squirrel brushes, (2) Glue brushes, (3) Paste brushes, (4) Paste bowls, (5) Glue pot, (6) Stove, (7) Degchi.

up. In case of home bindery 1 to 2 lit capacity *dexsy* alongwith a centigrade thermometer will serve the purpose. It is important not to over heat the glue. The stickiness may be reduced due to charing the paste.

Stove (Fig. 5.11)

One stove is required for preparation of paste and gold lettering which temperature can be controlled easily.

Glue Brushes (Fig. 5.11)

The best glue brushes are made from pig bristles, round in shape, and wire-bound. These are made in a variety of sizes and are sold by number.

The no. 2 is ¼ inch in diameter, no. 4, 3/8 inch, no. 8, 5/8 inch no. 14, 1 inch and so on. A range of sizes is desirable.

Paste Brushes (Fig. 5.11)

One inch flat paint brushes is required for binding and 1½ inches squarel soft brush or 1½ inches *chamel* brush is suitable for tissue lamination.

A stiff artist's brush about 4 inch in width is handy for small tip-on jobs.

Paste Bowls (Fig. 5.11)

Almost any type of bowl with a wide top that holds 400 to 500 gms paste is suitable in a small shop.

TOOLS FOR PARING LEATHER

Paring chesel/nishkarta (Fig. 5.12) these knives have a diagonal cutting edge. That is *bevelled* on the front or top and flat on the back or the side that rests

Fig. 5.12: Tools for Paring Leather. (1) French paring knife, (2) Spoke shave, (3) German or English paring knife (right and left handed), (4) Skife, (5) Lithographic stone.

can be ground for use with either the right or left hand. The Indian or German knife is usually equipped with wooden handle.

Indian Knife, Chesel/Niskarta

This is also *bevelled* round the top side of a wooden handle. Its rounded cutting edge is designed for use in the overall thining of a piece of leather.

Spoke Shave

It is a wood worker tool used by binder in the overall thining of leather. It has removable blade for case in sharpening. The depth of cut can be adjusted.

Skife

This is an all metal tool curved at one end. Its cutting edge consists of removable narrow razor blades.

SMALL TOOLS AND OTHER ITEMS

Backing Hammer (Fig. 5.13)

Some types of hammers with a rounded head is needed in the backing of book. These hammers are made in a variety of weights. Select one that feels comfortable in the hand. Small hammer should be used during backing of brittle old book.

Bone Folder (Fig. 5.13)

These are designed in a variety of sizes and shapes and have many uses. A large one is essential in the folding of laminated sheets, smoothing out slight wrinkles when pasting and gluing. Its small one is needed in turning corners, setting headcaps and in drawing off lines to be tooled.

Burnishers (Fig. 5.13)

Metal burnishers are used hot in ironing out small wrinkles, and polishing leather. One about one inch and half inches in width is a good average size for many jobs. Same purpose **Electric heater** at 70°–80°C temperature is also used for wrinkle free or water damaged document. It may save from Jamed pages.

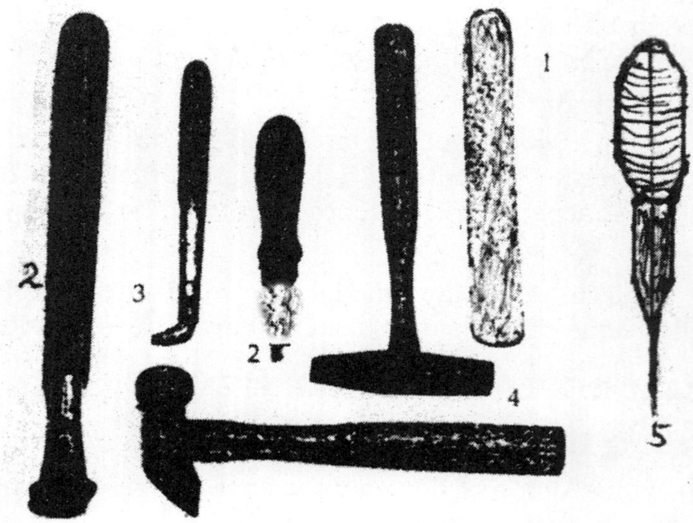

Fig. 5.13: General Tools. (1) Bonefolders, (2) Metal burnishers, (3) Agate burnishers, (4) Backing hammers, (5) Awls/Soa.

Dividers (Fig. 5.15)

A pair of 5 to 6 inches long with fine points and an adjustable screw for setting will serve most purposes. Those have many uses in checking corner during half binding, gold lettering for transferring measurements.

Knives (Fig. 5.14)

Variety of knives are required for restoration. A mat or utility knife (Fig. 5.14) is good for cutting paper and board its blades are easily changes or replaced.

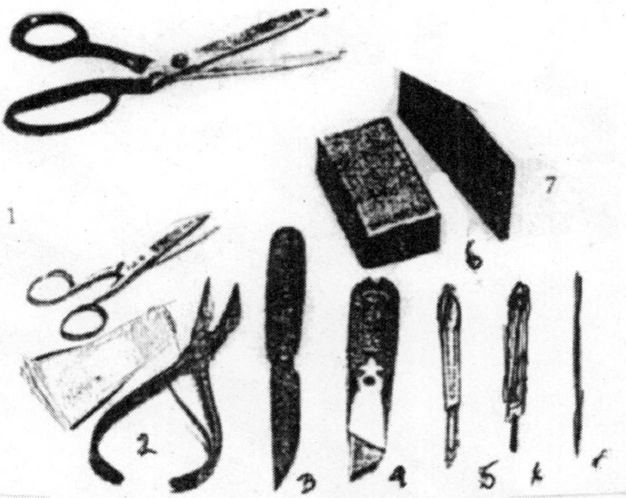

Fig. 5.14: General Tools. (1) Scissors, (2) Band nippers, (3) Bench knife, (4) Mat knife, (5) Scalpels, (6) Spatulas, (7) Weights (Brass, brick).

One round headed 8 inches knife is needed for deacidification of brittle documents and surgeon's scalpel (Fig. 5.14) also with replaceable blades, is excellent for jobs that require a thin, sharp blade. The no. 4 handle and a no. 23 blade make a serviceable combination. For safety in sake, scalpel blades should be changed with a pair of thin-nosed *pliers*. The traditional bench knife (Fig. 5.14) has many uses where extreme sharpness is not required, or of course, it can be ground to a very keen edge.

Scissors (Fig. 5.14)

It is a main equipment in the binding where both one foot long with wooden handle and 8½ inches are essential. One foot scissor is required for board cutting and 5–8½ inches for paper cutting.

Rulers (Fig. 5.15)

One 1' steel ruler graduation mark with centimeter and inch both sides is most useful and

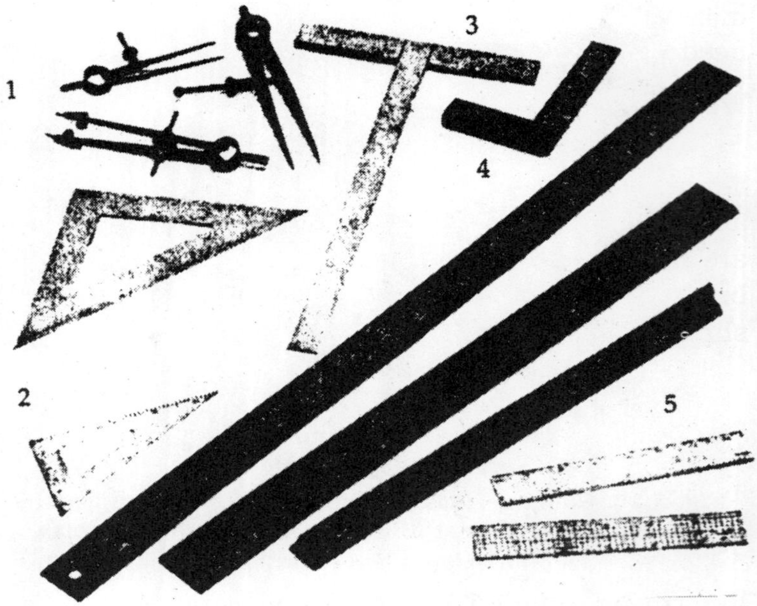

Fig. 5.15: Tool for Measuring. (1) Divider, (2) Triangle, (3) Right triangle, (5) Scale, (6) T-Square.

versatile. This can also serve as a straight edge in cutting.

Band Nippers (Fig. 5.14)

This is a *plier* like tool whose chief use is in shaping and sharpening raised cords after backing and raised bands after leather has been applied.

Triangles (Fig. 5.15)

A small right-angle one is especially useful in mitering corners, and if made of metal that can be used to cut against.

T-Square (Fig. 5.15)

It is useful in checking right angles, drawing parallel lines and if metal as a straight edge, spatulas (Fig. 5.14) several sizes are useful. Particularly in lifting materials where a rigid, thin blade with a dull edge is needed.

Weights (Fig. 5.14)

Different types of weights are needed after lamination and binding on it. Any stone 8" × 6" × 10" and or Lithographic stones make excellent weights and are also a good surface on which to pare leather. Small brick and lead also make good weights. The size and shape are not particularly important.

6

Basic Techniques: Grain and Gluing, Pairing of Leather

MEASURING SCALE

A steel ruler is the best tool for measurement. It has graduation mark in centimeter and inches fraction. With this desired size of binding cloth, hand-made paper, any type of preservative material of binding work can be executed successfully. During gold lettering measurement of margin and indent are required. The objective in measuring to make sure the material fit for the book. Divider are useful in transferring narrow measurement. These can be set at the desired width and the cutting point marked. These are useful in cutting guard strip with a knife.

It can be used to transfer of measurement. A strip of board cut to the desired length is an excellent way to determine the proper position for the material in a two-one binding. Once the position is decided, lay the strip even with the fore edge of the binder's board, mark it, and cut to the determined length. The strip can then be used to mark all cutting points on both front and back boards. A narrow strip of paper can also be used in determinig the exact width of a spine.

CUTTING

Before cutting of an object, a binder should determine the grain directly (*ara*) then start operation. Cutting technique is different from a few equipments and is explained in a nutshell. In every step of book binding, definite cutting is essential from an intact board, paper, cloth, etc. There are different types of cutting equipment from scissor to gigantic cutting machine.But appropriate tool should be used for better performance. Mark the corner or edge in some way to small pencil dot and mark all measurements using this as a point of departure. It is difficult to cut a piece of material accurately so as to given size without an accurate points from which to start. Cutting of an object with trimmer and board shares tool are ideal which depend on skill personel.

Trimmer is the best tool for cutting paper, photo cartridge in measured size. There are seales fix in vertical and horizontal position in the left edge of the trimmer by which 2.5 cm wide hand made paper guard can be cut easily. The glued position 1/4 inch can be cut down from the spine before deacidification and after lamination off side trimming is essential in order to bring back in shape.

The work execution needs considerable time where knife is only cutting tool. The best knife is the mat and round headed, in case of deacidification treatment of old book. A steel scale should accompany the knife. In cutting with a knife 2 points should be marked, 1 at each end of paper. Mark desired size at 2 points with a well-sharpened pencil holding it at some angle each time. The object is to be cut one some smooth glass top mending table. Place the scale on the object keeping it on the same side of each mark. Hold the scale firmly keeping off desired size, place the knife blade against it in a vertical position, and put it at about 30° angle.

GRAIN DIRECTION

Durability of hand binding material depends on the grain direction of material used. Almost all cellulose material have grain direction, but leather. In perchment and vellum have grain direction from head to tail. In cloth and other woven fabrics have grain direction which runs with the finished or selvage edge.

In hand-made paper the grain direction is determined by the way the Vatman who shakes the mold, he shakes the mold first from right to left and then from front to back. For this motion in both directions, the fibres are laid down in both directions. The right to left motion is more vigorous, and first, so the grain direction will be in the direction of the front-to-back direction.

In machine-made paper, the grain is more prominent. The screen on which the pulp is laid down moves forward, it is shaken mechanically from left to right or right to left, so the grain direction follow the forward motion of the screen.

The grain direction in paper can be determined in several ways. The first is the bending or rolling test. Fold the paper loosely, and with the hand press on it to test the resistance it gives to the pressure, repeat this in the other direction. The way that sets up the least resistance indicates the grain direction. (Fig. 6.1(a)].

Another way is to fold the paper sharply in one direction then the other. The fold made with the grain direction will usually be clean and smooth, the fold made against the grain will look rackly and uneven [Fig. 6.1 (b)]. The third way to test grain direction is to cut a swatch of the paper and cover it with hot glue, it will immediately curl with the grain direction. [Fig. 6.1(c)].

The forth test for determination of grain direction of paper is the folding and stensile strength test by the machine. Folding and stensile strength by machine is the best to achieve precise accurate result of the paper. More number of folding, stensile indicate the grain direction of the paper. Cross direction is less folding and stensile strength indicates in the machine.

The grain direction in binders board/photo cartridge can be determined by the bending test. The way it bends easiest indicates the directions of the grain. In making this test, however, be sure to use approximately the same length of board, for the longer the board the easier it will bend. A piece of board 5 inches long will be more strength to bend with the grain than will a piece 16 inches long against the grain. If uncertain, apply hot glue to the board; when it dries it will bend with the grain direction.

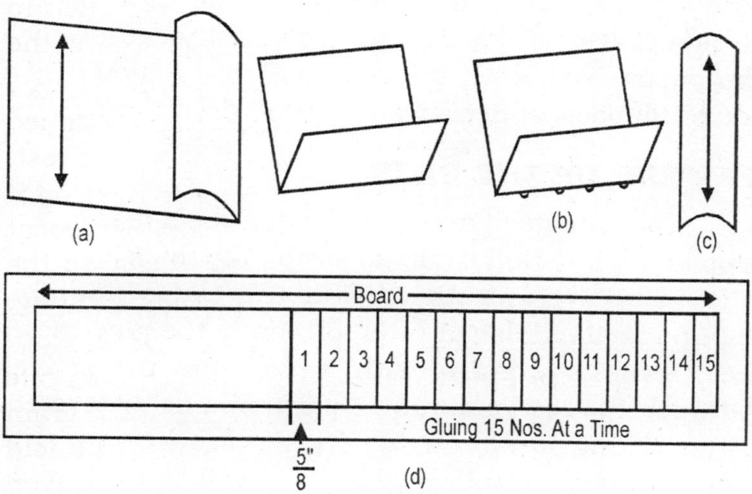

Fig. 6.1

PASTING AND GLUING

Professional binder adapts the gluing technique by their fingers. But in case of insecticide and fungicide added to glue, round brush should used. The objective is to have the adhesive evenly spread over the desired surface of a book while keeping the other side of the material completely clean. Eveness is particularly important when a water-soluble adhesive is used of for unless the material is uniform, moist wrinkles will develop.

Place the book to be pasted or glued on a piece of clean binder's desk and throw back the end paper. Take a piece of clean waste paper, and fold it to obtain a straight edge. Set up it on the book so that this straight edge is 1/8 inch a way from the back edge of the first section, and parallel to it. Paste along this 1/8 inch of the section left uncovered; remove the waste sheet, and bring over the end paper on to the book. Repeat the operation for the other endpaper, and immediately knock up the back of the book on the desk untill it is square, and the back edge of each endpaper flush with the backs of the section. Then keep the book under a weight untill dry.

PASTING UP THE BACK

The glue itself must be free of foreign matter and thin enough so that it spread easily. Too thick adhesive should be avoided otherwise it will cause ridges or bumps in the finished product. Apply the glue to the back evenly, working with it well into the spaces between the section untill no part remains uncovered. Then gluing it thoroughly with three fingers. The importance of rubbing the glue well it cannot be overstressed. It is not the quantity of glue that is applied which counts, so much as the amount that can be rubbed in between the section. The whole purpose is to hold the section in position during the operations to follow and unless this is achieved, rounding, backing and cutting cannot be successfully accomplished.

The book is not square in the press during the glue is applied, it is difficult to right it afterward. In completion of gluing up, the book must remain undisturbed untill the glue has set; but not untill it has dried. Craftsman should be aware that setting and drying of glue are different. After it has been applied to the back of a book called *cementing*, it begins to set and in doing so loses its stickiness, but not its elasticity. It is, therefore, important that the operation of rounding and backing shall be executed when the elasticity is present. The glue does not retain sufficient of this elasticity when it has dried. There is not the same urgency when prepared elastic glues are used. If, however, this is done it will be necessary to soften the glue (Astor) when the work is taken up again. This is done by applying paste, to the back with three fingers, and allowing it to stand for a few minutes.Then sponge off this paste, and allow the back to stand aside untill the stickiness has gone. Use the brush right away on the book, rubbing the back vigorously until most of the glue has been cleaned off. Repeat the rinsing of the brush if necessary, but do not overdo this washing off as damage may be done to the back of the section by too much moisture. In case of old books stain evolved which is sign of fungus attack. Same size 15 sheets are laid down one after another on the thick straw board. It is placed 5/8 inches margine at the right edge of the last sheet.

Press your hand on the scale which has been set up at the last sheet, keeping 5/8 inches off from the edge. Medium thick glue (Astor) is used with the fingure/brush all over the 15 sheets at a time. After a few minutes use the sheet for preparing of end leave.

A general method is that the adhesive should be applied to the thinner of the two materials to be put together. Starch-filled book cloth is glued (aster) because paste tends to dissolve the filling and the cloth become very limps and hard to handle.

Leather and paper are general pasted because they are easier to handle — particularly in large pieces. The time is longer and adjustment if necessary, can be made.

OUTLINE

- Hand binding
- Types of hand binding
- Case/gel binding
- Bradel/overcasting/lypeta
- Tube/sunken cord/tape
- Tight back binding

Types of Hand Binding

There are two types of hand bindings: a tight back (sometimes referred to as a fast back) and a hollow back. In a tight back binding, the covering material is attached firmely to the spine of the book. When the book is opened, the covering material on the spine arches with the spine of the book. In a hollow back binding, the covering material is free from the spine. When the book is opened, the spine of the book arches and the spines of the binding lies flat on the table. A case binding, a bradel, an English split board and a German tube are all hollow back binding.

Another distinction between types or styles of binding are those with a visible joint, or groove, in which the covering boards are offset from the edge of the spine and those that have no visible joint and with relatively little space between the edge of the spine and the edge of the board. Those with the visible joint include a case binding, a bradel and an split board. Those without the visible joint include the tight back and the cord/ tape the tube.

Still another variation is between the binding that is built up on the book step-by-step and the one that is prepared one series of steps and the cover made in a separate series, when book and cover are complete. These are brought together bindings built up on the book include bradel, English split board, tight back, and German tube. Only in a case of binding the book and the cover of prepared or constructed separately.

Case/Gel Binding

A case binding (sometimes called a *casing*) is a hollow back binding with a visible joint, or groove. It resembles a hard cover edition binding (one with stiff covers). The basic differences between a machine-edition binding and a hand-made case binding are in the treatment of the endsheets and in the sewing. In a hand casing, the endsheets are sewn along with the book tapes. In machine casing, the end sheets routinely consist of folded sheets, which are attached to the first and last signature of the book by a narrow line of adhesive, and the book is sewn if at all — without tapes.

The book is prepared in one series of steps, and the case or cover is made separately. The book is their attached in the case by hings or pasted-down board papers and pressed between brass-bound boards.

The protruding brass on these boards, along with the offset covering board, produces the visible joint.

A case binding is the simplest of hard cover

bindings. It is a suitable and adequate bindings for a large percentage of the books produced in the last half of the nineteenth century old book cannot bind with this method.

Bradel/Overcasting/Lypeta

A bradel binding resembles a case binding in that it has a hollow back and a visible joint. It is, however, built upon the book and is comparable in some respect in the spilit board binding.

This type of binding is considered to be stronger than case binding and thus more appropriate for heavy volumes such as reference books that will be subject to frequent and heavy dressing. It also is useful when a rounded spine is desired and the paper on which the book is printed is too soft or spongy to hold a normal rounding. Like case binding, the bradel can be executed in a variety of materials or combinations and sewn head band are not recommended.

Sunken Cord/Tape

It is a hollow back with no visible joint. It differs from other hollow backs primarily in the construction of the cord which is routinely made from durable sunken cord which more stronger than other cords. It can be executed with a smooth spine or raised bands, both the cord and the binding are built up on the book. Sewing is needed on the spine to insert a cord into it. The cord binding is suitable binding for book like the tight back. It is executed primarily in leather or vellum and its headbands are routinely sewn. Books bound in this style usually open is due to some extent to the quality of the paper on which it is printed. This is a durable well-constructed binding and appropriate for creative designs.

Tight Back Binding

A tight back binding, sometimes referred to as a fast back. It has covering material attached solidly to the spine and has no visible joint.

It is built up step-by-step on the book. The light back is considered by many people, including binders, to be the most durable of hand binding and considered by some to be the only true hand binding. The tight back is an appropriate binding for most books published over the last few centuries. It can have a smooth spine or raised bands, it is executed almost exclusively in leather or vellum and headbands are sewn or worked in either silk or linen thread.

Small, format books bound in this style do not open easily, so its use should generally be restricted to large volumes. The back bends itself well to tooled decorations inlays, onlays, and other ornamentation, xeroxing is not possible for modern reader's service.

THE STEPS FOLLOWED IN CASE OF OLD BOOK BINDING

Binding Comprises with Sewing and Dressing/ Covering

1. Examine the style of binding.
2. Segregate the cover of the book.
3. Clean the spine of the book.
4. Repair damaged leaves.
5. Take action for straightening the edges.
6. Knock out the grooves.
7. Paste up the front and back sections.
8. Paste up the end sections.
9. Collect the sections.

10. Put section in place.
11. Cut end papers according to the sizes.
12. Paste up end papers.
13. Mark on the spine for sewing.
14. Clamp up the book for sewing.
15. Cut the spine of the book at desired distance.
16. *Jog* the loose sections several times.
17. Mark the back of the book at head or tail for guarding against wrong sewing.
18. Fix up end papers by method of sewing.
19. Glue up the spine of the book.
20. *Jog* the head and back of the book.
21. Glue up the back of the book.
22. Cut by machine the head, tail and fore-edge.
23. Cut board according to the size of the book.
24. Apply the glue on the back of the book with a wet cloth.
25. Round the back of the book properly with the rounding machine.
26. Take action for backing with hammer in order to form of cylinder.
27. Prepare holes on the boards for inserting on cords.
28. Split up boards for inserting inside tape or cords when necessary.
29. Prepare head and tail bands.
30. Cut the bands according to the size.
31. Fix up the head and tail bands.
32. Prepare paper cylinder.
33. Cut the cylinder according to the size.
34. Fix up the cylinder on the back.

35. Paste down the paper.
36. Fix the boards.
37. Cut the canvas, cloth, corners according to size.
38. Apply glue and paste the clothes on the spine.
39. Trim cloth according to size.
40. Apply paste on the covering materials.
41. Fix the corners and to turn in.
42. Dress the covers and turn in.
43. Paste the end papers at the front and back.
44. Clean the book for removing excess paste and glue by cloth.
45. Keep the book under pressure properly over night.
46. Next gold finishing.

QUESTION FOR DISCUSSION

1. What is the best tool for cutting an old book pages?
2. How will you determine the grain and cross direction?
3. Describe pasting up the back?
4. How many types of hand binding?
5. Which is the best type of hand binding? Explain.
6. Name of the steps which will you use to complete a book by hand binding.

7

Techniques of Hand Binding

FIRST STAGE IN RE-BINDING

Book

1. Count leaves/checking
2. Work sheet
3. Remove cover/board
4. Separate signature
5. Remove backing ridge/groove
6. Remove glue
7. Delamination/patch remove.

Magazine

1. Index
2. Size of magazine
3. Advertising pages
4. Cumulative periodical binding

Technique of hand binding delt with about fourty five main steps almost followed by conservation methods with a view to up keep the cultural heritage, generally new book, edition and pamphlet laminated pages binding concerned with machine operation. The hand binding which involves the name basic operation as machine binding, but the manner of performing those is entirely different. Many additional operations are performed in hand binding that have no place in machine binding, only section stitching is the machine binding, style of cover/dressing and sewing both comprises with the hand binding. In small library, there is no such type of rare documents. In these categories of libraries only commercial binding is required for reader service. It begins at the starting point of checking the book till completeness, followed by technique that concern, pull the cover both sides, leather binding, end leaf, open section by section, repair top and bottom pages, delamination if needed patch remove, deacidification, Trimming the spine 1/8 inch lens tissue lamination repair torn page collation, sewing, hinging, inlaying, re-edging, guarding, wormhole, remove stain gluing (cementing), drying, cutting, rounding, backing, board setting Tajma/sunken cord/tape, end cutting, head band/tail band/ gluing, cylinder paper, dressing cloth/rexin/leather, where techniques varies for the four styles of binding described in this book.

According to condition of three categories of documents are segrigated for preparation of work sheet. In case of binding and mending work sheet should be included the name of author, tittle, publisher date of publication, condition of the book when received for restoration, style of binding, nature of covering/ dressing material, type of sewing, head bands, date of book received, date of work is started, work proposed or recommended, work actually done, width or number of filler used. This type of work sheet is useful to the National Library and other large libraries.

CHECKING AND PULLING A DOCUMENT

Examine the book for completeness is the first

step in rebinding a book. It is practically important, what extent it, the object is brittle wheather it is fit for sewing or not, if not, lamination is necessary then binding. In case of frazile document, pages may be displaced or broken into several parts where envelope should be prepared for each broken page before lamination. New pagination is done continuous top to bottom keeping the plates, maps, etc. in place.

Next step is the removal of fold cover. This cover board can be pulled from outside if spine and board joint by the Tajma (cloth) Fig. 7.1 (a). But in case sunken cord or tape used during stitching the spine and joint with board binding needs cutting with sharp knife: First one top side then bottom.

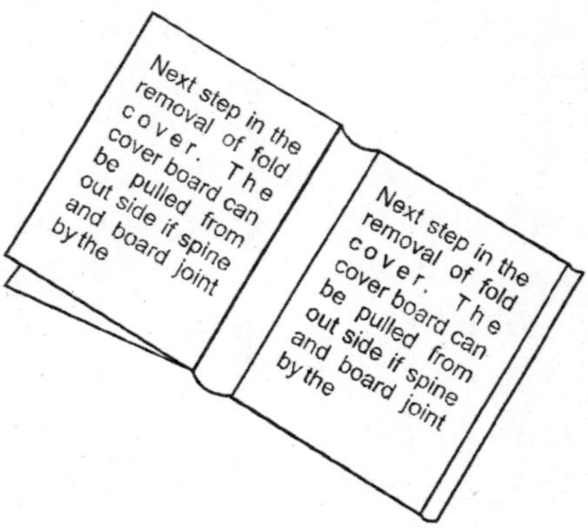

(a)

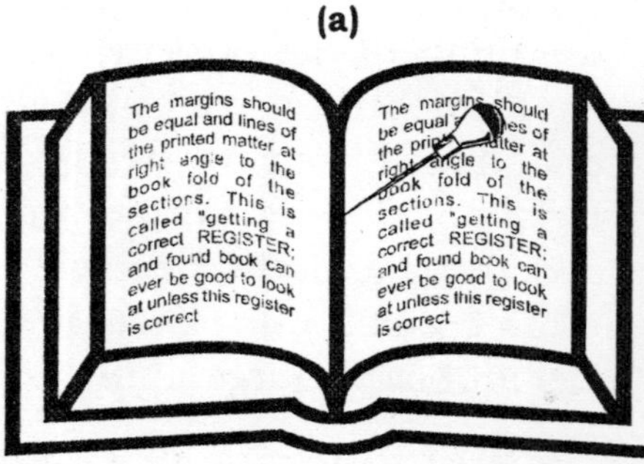

(b)

Fig. 7.1

This will free the book from its covers board, if it is a hollow back. If a tight back, it will free the covers but not the spine. Place the book between clean protective boards (The covers just removed will serve) and put it in a press with the spine exposed. Carefully remove from the spin as much of the lining material (tajma, paper cylinder) as possible in a dry state, prying it up with the point of a knife and pulling it way. In a hollow back, this usually consists of a piece of paper, a piece of lawn or Tajma (cloth), headbands, and a layer of glue, in a tight back, it will consist of the covering/ dressing material, some type of cylinder paper, durable paper, head-bands, and glue. If it is bound with hollow back, the hollow is split to remove the old leather and paper cylinder is scraped from the back. If it is old case-bound-book, the case can sometimes be removed with the back lining at one operation. To execute work, the boards are folded back and grasped in the left hand, while the book is held in the right hand. A steady pull will usually completely strip the old back lining from the book.

Find the middle of the first section, and carefully cut the sewing thread seen down the fold. Go on turning the pages the signature of the next section is seen. From the information already given on signature, it should be clear that the beginning of the next section has been reached. Hold the book firmly on the bench with the right hand, in case of the first section gently with the left. A thin folder inserted between the sections is often helpful in difficult cares. Remove all the sections in this way, and keep them in the right order by turning each one face down in a pile as they are detached (Fig. 7.2).

Fig. 7.2

Break down the old glue and muslin with the left thumb as the section are taken off. This helps the removal of the sections.

If it is not possible to remove these materials in their dry state, use a knife to carefully scrape away as much as can safely be removed. In case of leather binding, it is difficult to remove from back, on the other hand, spine of the old book becomes brittle due to accumulation of acidity, account of use of conventional adhesive wheat paste with copper sulphate but not in case bone glue.

Instead of wheat paste cloth/cotton *swab weted* with lime water should be absorbed for 5 to 10 minutes the leather has been soaked through cotton. It will then possible to remove the leather. This is called *pitch panee*. In case of, case binding where the glue on the back of the section proves difficult to remove, *i.e.* if it is impossible to take the sections apart without considerable damage, then apply lime water with soft cloth/cotton swab and allow to soak. Scrape off and pull the book. It is very important that the pulling should be done while the book is damp. If it is not pull in just time, it will become hard and difficult to remove. During this pitch panee process lime water gradually absorb and enter into gutter margins which can result little bit stain. Jet of steam is a good method of removing old glue, if it is used with care. The gutter margin is the left-hand margin, or the margin nearest the spine.

All the pieces of old glue and thread are removed from the backs of the sections and none of these discarded material should be allowed to become lodged between the pages or sections. All plates, maps or single leaves which have been tipped should replace loose. If these are left projecting a little at the head. These will not be overlooked when the time comes to guard those back into the sections.

The signature, specially those near the front and back of the book, will have a crease near the back fold caused by the backing. To remove this backing ridge or groove, the signatures are placed a few at a time on an iron block and a hammer is used to beat out the ridge or groove.

If hammer is used, care should be taken not to beat the spine so hard that it will be mashed down thinner than the fore edge. If the book is very old, the paper may be so brittle that direct blows from the hammer will break it, so the section should be placed between layers of binder's board before they are beaten.

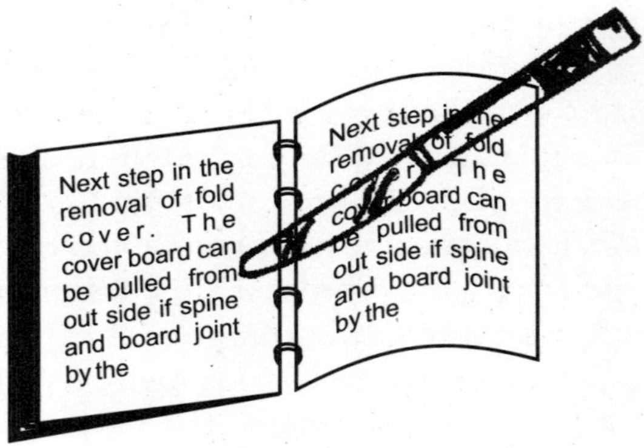

(a)

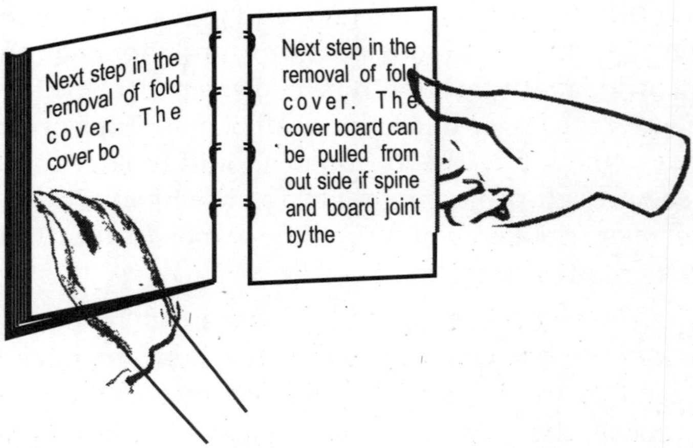

(b)

Fig. 7.3

When the spine is clean, remove the book from the Press, "Pull" the book to take it apart for signature. Threads from the sewing will be exposed in the center of the signature. Cut the threads (Fig. 7.4). Count off the same number of pages on the other side of the sewing. This should be all of the pages in the last signature.

When the signature is not marked, another way to check the number of pages in a signature is to count the leaves between the center of one signature and the center of the next. If there are 8 leaves, that is the number to a signature-4 on each side of the center. Unless the total number of pages in the book is evenly divisible by the number of pages in a signature, either the first or last signature of the book will probably not have the same number of the pages as the other signature. Proceed with caution until the number of pages in the full of signature is definitely ascertained. The separating or tearing a part of a few pages in a given signature is no great tragedy, but it does mark additional work in the repair.

The last page of one signature and the first page of the next are attached at the gutter margin. This is the result of the original gluing. Hold the book firmly with one hand, grasp the center signature to be removed in the otherhand, and gradually case it free (Fig. 7.5). Continue until all signatures are separated.

Next take the signatures one at a time, lay them on a piece of waste board in their folded state, and with a sharp knife. Push off any remaining glue. First do this on one side, then turn the signature over and repeat (Fig. 7.6). If glue is embedded in the holes made by the earlier sewing, pull it out with the point of a knife or the fingers.

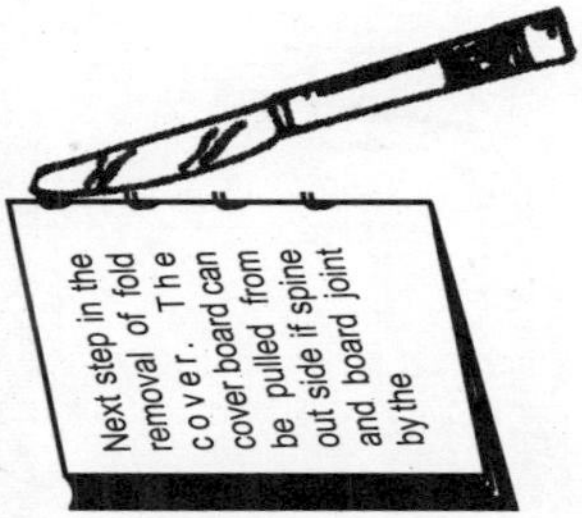

Fig. 7.4

Books are often issued in parts, and each issues are frequently found together by wire stitches or staples. For putting, a knife and a pair of pincers are needed. The lifting of the staples should be done with great care, as the leaves can be badly damaged in the process. When the two ends of the wire have been lifted by the knife, they should be nipped off close to the book with the pincers, and a section or two detached. As the sections are taken off it is best to nip off more of the wire. Another method is used where by the ends are first lifted, and then the whole of the staple withdrawn from the other side with the pincers.

It is usual to find that the section have been stapled in such a way that the two ends of the wire are turned over at the end of the book, and not at the first sections. This means that pulling begins with the last section. If the old glue on the backs of the sections can not be removed by using the finger and thumb, lay the section down with its back along the edge of the bench. Then take a very sharp knife, and work is along the section behind the pieces of glue, keeping it as flat as possible on the paper with care then it will be possible to avoid cutting the paper.

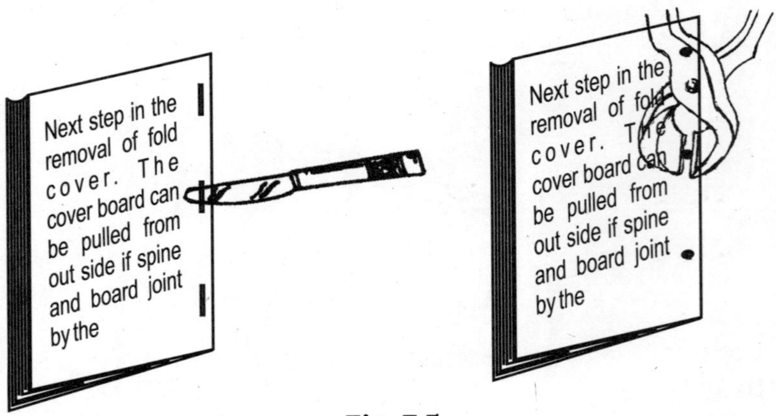

Fig. 7.5

Work out or flatten the fold or crease made when the book was originally backed. Backing is the fanning out of the signatures to create a shoulder or joint against which the covering boards rest. If it is not too pronounced, flatten it first by bending the creases in reverse and rubbling it on a flat surface with a bone folder or end of knife handle.

When press the book as follows lay a few signatures 4 or 5 on a pressboard add another board, a few more signatures with the spine or folded edge oriented in the opposite direction. For proper pressing the signatures should be piled exactly on top of each other. Continue until the entire book is between boards. Place it in the press and screw the press down tight. Leave under pressure, preferably overnight, but at least 2 hours. If sufficient press boards are not available, or the clearance of the press is in adequate, the pressing can be done in stages. Sometimes a book has been overbacked and folded edges of the signatures are badly creased and wrinkled. In that case as they are piled up for pressing, moisten the wrinkled area with a piece of damp cotton (Fig. 7.6), only the outside pages of each signature have to be moisten.

Fig. 7.6

The leather is difficult to remove from back, on the other hand spine of old book becomes brittle (due to gather acidity). It is on account of conventional adhesive used which is prepared by wheat paste and copper sulphate. Lime water (calcium hydroxide) wetted cloth/cotton swab should be absorbed continuously for 5 to 10 minutes, until the leather has been soaked through cotton. It will then possible to remove the leather. This process is called **Pitch Panee** (Bengali).

Repair the tear portions of a leave with patch before re-binding elaborate discussion will be in the next chapters. Missing corner should be replaced by durable paper.

Generally fly leaves, old end sheets are made of the same paper should be pulledoff because these papers become acidic and brittle, on account of brittleness sewing cannot stand for which durable new paper should be used. If the colour of old books do not match with patch, durable while paper patch/end leave should be deep on into the tea/coffee, liqueur.

In the National Library, Kolkata huge number of rare documents were laminated with starch contain quality Tribanee and Padamjee tissue paper with starch paste. The starch laminated pages become yellow, hazzy, illegible on account of chemical oxidation in presence of *nacent* oxygen as a result lignin in paper break down into aromatic acid like benzoic acid. Delamination is being done in warm water (50°C) tray. The tissue paper is pulled out from document by the sharp pointed knife and dry it for re-lamination and re-binding. It is long process but reversible. Repair can be made with care, librarian are interested to get back same form document after restoration, but it is an operational method of conservation of old frazile rare antique, so to some extent it will be changed at the end of restoration beacuse "an old man cannot be young after proper treatement".

When the corner has been turn off, the edge of

the paper should be pared or tapered by shaving it with a knife/scissor. Broken portion should be used with filler and laminate both sides. This operation is known as *skiving*. The edge of the replacement corner should be pared also and the pared edges pasted, joined together and pressed between sheets of waxed paper.

If the paring is well done, the top of the patch on to the leaf of the book will be no thicker than the leaf itself. Pairing requires a very sharp knife. The material to be pared is laid on a piece of glass top table or flask wood held firmly with the left hand. The knife is held at an angle with the right hand and pushed along the edge of the material to taper it.

If any of the folded sheets were torn apart at the fold when they were removed from the book, they should be joined together with a narrow strip of matching paper. It is sometimes better to use a strip of very thin tough paper so that it will not build up a swell in the back.

Tears in the pages are repaired with tissue paper. When paper is torn, the edges always have a slight overlap. Paste is applied to the overlap and the edges processed together. A piece of tissue is then placed over the tear on each side of the leaf and it is pressed between sheets of waxed paper. Enough paste will squeeze out the tear to stick the tissue and when the repair is dry, the excess tissue is pulled away. The fibres of the tissue that stick to the tear will provide an almost invisible reinforcement.

Generally, books are mended first top two pages and bottom two pages of a book with bond paper strip wide 3/4 inches which is overlapping between strip of bond paper and leaf.

The mending methods that have just been

described only for commercial library binding. Detailed repair and rehabilitation of rare valuable documents will be discussed in the next chapter.

The book should be checked that all plates, maps are in their correct places and firmly affixed to the signature. Inserts that are tipped to the signatures may be reinforced by fastening them to guards tipped around the signature so that they will be sewing in place.

Different methods must be used to prepare magazines for permanent bindings because generally they are wire stitched. The number of issues to be bound is one volume depends on several factors.

Many periodicals have an index and title page printed by the publisher. Since the index covers a certain definite number of issues which are listed on the title page, it is obvious that those issues must make up in one volume. The publisher usually takes into account the size of the magazines so that the finished volume is a convenient size to handle.

When no index or title page is published for magazine, the number of issues to be placed in a volume depends largely upon their size. It would be poor policy to bind together. So many numbers that the volume would be too heavy and bulky for convenient reference. On the other hand, if the volumes are too small, the result will be unnecessary incurred expense for binding. Even though no index appears, the publisher usually assigns a new volume number at regular intervals, generally once a year. The bindings should be so arranged that the first issue of each new publishers volume is the first issue of a bound volume. The change from one publishers volume number to the text should not occur in the middle of a bound volume, unless two or more such volumes are bound together.

No librarian desires to remove advertising pages from magazine. The back folds are removed by taking a very small cut in the cutting machine or by using a book sander, and the binding edge is then glued. After the glue is dry, the sheets are separated into sections of suitable thickness to be oversewn.

The wire stitches must be removed by cutting off the folded legs of the stitches, with diagonal cutters. Pincer can be used to pull out the stitches. Broken pieces of wire must not be allowed to remain in the magazine, because the knife will be badly damaged. The wire may cause iron stain in the magazine.

QUESTIONS FOR DISCUSSION

1. What is Pulling?
2. By what are means covers removed from books?
3. What care should be taken when the section are being separated?
4. How is the backing, ridge removed?
5. How is the wire stitch or staple removed?
6. Why must different binding methods be used for magazines?
7. What are the factors which determine the number of magazine to bound in one volume?
8. What adjustment must be made when the advertizing pages are removed?
9. What is Pitch Panee?
10. What is Skiving?

8

Repairing through Chemical Treatment

CLEANING

The pulling of a book is completed section by section. Next, it is examined the brittleness for possible washing, deacidification, trimming, mending, guarding and inlaying, etc. If the document is too brittle, treatment should be done dry deacidification. "Many marks/stains found on the document will respond to treatment by dry cleaning and these methods can be followed first. Generally, soft cotton/cloth, very fine sandpaper, soft rubber, ether, petrol and similar materials are needed for the too brittle documents. Ink can be treated carefully with 1% oxadic acid keeping the document on the blotting paper. Where grease stain is found on the leave must be placed on a sheet of clean blotting paper and the grease mark washed with benzene and 1% citric acid. The solution should be poured through dropper round the spot, gradually absorb most of the solution on the spot. The blotting paper absorbs most of the grease. The stain on paper due to oil, fat and tar can be vanished with the petrol or benzene.

The marks on document with tea, coffee, can be dissolved by hydrogen peroxide, or amonia. Sometimes old books show brownish spots on the leaves due to attack of mildew, foxing, fungus which can be destroyed with thymol 2% in methanol solution.

On account of prolong use of valuable rare books become soft and woolly, it is a sign of lost most of the original size.

The Barrow's method of wet deacidification of valuable rare documents gives buffer action and sizing simultaneously acts on the object. This method of deacidification is followed in the National Library, India. It is a full prove of two shorts wet deacidification process. After deacidification brittle paper gets to some extent of strength due to repair of cellulose structure.

WASHING

In case of mass production of old document treatment, stain can be removed by merely passing the sheets through clear warm water at (60°C) which has been added a little alum (if the water is hard). Ink and similar yellow stains require rather more special treatment. A tray is prepared containing of weak little chlorine water and through this solution the sheets are *imergged* at least 15 minutes. These treated sheets should be washed with clear water at least three times, until residual chlorine remains in the paper (white precipitate which does not appear). But too brittle document cannot persist this solution. Residual chlorine test in paper can be done with dilute 2 to 4 drops silver nitrate solution. This process should be carried out by restorer (skill hand).

BARROW'S DEACIDIFICATIONS

W. J. Barrow investigated extensively into the

causes of deterioration of paper of the eighteenth and nineteenth centuries and confirmed that nearly all the deteriorated papers were highly acidic. Even if ideal storage conditions, temperature 20 ± 1°C and relative humidity 45–55% per cent are maintained in the record repository. Gradual increase of brittleness due to the inherent acidity in the paper is dynamic process. The acidity in document is accumulated partly to the treatment rendered to the pulp during manufacturer of paper and partly due to absorption from the environmental atmosphere and absorption from acidic material in contact. Acidic nature of ink (iron gal ink) used for acidic material in contact. Acidic nature of ink (iron gal ink) used for writing also deteriorate the paper appreciably.

WET METHOD

Accessory	Plastic drum
	Enamel tray 2' × 3' × 3"
	Keeps apparatus for preparation of CO_2
Wax Paper	Enamel Mug 1 Liter
Stainles steel wire frame (net)	
	Round headed knife
	Calcium hydroxide 0.15%
	Calcium bicarbonate 0.15%
	Sulphuric acid concentrate and pumic stone.

Preparation of Calcium Hydroxide Solution I

Approximate half kilogram of Calcium oxide (lime) dissolved in 10 liters water in a plastic drum or enamel container whose capacity is 30 liters. Stir it well and add more pure water gradually till 25 liters. Settle it down for half an hour. During these processes, considerable heat is evolved and uniform. After the excess of calcium oxide (supernatural lime) has settled at the bottom. The clear lime water is pour in a tray through 1 liter mug. 10 liters lime water is sufficient to make acid free from 40–50 sheets of normal size book. During this treatment, the sheet in different trays it is necessary that the solution are agitated tightly by raising and lowering the end of the trays. After 15 minutes drain out all the used lime water and add more 25 liter pure water. With residual lime which is again used. In this manner, the same lime can be used as calcium hydroxide solution 20 times. But every time settled lime should be stirred. pH of the lime water should not be more than pH. Which can be tested by pH paper. If pH more than desire level, add a little quantity of waters. Then shift the sheets to second solution calcium bicarbonate.

Preparation of Calcium Bicarbonate (Solution II)

It can be prepared by dissolving half kilogram calcium carbonate in a 30 liter enamelled jar or plastic drum and passing carbon dioxide gas through the solution for 15 minutes. The solution is kept well stirred.

Alternatively the solution (0.15%) can be prepared by passing carbondioxide in a solution of calcium hydroxide in water (1 solution). At first, a milky suspension of calcium carbonate is formed. On continued 20 minutes passing of carbon dioxide from keep's apparition/carbon dioxide gas from cylinder, it changes clear solution of calcium bicarbonate. Therefore, the clear solution of calcium hydroxide obtain from solution I is taken and diluted to twice its volume. During the passing of carbondioxide constant stirring till the white precipitate of calcium carbonate again dissolves to give clear solution.

Anne and Jacob have shown the rise of pH which was much less after treatment with calcium carbonate treatment than with calcium hydroxide alone. It is, therefore, better to air dry the acidified document after calcium hydroxide treatment, alternatively in atmosphere of carbon dioxide for rapid conversion to calcium bicarbonate. But treatment of old paper with Solution I calcium hydroxide and calcium bicarbonate Solution II successively gives buffer action. Calcium carbonate deposit on the paper which heal up the even surface of on the other hand it gives buffer action. Buffer action is neither increase acidity nor increase alkalinity. Both excess are harmful toward the paper.

DRY DEACIDIFICATION

Barium Hydroxide–Octahydrate

Barrow's wet method do not permit to deacidify the too brittle and frazile rare document, in this case, dry deacidification with barium hydroxide in methanol is best method. A solution of 1 : 10, *i.e.*, one gram barium hydroxide and 10 c.c. of methanol. The solution is applied on the brittle document by brushing. Methanol takes the hydroxide into the paper where it is gradually converted to barium carbonate raising the pH to about 7.6

Degraded harmful material cannot be removed through this method. Methanol is highly volatile liquid. Therefore, deacidification with this solution should be completed at a time. Methanol is dangerous one and toxic, while barium carbonate precipitate the paper is poisonous on ingestion. Technical personnel should use carefuly to this solution.

There are so many deacidification processes which are discussed in "Preservation of Documents."

9

Mending and Lamination

Generally book tear due to prolong use and broken into pieces for brittleness, frayed edge or defective leave call for care, time and patients of a skill personnel. These are special type of job needs preservative materials besides binding work. The writer has achieved very highly skilled delicate, precise work in the National Library Kolkata, during his service as chemist.

Required Material

Glass top table	Lawn cloth
Curry pot	Sulpher paper
1½ inches soft brush	Blunt knife
Lens tissue paper (imported)	Scissor
Bond paper	C.M.C & jebanjor 10 : 0.5
Hand-made paper (Thick & Thin)	Methyl cellulose
Nepalise tissue paper	Wax paper

It is observed that most of the fly leaves are brittle though colour matching with the document should not re-bind. Hand-made paper, bond paper or cartridge is required to use. Rice or wheat paste should be discarded. Because it is a delicious insect food, on the other hand, if one uses copper sulphate as insecticide in the paste that is also harmful. Synthetic adhesive like sodium salt of carboxy methyl cellulose, with Jebanjor (epoxirasin) or methyl cellulose. All these are transparent white which is fit for tissue lamination.

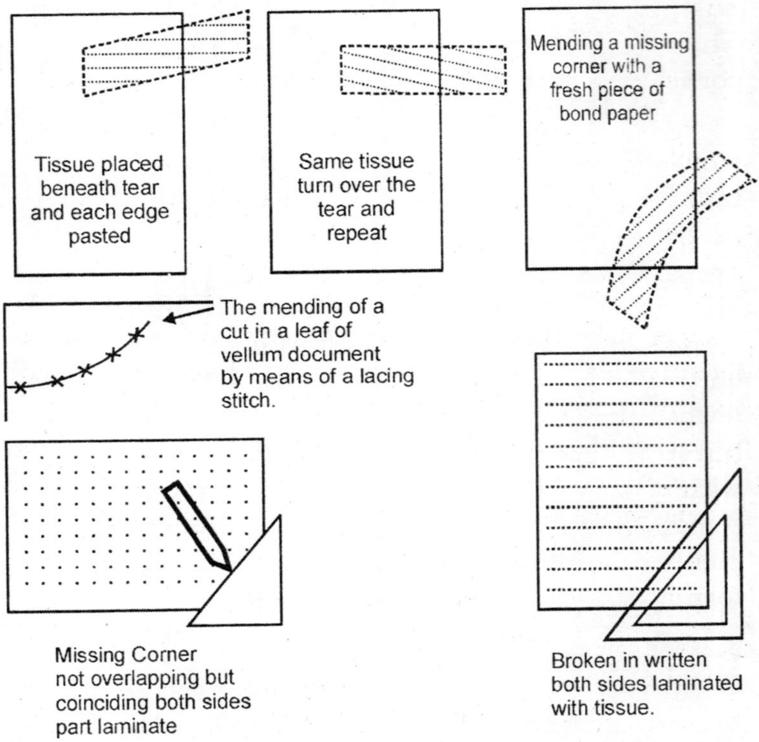

It is observed that paper usually tears in such a way as to give two frayed edges which overlap each other. Cut a tissue paper a little bit more than double of the torn length and width will be half inch + half inch = one inch. Carefully paste the tissue paper through small brush the double length, place the document on the glass top table and lay down the adhesive tissue paper on the document underneath. Then turn over the leave along with pasted tissue paper and set up on the torn place and rub down very gently with cotton snab. It must now be set aside until it is completely dry, when the superflows double tissue paper can be cut with scissor, thus, leave a good joint which is practically invisible.

In case of a leave, the corner of which is broken but present. Cut the tissue paper two fold triangle which is more than inner side length of the broken corner and process is same as previous.

In case of a leave, the corner or side portion of which are missing, a piece of bond paper thickness must be found to match the colour of old book paper as nearly as possible. The matching colour can be prepared by deep a bond paper in tea liqueur and dry. This must be placed underneath the torn edge of the leaf, and a folder point run carefully along to mark it on the new piece of paper to tear, the latter about 1/4 away from the line. This should give a thin frayed edge, but it will be improved if it is pared down very slightly with a very sharp knife on the glass plate. It only remains now to treat the torn corner and the new pared piece of paper. Then laminate with part tissue over the torn area coincide the both missing portion and leave.

As a result 1/4 inch written position will not overlap. The diagram will make the matter clear.

If a sheet of Vellum has been cut, the best-way to repair it is to use the lacing stitch as shown in the sketch. A very fine silk must be used in the matter.

Sometimes, old books have defects in the way of small holes made in the pages by book worms. If these have to be made good, mix up a little clean white blotting paper with size until a pulp is obtained, and fill the holes with this pulp mixture. Press it into the holes with a knife handle. When dry it can be smoothing off with very fine sandpaper. If a page is very badly damaged, it is often possible to try and obtain a second copy, and extract whole leaves from it to insert in the book in process of being repaired.

LAMINATING A FRAYED EDGES

When a sheet is damaged with multiple tears, frayed edges, missing portions, and the like, it can be preserved by laminating. This means covering the pages on both sides with a thin, transparent white tissue.

Laminating with lens tissue of a brittle rare manuscript is the best method. Methyl cellulose may be used as adhesive. The lens tissue paper is manufacturing by M/s James R. Cromption & Bros. Ltd. Eltron Paper Mills, Burry Lancashire, England. Five Ply solvent lamination is best method of frayed edged tear documents. First lens tissue, 2nd cellulose accetate foil, 3rd in the middle document, 4th cellulose accetate foils and 5th tissue paper, is the five ply lamination. It is a reversible process of lamination which is ethic of conservation.

Material Required

Glass top table: 3 ft × 5 ft any size of map, diagram, etc.

Lens tissue Alpha cellulose contain 90% weight. 9 to 10 gms/square meter

Ash content not more than 0.5%.

pH not less than 6, Free from oily and waxy constituent, Chinese/Indian fine tissue paper with methyl cellulose, may be used as paste and carboxy methyl cellulose also.

0.4 to 0.5 : 10, Jebanjor: methyl cellulose or carboxy methyl cellulose.

Blotting paper, one-guard strip hand-made paper.

Most of the title, preface pages of a manuscript become frayed edged, torn which needs restoration. In order to upkeep it, guard, filler and patch etc. are

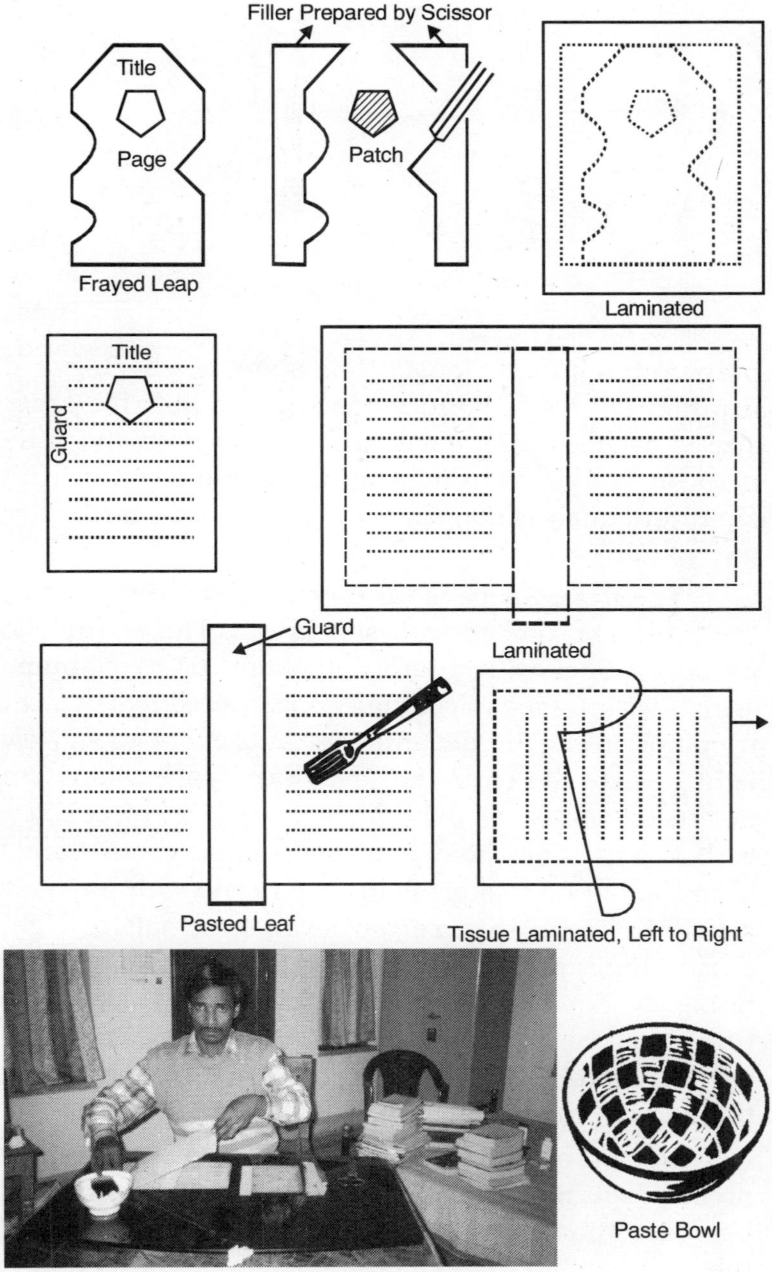
Filler Prepared by Scissor
Title
Page
Frayed Leap
Patch
Laminated
Title
Guard
Laminated
Guard
Pasted Leaf
Tissue Laminated, Left to Right
Paste Bowl

Fig. 9.1

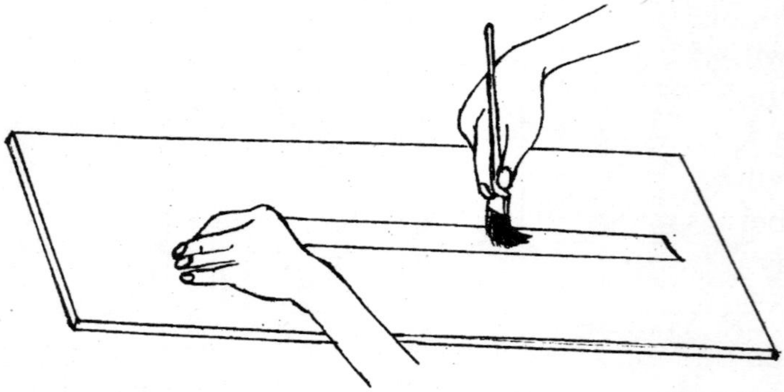

prepared. A little bit longer than spine of a book guard is prepared. A thin hand-made paper, a little bit larger size is taken on the glass and lay down on the tittle broken page. Then penciling and trimming simultaneously is done in order to prepare guard, filler and patch.

The frayed page is lay down on the wetted glass top table and pasted with soft brush. The set up the prepared filler with guard coinciding or overlapping 1 inch with frayed edged page and pasted it. Then set up patch in the middle and filler at the fore edge. Now lightly paste the entire surface of the page taking are not to move any of the added pieces out of position with brush. Next hold the tissue paper both hands from the left hand start fixing the tissue with the page slowly and rub with cotton swab from left to right during the lamination, care should be taken that air buble do not left inside the lamination whole set is turn down carefully pasted with brush horizontal and vertical direction lightly lay down the tissue paper on the page in the same fashion, i.e. left to right.

In case of double leave lamination at a time same process will be taken place, but only guard strip will be wider than previous. It will according to width of the book such as 1.5 inches, 1.25 inch, 1 inch etc.

First leaf lay down on the wetted glass and pasted it with soft 1.5 inches wide brush. Next set up 1.5 inches hand-made paper guard strip coinciding with the first leaf gutter margin if fiberalation is proper, swelling will not appear. Otherwise overlaping 0.1 inch in between leaf and guard. In this case little bit swelling may be occurred.

Then lay down second leaf coinciding with guard. Then pasted with all sections at a time by soft brush. Lay the second piece of lens tissue paper on top of the paper, brushing it lightly with water in the same manner as the first tissue was put down on the working surface. Next carefully set up long size tissue paper on the pasted both leaves and simultaneously press it with soft cloth/cotton swab. It is kept in blotting paper over night for air dry. At last the laminated sheet is inserted in a hot press for proper setting of tissue without air gap and transparency.

QUESTIONS FOR DISCUSSION

1. If you keep a few papers in open space, will it be deteriorated?
2. Why a book becomes brittle?
3. What is the need of acid free paper?
4. Fungus grow due to acidity in paper?
5. How many types of deacidification? What are these?
6. What type of acidification method will one adapt's in case of too brittle book?
7. How are tears crumble leaves repair?
8. How will you repair Wrinkled Pages?
9. What materials are required for wet deacidification and dry deacidification?

10

Guarding

Generally all frayed edged, tear, damaged book are essential guarding, for rebinding. Every old book top five pages and bottom five pages become damaged which is required guarding in order to strengthening of the stitch and spine. It is observed that damaged caused by pulling, and all loose pages and plates also must now be guarded. This means that the leave damaged down the back fold must be strengthened with strip of paper called *guard.* The paper must be durable and thin from the conservation point of view. The National Library, Kolkata using thin hand-made paper for this purpose. Ordinary re-binding bond paper may be used as guard of which thinkness is almost identical thickness of book leaf. Preparation guard: About 4 and 1/8 inches hand-made paper is taken on a glass top make it first two fold it will become 2 and 1/16 inches and 2nd fold it will become 1 and 1/32 inches, i.e. 1 inches width guard. Width of the guard is decided according to width of the volume 1, 1¼ and 1½ inches etc. A ¾ inch guard is required in case of single leave and its length is little bit longer from head to tail of the book spine. If two leaves are completely separated to make these pair into a folded sheet again at the same time keeping bulking in the spine area a minimum. This double of triple folded hand-made paper is cut with a blunt knife so as to come out of the long fibre which will form strong bond with leaves and paste. This fibre is also overlap with pages as a result swelling does not take place. At a time large number of guard as for lamination of book can be prepared. The best method of fiberalation guard is prepared by tearing two or three fold measured thin hand-made paper by the both hands.

A book is laminated with double pages is different from a single pages, only outside or inside pairing guard should be overlapping on the document or ½ inch overlapping with gutter margin and single guard strip. The spine of old book gets acidity and become more brittle for that reason ½ inch gutter margin is trimmed out and lay down 1½ inch wide guard for double pages

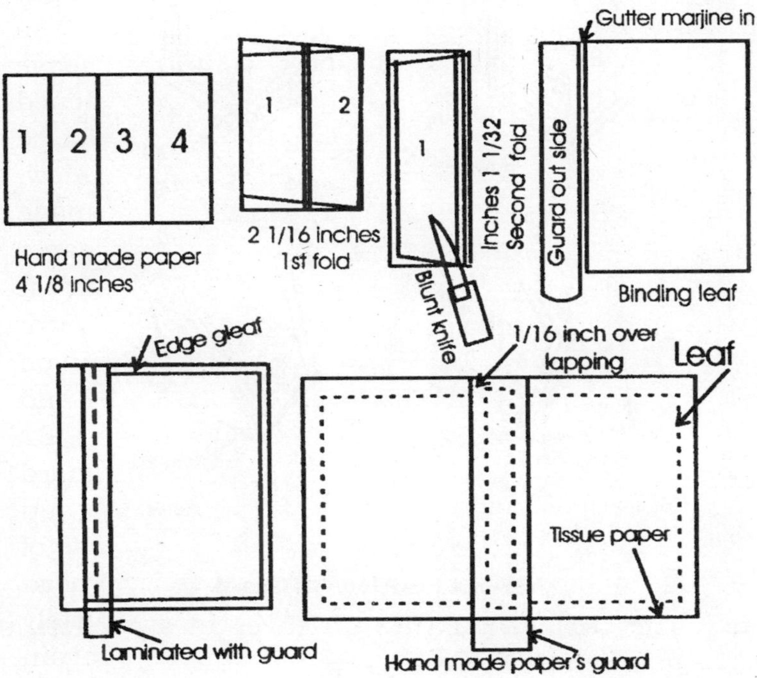

lamination coinciding in case of proper fiberalation or 1/16 inch overlapping if sharp cutting guard is used.

A few points arise at the time of guarding which is given below:

1. The sewing thread must always pass through CENTER of guard.
2. During pesting the guards is unstretched or when set up on those on the leaves. It will cause "crinkling" of the pages due to preparation of the guard when drying.
3. The guard is pasted throughly and uniformly. It is very trouble some to find guards which have not adhered properly and partially loose leaf will spoil the whole of the work when bound.

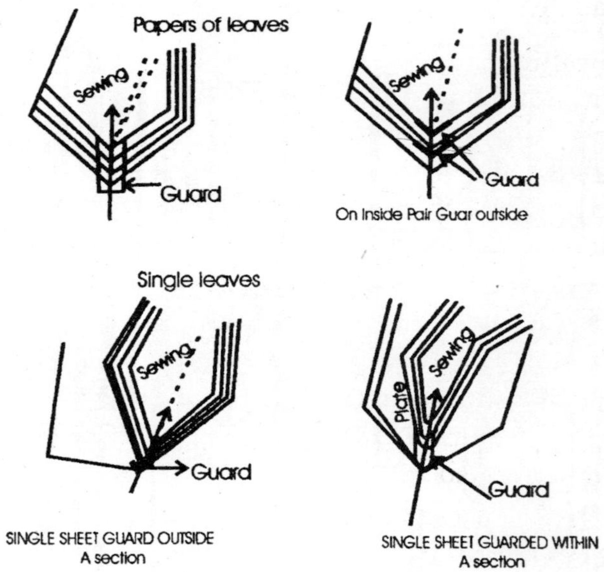

Various Positions of Guard

4. The OUTSIDE PAIRS of leaves in a section is guarded INSIDE.

5. The INSIDE PAIRS of leaves are guarded OUTSIDE.
6. SINGLE LEAVES outside a section must be guarded on the outside.
7. SINGLE LEAVES occurring inside a section must be guarded in such a way that the sewing will always pass through the middle of the guard. Plates usually come under this rule.

Guarding is of little use unless the actual sewing thread passes through the centre. A binder can solve any problem if this rule borne in his mind. When plates are being guarded every attempt should be made to have the guard on a back of the plate, but this rule does not obey always. No book should be guarded any more than is absolutely necessary, as these cause too much swell in the back of the book. In order to minimise the swelling, guard should be coincide with gutter margin. This guard must be fiberalated of thin hand-made paper when both sides partly or full tissue laminated. Otherwise swelling caused space problem in the library as the library is a growing organism. This method follow the National Library, Kolkata. But in case of only binding guard should not use too many pages.

Generally a section composed of only two leaves, *i.e.*, four printed pages. These are called 'Q Section' and they should ALWAYS be guarded as for an outside pair of leaves so as to strengthen to the back fold.

The OUTER PAIR is guarded INSIDE, while INNER PAIR are guard OUTSIDE. The outer pair could be guarded outside and still they obey the rule, but in doing so a new clean spine will be given to the section. If it is guarded inside, the roughness of the fold of the section, due to defects and its previous gluing, will give an added 'key' when re-gluing after sewing. In the case of the inner pairs, it will be found that guard placed on the outside are less obtrusive when the book is bound. In practice such guarding of the inner pairs is not often necessary, damage usually being confined to the outer pairs. During examining whether a guard is necessary, hold the pairs of leaves up to the light and any 'Splits' or very week places or tear in the fold of the leaves will ready to be seen. If such are present a guard is needed, but ignore the presence of the 'Stitch holes' caused by the previous sewing. These will be filled by the gluing-up after sewing. The guarded work must not be allowed to dry out half before being refolded and replaced in the section otherwise great care must be exercised in seeing that no paste is squeezed out from the guard. This will be avoided if, when pasting a guard, the paste is spread evenly but thinly, it just sufficient to make guard adhere and no more.

GUARDING OF PLATES

Plates that are attached with a thin line of paste to the adjoining page of original binding should be removed and hinged. This will allow those to open more freely and will remove any strain from the page to which they are attached. Before removing the plates, check those proper position, in the book is indicated on the plates, or a list of plates, giving their position, appears along with the table of contents. Suppose contents of the page damaged due to prolong use and plates are number less. In this case, mark lightly on the back of the each plate with pencil. If the plates position are after 20, 55 printed pages then mark it 20A, 55A, respectively.

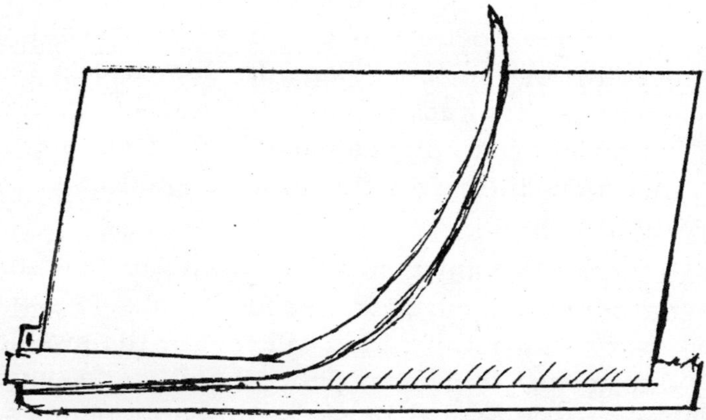

Cut the thin hand-made paper/tissue hinges about 1 inch in width and 1 inch longer than plate (grain direction running with the vertical measurement of the page). Attach the hinge to the back of the plate. Lay the plate face down on a strip of clean paper, lay a second strip of paper ¼ inch in from spine edge of the plate and apply the adhesive to this area of the plate. Discard the waste strips, lay the pasted edge of the plate face up on a glass top/stip of wax paper and place the hinge on the pasted area shown above cover with wax paper and use hot press/weight with a board and a brick. When dry, cut away the excess tissue/hand-made paper head and tail.

(a) Put the plate in the proper position in the book and fold the hinge arround the spine edge of the page next to it. If the plate falls in the centre of a signature, fold the hinge back on itself at the edge of the plate. The entire hinge, both the position attached to the plate and the position that is free, will remain on the back side of the plate, and the plate will be sewn into the book through the fold in the hinge. The free portion of all hinges can be left free or they can be pasted down to the pages that they fold arround or adjoin.

(b) In spite of proper care and process followed for stitch of a document, one page comes out on account of short size page. In this case ¼ inch guard is required to be pasted and inserted by round headed knife causiously. To facilitate the insertion into pages the guard should be cut at stitch points.

(c) If there are many plates to guard it will be wise to pare the back edges on a sheet of plate glass with a very sharp knife. This will reduce the swelling due to use thin bond paper/hand-made paper. Time will be saved where a number of plates are to be guarded by pasting a few at a time together. 1/8 inch of each plate should be pasted up ward to down. The remaining half of the guard must be bent round the back of section or pair of leaves to which it belongs, and the sewing will complete the work of binding the plates into the book.

(d) Plates made of cartridge/card need two paper/ linen guard—one on the front and one of the back.

(e) If a book is made entirely of plates, a decision must be made as to how many plates are going to be taken to make up each section. This also applies to single sheets of printed matter. Each section must be arranged in the appropriate pairs of leaves and guarded in the usual way, but where the leaves are thick hinge there as in (a) In dealing with books of single leaves a little thought must be given to the nature and purpose of the book. Guarding it may causes for two, much swell in the back, and it is better to laminate both sides of the leaves.

QUESTIONS FOR DISCUSSION

1. What is guard?
2. What are the guarding rules?
3. The sewing thread must always pass through.
4. What is stitch hole? How will it be filled up?
5. How much width of guard will be needed in case of single leave?
6. What is quarter section? How will it be guarded?
7. How will you tear/cut the thin hand-made paper/bond paper for preparation of guard?

11

Throwing out Maps, Diagrams Inlaying

REQUIRED MATERIAL

- Nepalese hand-made paper
- Hand-made paper
- Tissue paper
- Lawan cloth/jaconet
- Wooden table (3 ft by 5 ft)
- Adhesive
- Processed Tamarind seed powder
- Jebanjor 10 : 0.5
- Methyl cellulose, etc.

THROWING OUT MAPS AND DIAGRAMS

Maps, pliograms and illustrations are included in the text of a book, which is very convenient for the reader if these are **"Thrown out"**. This means that it is possible to bind the map into the book so that it can be opened out beyond the pages, and remain in constant view during the reading proceeds. The guard to which the diagram is attached must be as wide as the pages of the book, and when this sewn in, the joint where the map is folded will then be somewhat inside the fore-edge. This will prevent the cutting of the map when the edge is trimmed. Usually such maps or diagrams are placed at the end of the book, as shown in the diagram. In case of one or two folds may be in place of the books, where hand-made paper guard should be used. When the map is closed its total thickness must be noted, and sufficient ordinary folded guards paved inside each other to level up the thickness at the back of the book. If this is not properly done the book will not close satisfactorily.

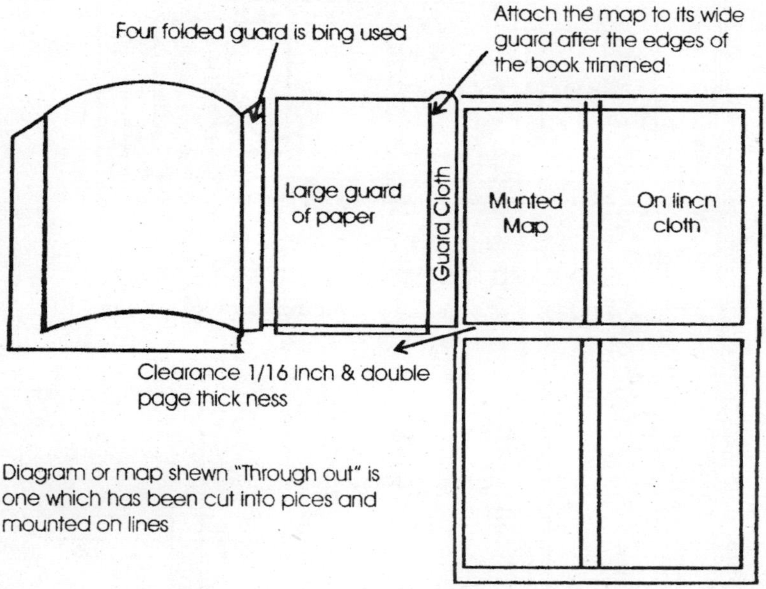

Fig. 11.1

If the map and illustration is small, i.e., one fold only tissue paper lamination can permit, using guard at the joint and the gutter margine. It will be folded 1/8 inch less than a book size. If the object is two or three folds one Nepalese hand-made paper (acid free) can be used as guard which turn in upward from back fold so as to adjust the level of thickness. Stitch will run at the centre of the back fold (Fig. 11.1).

If the map or illustration is a large one with several folds, it will be necessary to mount it on fine mesh cloth/linen (acid free unbleached) called *Jaconet.* A large piece lawn cloth about 1.5 meters length and

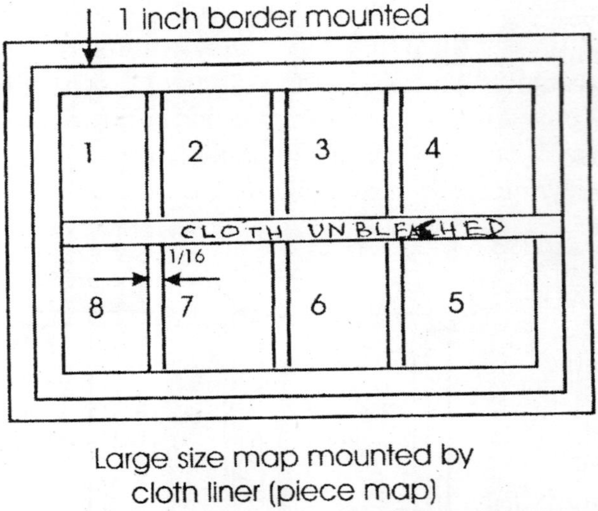

Fig. 11.2: Large size map mounted by cloth linen (piece by piece map)

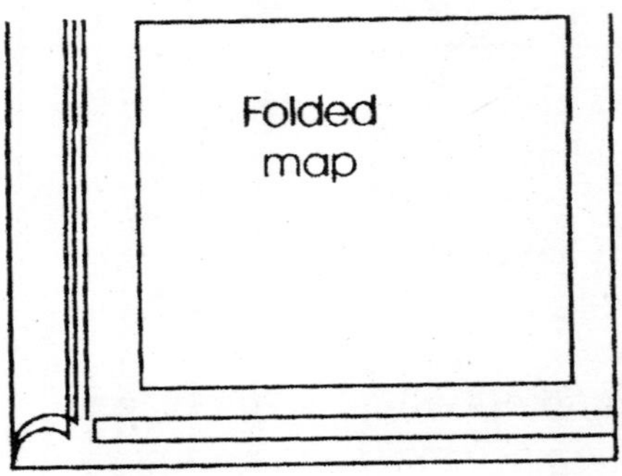

Fig. 11.3: Sufficient guards are inserted to equalise the thickness of the folded map.

one meter breath (Fig. 11.2) enough for the whole map is wetted slightly. It is placed on a flat wooden table which is board pinned down all around the edges of course. It has number 1 to 8 pieces during pulling the map. Paste the map in the back with thin paste, lay it keeping 1/32 inch clearance on the end rub it well down under clean paper. In order to spread the paste evenly, first heavy pressure on the paste brush is exerted then decrease the pressure gradually on the brush. Last of all the brush is merely, runing over the back side of the map very lightly. Now the pasting is evenly completed. 3/4 inches hand-made paper border over the map is set up for easy handling of map when dry, the map is trimmed in case of individual map Fig. 11.2. In case of Fig. 11.1 map is folded and guarded to the whole page guard. Cautions may be taken which pasting these pieces to spend approximately the same time on each. This will avoid uneven stretching of the pieces which makes it difficult to get the "Joints" straight all over the map. In case of old book, before finally tightening in the cutting press, to insert narrow strip of card such as straw board, down to the edge of the map and of the same thickness as its folds. They can forward a little above the level of the pages and be cut as the edge is trimmed.

INLAYING

Now and then small size leaf and plate observed in the large volume of an old book. That object is placed on a durable paper which is same size and colour of book page, and its corners make ornamental is called *inlaying.* A piece of hand-made paper is prepared as tea colour (deep tea liqueur) and trimmed it same size of book page. The small leaf/plate is then laid upon the large one in such a position as shown in below figure. To make it ornamental album corner may be set at the four corners or mark the corners of the smaller sheet with bone folder and remove it. Now mark again about 1/8 inch inside the first marks, and trimmed it rectangle formed by these later points. Turn the plate over on a sheet of glass, and very carefully *pare* the edges all round with a very sharp knife. Do the same with the upper edges of the frame. Both pared edges should there be pasted and the leaf to be inlaid placed in position on the first folder marks. Rub gently down under a sheet of clean paper/cotton swal, and put under light pressure until dry. The new page is then guarded into the book in the usual ways.

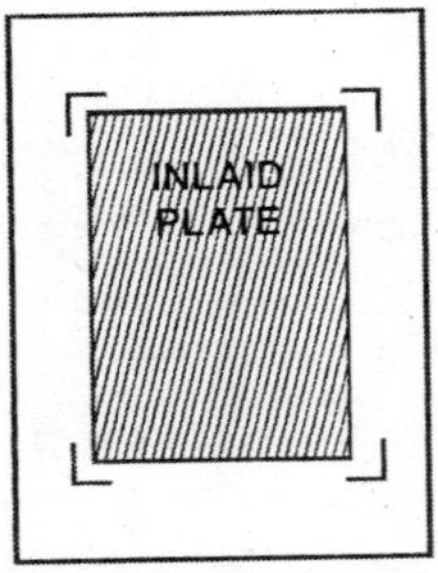

Folder Marks
Shewing size of
Plate to be inlaid

Fig. 11.4

QUESTIONS FOR DISCUSSION

1. What is thrown out?
2. How many folder map can be accommodated inside book?
3. What kind of cloth or hand-made paper will be used in case of large or medium size maps?
4. What type of paper will be setup at the border of medium size map?
5. Discuss about the precaution will be taken of an old book before tightening of cutting machine.
6. Define inlaying.

12

Inner Hinges

There are two types of inner hinges first one attached to the first and last signature (sewing) of a book and second one to which the endsheet sections are attached after the book is sewn. Several binders take credit for the development of the new technique. It replaces or is an alternative to the traditional, older technique of tipping (pasting or gluing a narrow area) the endsheet sections directly to the first and last pages of the book.

These hinges have several advantages over the older method. They permit the first few pages of the book, both back and front to open more freely, the front hinge eliminates the riding up of the first (or last) page of the book when it is opened, which invariably happens when the earlier technique is used, and most important, those remove all strain from the first and last pages of the book.

MATERIALS REQUIRED

Napalese tissue strong and thick (cream colour) or unbleached mark in cloth or hand-made paper (white) is good for white book pages. Strips ¾ inches wide, ½ inch longer than spine of book (grain direction with length).

- Wax paper 4 pieces
- Glass top table 3 ft. by 5 ft.
- Stone block or brick
- Mixture Tamarind seed paste and synthetic adhesive, Jebanjor 10 : 1

One hinge is attached to the last page of the first signature of the book, the other to the first page of the last signature. Lay the first signature face down with the folded edge resting on a glass top table and the last page of the first signature will be up, or exposed. Place a second strip of paper the entire length of the book page 1/8 inch from the fold. Apply paste to the area. Place the signature on a glass top and lay 1 edge of the hinge on the pasted area, placing it so that both ends of the tissue extend beyond the top and bottom of the page. Cover with a strip of wax paper and weight down with the stone/brick. Repeat this process on the last signature.

This time the last page of the book will be on glass top and then the first page of the last signature will be face up leave under the weight of Brick/Stone for about 15 minutes or until dry. When dry, fold the hinges arround the folds of the signature and leave these free meaning that this portion of the hinge is to have no adhesive applied to it at this time. When dry, cut the hinge even with the top and bottom of the signature and fold it flat onto the first or last page of the signature. Run the sewing at the centre of the cloth/ tissue ¾ inches strip first and last section which is attached with spine of the book. This signature is shown in the Fig. 12.1.

Sunken cord is a method of binding. In order to execute this method two places sewing is done in the spine of the book (Fig. 12.1). Next place the sunken

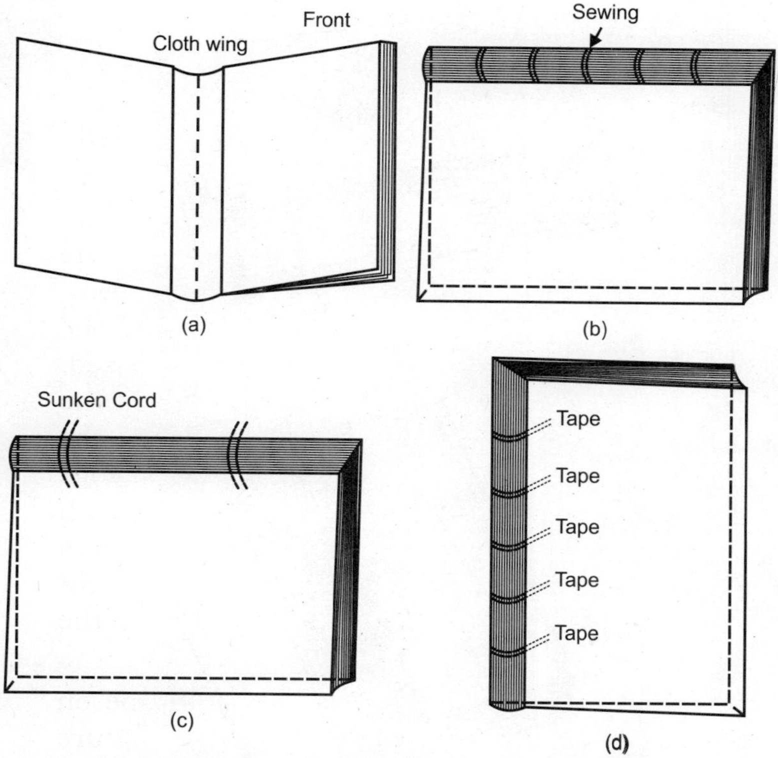

Fig. 12.1. Large size map mounted by cloth linen (piece by piece map)

cord hinge in the groove/hole which is prepared by sewing. Now start the lypeta section stitch along with cord, so that cord hinge cannot move both sides, leave 1½ inches cord both the sides which is shown in Fig. 12 (c). Then place D.B. Board both sides front and back where two holes are inside the boards to set up the cord hinge are inserted as shown in Fig. 12.1(d).

There is another type of hinge which is called tape hinge. It is made of ½ inch tape which is set up on the plane spine. These three tape hinges are attached with sectional lypeta stitch as shown in figure. These tapes are fixed and cannot move both sides. They can

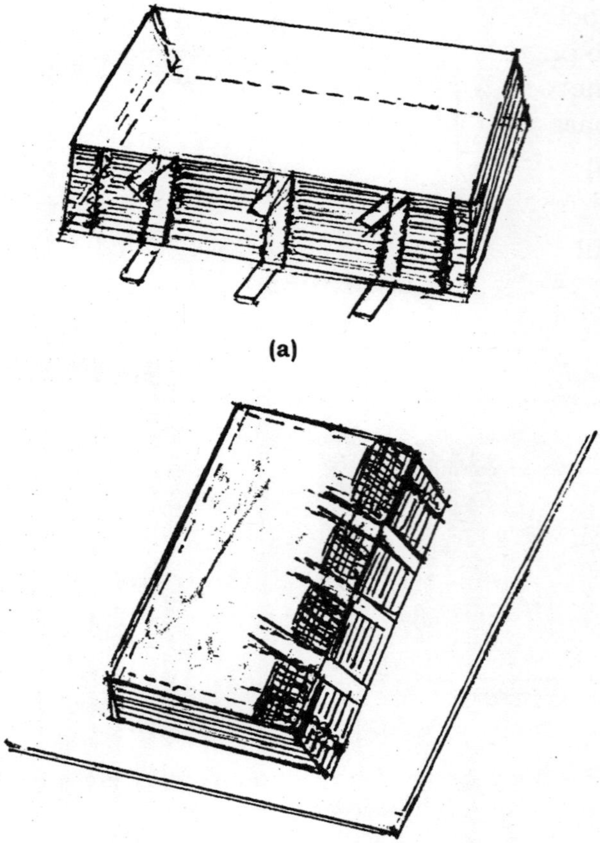

(b)

Fig. 12.2

protrude 1½ inches both the sides which is pasted inside the D.B. board. It is a very common easy method of inner hinge than the sunken cord hinge.

Nowadays this type of hinge is used in the National Library, Kolkata, the Asiatic Society, Kolkata, besides commercial binding. It is called *special binding of manuscript.*

Strengthening of crumble vellum leaves Vellum is an ideal writing material in ancient time. It is apt to cockle if exposed to dampness. But it is much difficult to preserve those vellum as these become cockled. The method is enunciated detailed under the following paragraphs :

(i) A book is taken to make it into pieces, and clean out the folds.

(ii) A sufficient number of sheets of clean white paper is taken, and double the number of sheets of clean blotting paper. The number of sheets of blotting paper required will be the same as the number of vellum sheets. Wet all the sheets of paper with a sponge and place a sheet of blotting on the bench. On this place a wet sheet of paper, then two pieces of blotting another wetted paper, and so on until the whole of the blotting and wetted papers have been interleaved.

Place the whole pile between clean pressing boards, and leave in a press for one and half hour. On removing from the press it will be found that the blotting paper is slightly but evenly dampened.

(iii) In order to make a pile of vellum and blotting paper interleaved, place vellum and damp blotting papers both alternatively. This will dampen and soften the vellum, and in this state the whole pile may be put into a press and left for 12 hours.

(iv) Next day all the pieces of damp blotting paper must be replaced by dry ones. This process must be repeated at intervals of 2 or 3 days until the vellum is perfectly dry.

(v) Any illustrated, miniature painting picture and other forms of painted decoration found on the pages that may be carefully covered with waxed paper or cellophone to prevent damage from the damp blotting paper. The pressure on the vellum will less, just for keep the sheets straight. High humidity, temperature and thickness are the factors of vellum deterioration. The author has never seen damaged vellum in the National Library, Kolkata which needs conservation, because of the ideal storage area. *Vellum binding will be discussed in 19th chapter.*

PRESSING

It is a very important mechanism with a view to make transparency of laminated sheets. At least two time operations are required through this process for restoration. As a result of before sewing the section become "solid". In the first operation, laminated sheets are placed in the press, first light press is applied then heavy light press simultaneously for 6 hours. Next take out sections from the press and trimmed it, three sides fold it, since it is a double sheet lamination. Then collect the sections wise all the pages for second operation in the press. The arrangement of sections in the press should be alternatively spine and fore edge as shown in as a result same level will attained, there will be no difficulty in order to binding a book. At least three pressing boards a little larger than the book and hand-made paper are required. Place one of the pressing hard boards on the bench, and pick up the first three or four sections. Knock them up square at the head and back; and place in the centre of the board. Place blotting paper where newly printed colour pages. Take the next few sections, knock them up and place in the middle of the next hard board; but this time the opposite way round, *i.e.*, the backs of the sections facing in the opposite direction from the first lot. Half portion of the book pages set up another D.B. hardboard. The process is repeated until all the section have been arranged in the above, any way and third pressing board placed on top. Pressing boards at bottom and top must be hard and thick so that iron stain cannot evolve. It must be remembered that before any pressing takes place all guarding, interleaving and repairing must be thoroughly dry. Otherwise excess adhesive will squeez out in pressing and jamed the pages. In case of full tissue laminated pages, half dry condition should be placed in the press for 3 hours, for better bonding of adhesive and proper setting of tissue for which transparency increase at least 10% more and air gap in the laminated pages will come out at certain pressure. This is the practical experience in the National Library, Kolkata of the author.

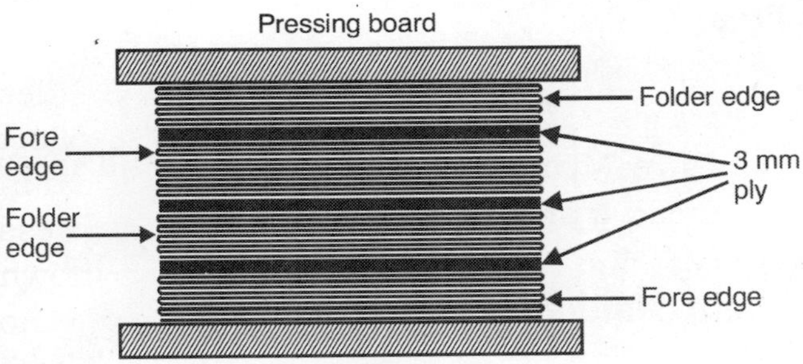

Fig. 12.3

QUESTIONS FOR DISCUSSION

1. How will you save the map from the cutting?
2. What is map's setting position in a re-binding book?
3. What is inlaying and inner hinge?
4. Describe the operation of hand sewing on raised cord of sunken cords?
5. What are factors of Vellum deterioration?
6. What procedure will you adapt in order to achieve proper transparency of lamination?

13

Hand Binding: End Sheet Section

MATERIALS REQUIRED

- Press board
- Brick or stone
- Fly leaves 2, folded
- Adhesive: Mixture of processed tamarind seed and synthetic adhesive (Jebanjor) 10 : 1
- Hinges, one it should be lan cloth, (unbleached cloth), leather, silk, jaconet, shatin, etc.
- Doublure waste paper, 2 clean sheets, leather or hand-made paper, cover material, Nepalese tissue paper, photo cartridge thin, bond paper, craft paper is used in lieu of marble coloured paper, glass top table or wax paper sheet
- Trimmer 18" which will work as trimmer and right angle triangle.

Long back, binders observed that on account of constant wear and tear first page and last page of a document/book dragging away are damaged. In order to prevent the same, damage end sheet was replaced by new one. The introduction of end sheet various methods were tried as attaching end sheets to the book, but the one which has been most successfully accepted is the end sheet are sewn on. These are composed of the fly leaves, end leaves, hinges and protection sheets. The fly leave should match as early as possible in both colour and texture paper on which the book is printed. The end leaves should be permanent paper, *i.e.*, hand-made paper, Nepalese tissue or photo cartridge, Board paper should be used as craft paper. These papers are acid free. Marble paper is being used as a board paper and another which is for beautiful, decorative and ornamental binding. Since binding is an art, it is known that coloured marble paper is acidic in nature, because, dye is acid base which is used during the manufacturing of colour paper. The hinges are unbleached cloth/lan cloth, leather, shatin, silk, etc.

The paper used should be permanent and durable, and a cartridge paper between 18 kg and 23 kg to the ream gives about the right thickness. 'Offset cartridge' used in lithography is a most satisfying paper to have, as it is usually 'double-faced', *i.e.*, both sides are alike in appearance and texture. A knife handle must always be at hand in the preparation of endpapers in order that good sharp creases may be ruled.

The advantage of these sections is that these are incorporated in the sewing of the book. It is a stronger form of construction than that of edition binding. Cloth or leather hinges also add strength to the binding. Since those have come into general use during this century. These are not recommended for older works or in conservation work, unlike these were used in the original binding.

There are a number of ways preparing of these end leave section. The method described here is simply constructed practical and durable.

Cutting the Material: Paper should be cut

according to grain direction runs parallel with the vertical measurement of the book. Cut the hand-made paper as folded fly leave, craft paper as board paper and protected sheets approximately ½ inch larger than the book page in both length and breadth. The hinges should be ½ inch larger than book spine and breath should be 1½ inches, waste paper strips must be bond paper, 1 inch longer than books spine and 1½ inches breath.

Assembling the Sections: Place the folded edges of the fly leaves—on at a time—on a strip/lining of the waste paper or doublure. Lay a second strip of paper on the fly leaf 1/8 inch in from folded edge, pasted the mixture adhesive to the area. Remove the strip of the paper from the top; transfer the fly leaves from the wastepaper to a strip of the wax paper from the top, lay 1 edge of the craft paper (colour paper) right side—if the sides differ, face up—on the pasted area [Fig 13.1(a)]. Cover the area where the two pages are attached with wax paper and weight down with the press board and brick until dry (about 25 minutes). Repeat the process with the second fly leaf. For drying, it can be placed on the top of the first one, if the two pages are separated by wax paper, and weighted with the same board and brick. When dry, place the straight edge along the folded edge of the fly leaf, and with the knife's handle fold the craft paper sheet around the fly leaf [Fig. 13.1 (b)]. The two additional craft papers are put aside to be used as board papers when needed hinges. Both the hinges are connected to the sections using the same pasting procedure as above. The area to be pasted is the 1/4 inch of craft paper that is exposed at the book side, of the section. One edge of the hinge should be laid on the pasted area with the right side of the material facing down. Weight down as previously described, and when dry, fold the hinge around the folded edge of the section. When folded, the right side of the material will be facing the right side of the craft paper end leaf. [Fig. 13.1 (c)].

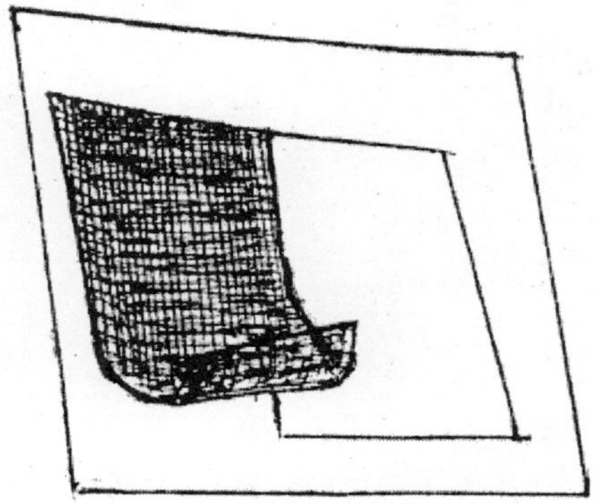

(a)

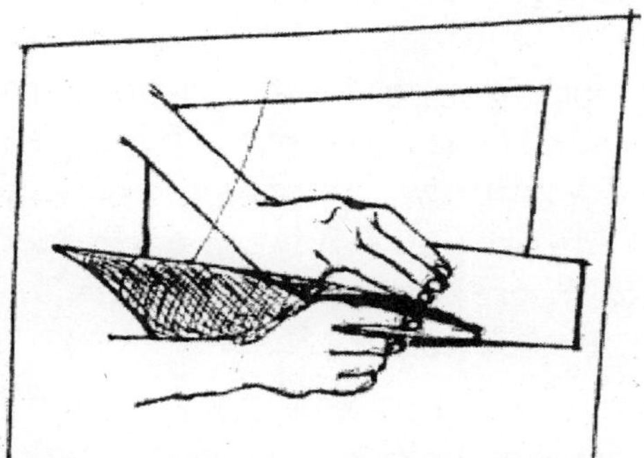

(b)

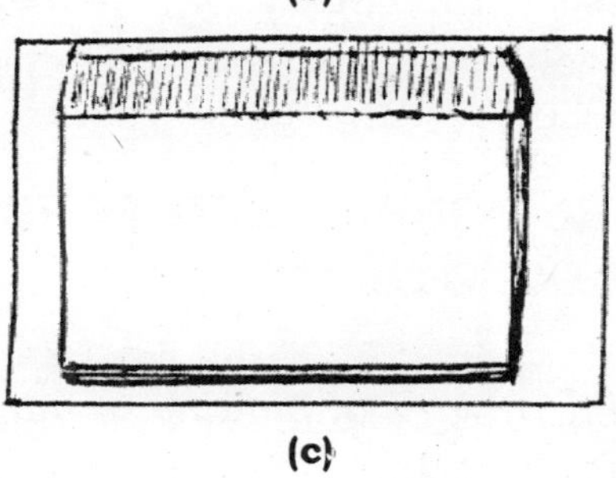

(c)

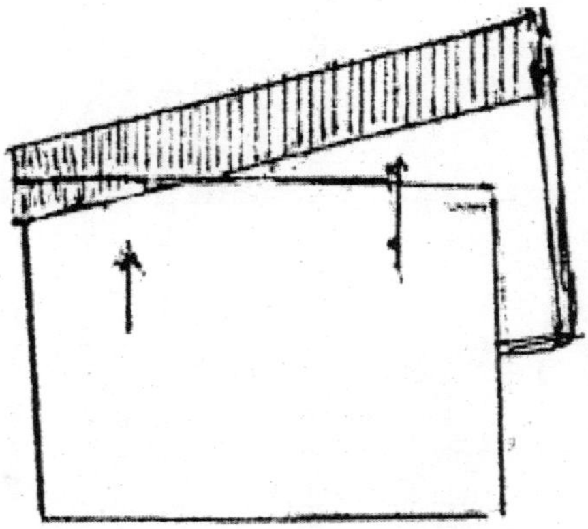

(d)

Fig. 13.1

Protection Sheets: Insert one protection sheet between the Craft Paper end leaf and hinge of each section [Fig. 13.1 (d)]. Secure in position with two short strips of masking tape. Pressing, place the prepared end leave sections between press board and put in the press for a few minutes, screwing the press down firmly. These sections are now ready to be trimmed to the size of the book. There are several reasons to be little bit larger than book size.

The book may not be a true rectangular; some of the materials may have slipped a bit in the process of attaching those to each other. The measurements may not have entirely accurate and when trimmed to the exact size as a unit, it makes for neater work.

THE "W" OR DOUBLE END PAPER LIBRARY STYLE WITH CLOTH JOINT

Endsheet is an important part of binding. It is known as *Library style of binding of manuscripts.* The books are for reader service therefore, need a considerable amount of protection from wear and tear.

Such as those are to be found in the National Library, Kolkata. The material required for this type are as follows:

(a) Waste paper (doublure), 1" wide photo cartridge, bond paper, every sheet is a little bit larger than book's spine.

(b) Two sheets craft paper which attached with board.

(c) Two fold four sheets bond paper thin which remain just on the book page.

(d) Two fold four sheets hand-made paper/cartridge/ Nepalese tissue paper.

(e) Paste/glue tamarind seed paste Jebanjor. (as insecticide) 10 : 1.

Take a 3/4 inches width waste paper (bond paper) strip (a) and pasted it all over thoroughly keeping on the glass top table. Place a craft paper (b) over, ½ portion from left side of waste paper and joint/coincide another ½ portion which is folded (two sheets) bond paper (c) on the right side of the waste sheet. Turn the whole over and rub the waste sheet down the thoroughly under a sheet of clean paper until paste is set up (d). Now take a lawn cloth hinge 1 inch width (e) which is pasted all over thoroughly keeping, on the glass top table. Lace the pasted cloth hinge on the joint of craft paper and folded edge bond paper. Rub with slight pressure over the cloth joint when the joint is dry. Take 2 sheets hand-made paper/photo cartridge/ Nepalese tissue which is available with the binders. Pasted all over thoroughly left side of craft paper and along with 1/3 portion cloth hinge from the left side. (f) Next pasted upper sheet right side thin bond paper all over thoroughly along with 1/3 portion cloth hinge right side. Then lay down one sheet and made paper/ photo cartridge over the pasted area both cloth and bond paper covering 1/3 portion from right side cloth hinge keeping gap 1/3 portion in the middle (g) Turn the whole set over and rub the cloth down thoroughly under a sheet of clean waste until the glue is set. One end of hand-made paper placed over the craft paper which is attached with board on the left side. Fold the two sides over so that the cloth is inside a crease the cloth well with folder. It will be seen that crease is middle of the gap 1/3 portion cloth hinge where signature will be made. Let it dry and trimming successively.

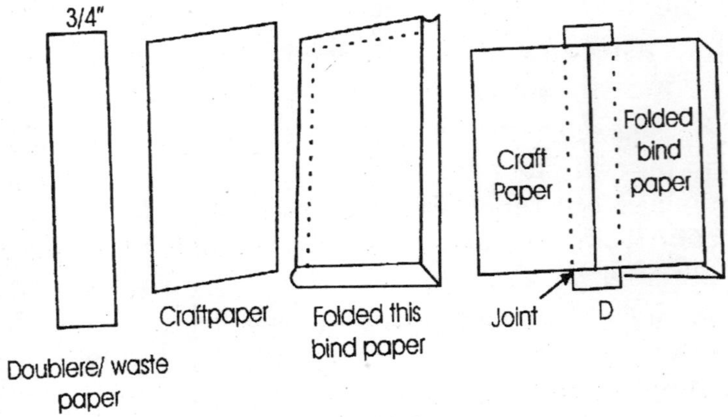

Fig. 13.2

THE "V" END PAPER WITH CLOTH JOINT

It is a very easy commercial method "V" shape single end sheet. Take a thin bond paper folded sheet (two sheets) and creased it at the middle with bond folder/knife's handle. The folded bond paper is a little bit larger in dimension than book size.

Now take a one inch width lawn cloth strip which is a little bit longer than spine of the book. Kipping it on the glass top table pasted all over uniformly. The pasted lawn cloth is attached inside in the middle of the folded sheet. Care should be taken oozing of

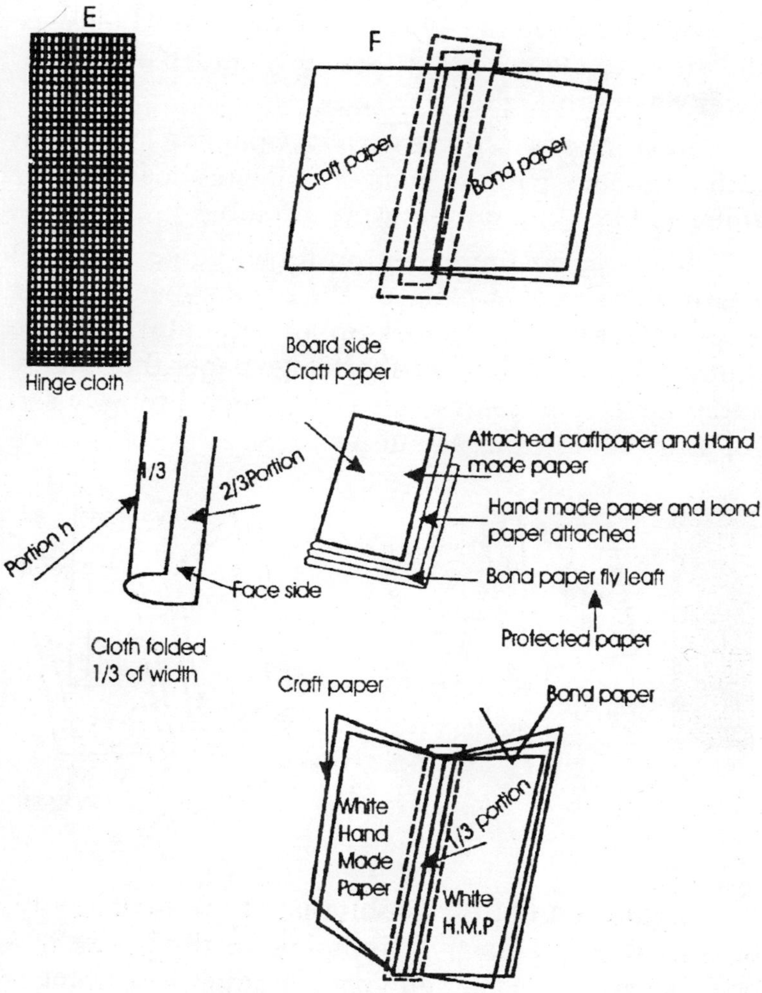

This is called five sheets end leave.

Above material and method are for one endleave only two such endsheets will be required.

(a) Craft paper or board paper

(b) Hand-made paper/photo cartridge

(c) Hand-made paper/photo cartridge

(d) Next bond paper (thin)

(e) Thin bond paper (fly leave)

adhesive does not take place. Turn over the whole over and rub the cloth down thoroughly under a sheet of clean waste until glue is set.

Next take two sheets cartridge paper a little bit in both dimensions of the book size. Paste those all over uniformly keeping on the glass top table.

Keeping on the glass top table, paste those all over uniformly. Now place on the bond paper covering from left side 1/3 portion of the cloth hinge simultaneously rub on the cartridge paper thoroughly under a sheet of clean waste until glue is properly set. Let it dry and trimming successively.

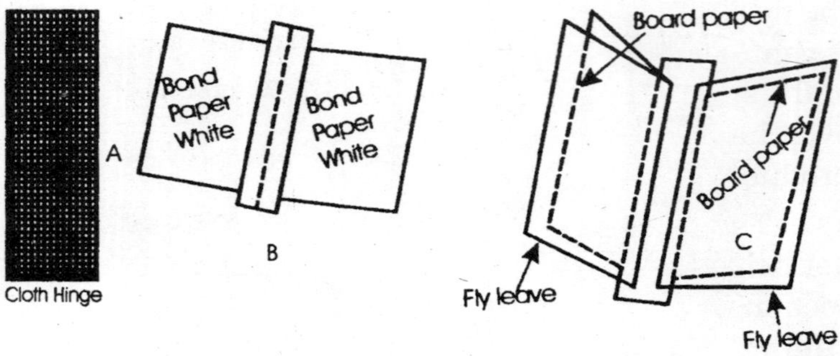

Fig. 13.3

Leather and Silk Doublures: The term doublure, broadly defined, means the lining on the inside of a book cover. Mainly in hand book binding, this lining is not referred to as a doublure unless it is made of leather or vellum that has been pared or pointed or of a silk fibre. The use of these material can be confined to the board, in which case the end leaf would be paper and the hinge would be made of the material that had been selected for the covering material. The techniques in their fabrication are the same as those previously describe V and W shape end leave. If the end leaves are to be Vellum of these can be treated in the same fashion as described for a craft/bond paper.

Where leather is to be used as end leaves, it will require over all thining and should not be attached in the end sheet section until after the edges of the book have been cut—if those are to be cut—but before the edges are gitted. The edges of the leather should be pared very thin. First, cut the piece of leather slightly larger in both dimensions than the fly leave (about 1/8 both sides) then pare the edges. Attatched the leather strongly to the first fly leaf of the front end sheet section and to the last fly leaf of the back end sheet section by applying tamarind seed paste to both the leather and the fly leave. Place this between clean pulp boards and weighted down until dry. Then, using a sharp knife and a straight edge, carefuly, cut away any leather that over hangs the edges of the fly leave. This should produce an even, clean edge.

The silk end leave is similar with leather, should not be contained into one substance in the end sheet section until all cutting of the edges is done and before **gilding**. The raw edges of silk are likely to wear off by rubbing in a short time, producing any thing but graceful appearance, which is the primary reason for it use. To eliminate any raw edges, these should all be turned in, this is done over a sheet of paper. Cut 2 pieces of paper (the same paper used for the fly leaves is good) the size of the fly leaves less the estimated thickness of the silk. In both length and width. Two thickness of the silk have to be reckoned with. The best way to arrive at the proper amount by which these sheets should be reduced in size is to make up a small sample. It is dependent on something else entirely on the thickness of the material selected. Once these sheets are cut to proper size and the material has been ironed—if it was wrinkled or creased—cut the material 1 inch larger in both dimensions length to breath than the sheet of paper. Lay the material, right side facedown, on a smooth clean surface, place the sheet of paper on the material so that 1/2 inch of the material extends beyond the edges of the paper on all 4 sides. Weighted the paper down so that it will not shift, and cut the corners to make neat corners some of the materials at these points is cut away. The cut is slightly curved and it is important to leave at the right angle of the board slightly more cloth than the thickness of the board. So when the material is folded around the paper, the cloth will come together as a marginal corner and there will be no surplus to make unsightly bumps.

Apply paste to about 1/4 inch of each edge of the paper top and bottom, then the sides and turn the cloth over the edge of the paper on the pasted area. Care should be taken to keep the cloth smooth, while at the same time not pulling it to the extent that it buckles the paper. When all edges are turned, place between pulpboard and weighted down until dry. These are then attached to the first and last fly leaves. First check to be sure that those are exactly the size and shape of fly leaves. If those are slip a piece of wax paper. If those are slip a piece of wax paper under the first fly leave in the fold, in other words and put a line of mixture about 1/8 inch wide on all 3 edges and in the spine area, lay the silk **doublure** in position on the fly leaf, checking it carefully to be sure that all edges are properly lined up. Cover with pulp board and pressure weight down until dry.

ENDSHEET VARIATION

There are so many variations of endsheet beside V style single and W style double sheet end leave which are described below. When craft paper (colour paper) endleave and board paper are not required, simply eliminate them and attach the hinges directly to the folded edge of the fly leaves. Lay aside 2 pieces of the paper chosen for the fly leave for the board papers. A third fly leaf can be added by using a single sheet of paper and attaching it to the folded sheet.

Traditionally, the end leaves and board papers are made from the same sheet of paper. In case where neither cloth nor leather hinges are appropriate or desirable, the hinges can be made of the same paper selected for the end leaves and board papers. A hinge made from some chosely woven fabric such as jaconet or linen should be attached as a reinforcement to the paper.

This same effect can be obtained by making the endleaves and board papers a folded sheet instead of 2 single sheets. In this case, the folded edge is attached to the folded edge of the fly leaves and the whole folded around the fly leaves.

If the book is not slightly square, or crooked its covers, the board papers will not be properly centered, and if the board papers stretch when those are pasted and those are likely to be too long on the fore edge and protrude beyond the book pages. These problems can be remedied by careful trimming.

If a folded sheet is used in either visible joint binding the board paper should be made 1/4 inch wider than the other sheet that make up the end sheet section. This must be taken into consideration in the cutting of these section to size. This can be done by rolling those back free of the cutting action. When either paper hinges or folded sheets are used care should be taken in selecting a paper that is strong enough to stand the wear that it will receive in the opening and closing of the book. For this purpose hand-made paper/ Nepalese hand-made paper is the best which has discussed earlier.

Fig. 13.4. Sewing Machine

For bindings to be covered with leather, it is customary to make the hinges of the same leather. These section are made up in the same way as previously described with 2 exceptions. The leather should be pared or thinned and the protections sheets are attached solidly to the 1/8 inch area of the materials that were pasted on the fly leaves and are folded around the entire section. This 1/8 inch of the protection sheet remains permanently in the book. For this reason, these sheets should be a good grade of medium weight bond paper, thin hand made paper, from conservation point of view it should be acid free.

It is advisable to test an unfamiliar fabric before use. If the adhesive comes through the material and stains it, try to use a little less adhesive or let it set a little longer before attaching the cloth.

QUESTIONS FOR DISCUSSION

1. What is utility of endleaf?
2. How many types of main end sheet, what are they?
3. What is mean by doublure?
4. What is satisfactory end sheet?
5. What category of paper is fit for end leaf?
6. What are normal variation of end leaf?
7. What are difference between fly leaves and end leaves?

14
Trimming

MATERIALS NEEDED

- Trimmer 14 inches, 18 inches
- Cuttting machine (guillotine)
- Finishing press/*putuly kath* (Bengali)
- Sand paper 80, 120 number.
- Cloth
- Pulp board

Repair and rehabilitation is an operational method, therefore, addition and alteration of acidic unwritten a little fit blank portion omission is permitted for prosperity of the cultural heritage. There are many process of edge treatment which are depend on the edges margine and brittleness of document : Maximum two folds at a time map and chart which are 1/4 inch small in size than book can be cut with the trimmer. The books are not cut when original bound and volume with deckled edges. Eraser should be used where cutting for alteration is not possible and that is free of abrasive material. A rare book needs three times edge treatment first two times trimming with trimmer and third cutting by cutting machine use are given below:

(a) Pulling by section an old book ¼ inch trimming

from the spine is required in order to get straight edge. This straight edge will facilitate tissue lamination.

(b) Drying up and pressing the laminated pages need trimming with trimmer.

(c) Final cutting with cutting machine has been done smoothly after stitching the book attached with prepared endsheet.

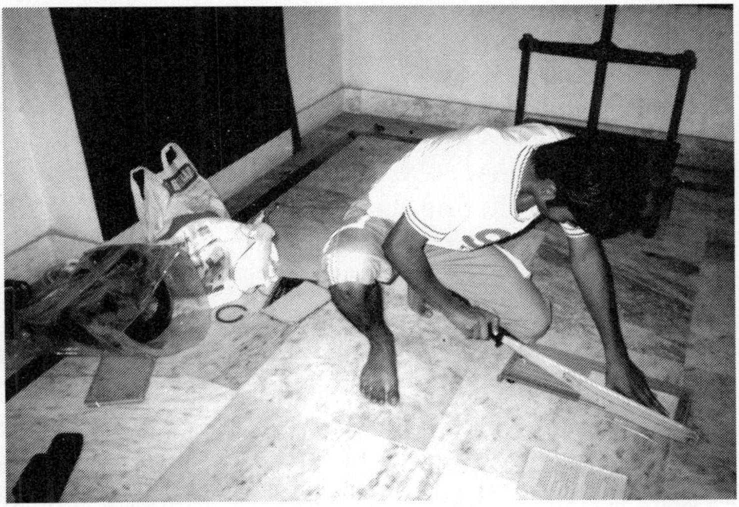

Fig. 14.1: Trimmer

Sanding the Edge: Sanding is another method of cleaning up the edges when cutting does not permit on account of narrow margin or too brittle book and unwanted coloured edges. Sanding can be done more quickly before the book is taken apart or pulled.

Place the book in any kind of finishing press or *putuly kath* (Bengali) which is suitable for rubbing with sand papers. Start the sanding with a 80 number graner paper (medium-grit sand paper) and finish with very fine paper such as 120 number graner.

Wrap a piece of paper arround a small, smooth block of wood and keep it flat or horizontal while in motion on the head and tail. Sand these 2 edges from spine to fore edge, not across the book from front to back, if the book is still in its rounded state and the fore edge. Concave, but results can be obtained by wrapping the sand paper around a rounded object that can be handled easily and that is large or small enough to fit into the concavity of the fore edge. Another simple method is this that holding the object by left hand finger sanding is done easily.

Cutting on Guillotine: Nowadays trimming is done with a guillotine cutter. The National Library, Kolkata, Posseses Polar, mark German made and Indian made guillotine cutting machine. Two to four normal sizes books can be cut at a time. It is indigenous best efficient electrical operated board and book cutting machines. The most common method is to trim the books in the rectangular and then backing and rounding. The back edge is placed against the back guides to trim the fore edge, which is these placed against the side guide to trim the head and tail. Some operators prefer to keep the back against the guides for all cuts. The book should be placed against the back edge to avoid breaking pieces out of the folds. If the book has such sewing swell, it may be necessary to build up under the cutter clamp to compensate for the swell.

Check the knife, that it is held firmly in its safety position before cutting.

There is another cause of cutting edges besides clearing and smooth that acid gathers in the all edges due to air pollution. Therefore, two times successive 1/8 inch acid portion of edges can be trimmed for two times rebinding and 3rd and 4th time of an old book sanding can be done, only keeping with minimum margine. Mark the cutting point with a pencil. Short pages have a ragged edge, due to their lack of support. When the knife strikes unsupported pages, the pressure tends to bend them and tear off. A few isolated short pages, will cause no trouble. To get even pressure in the area to be cut, build the book up on both front and back to compensate for the swell in the spine area.

Place several pulp boards on both sides of the book, offsetting them about 1/4 inch is from the spine. Press down on the fore edge and check to see if its height is equal to that of the spine. The number of boards (or packing) required will depend on the extent of the swell. When this process is completed, remove the boards from the top of the book, place an additional piece of pulpboard under the entire book on the bottom, and put it into the guillotine, head against the guage. Adjust the guage to bring, the book into the position where the cutting point previously marked is just visible when the pressure bar is lowered. When properly positioned, raise the pressure bar and add the packing to the upper side of the book and cover the entire book with an additional piece of board. Hold the book firmly in position with one hand and tighten the pressure bar with the other. If the pressure pulls the head of the book away from the guage, raise the pressure bar, add more packing, and try again.

There is another precautionary point: The head of the book and photo cutting to be sure that it is at a right angle with the spine.

If the head is off-square and is placed solidly against the guage, the whole book will end up with uneven margin on the tail. If such in the case, place a right-angle triangle or square against the guage and line the spine of the book up against the right-angle triangle or square. This would mean that the head of the book would be touching the guage only partially or only one point. When everything seems in order, make the cut on the tail.

Remove the book and check the margin on the tail on a number of pages and to be sure that the space between the last time of printing and the bottom of the pages is the same from spine to fore edge. If the tail is having sufficient margin, the head can be cut the same procedure, i.e. at this moment the tail can rest strongly against the guage on the fore edge cut, the packing need not be so carefully positioned. It is sure that each piece of board is as long as the book, wider than the pressure bar from front to back, and the spine of the book is resting squarely against the guage.

QUESTIONS FOR DISCUSSION

1. How many times of an old book edges permits to trimming?
2. What are cleaning and smoothen process?
3. In what condition of an old book needs sanding/erasing?
4. How will you get rectangle or right angle triangle shape which needs cutting the book smoothly?
5. Where will you use trimmer, scissor, cutting machine and sanding?

15

Handbinding: Sewing

Kinds of Sewing

1. Folded sections or *Juse* (Bengali) *Tajma* (cloth)
2. Lypeta/overcasting and sewing (Bagha Petchi)
3. Direct stitch sewing

Tapes or Cord

1. Raised
2. Sunken
3. All-along
4. Two-on
5. Philadelphia patent-back guards.

Sewing Procedure

1. Sewing on tape
2. Sewing on cords
3. Sewing on double cords
4. Sewing a single signature book.
5. Stitching of single pages.

Sewing plays a very important role to constitute a book together of preserving and facilitated the readers service. There are three types of old book hand binding such as juse or folded section sewing, lypeta or overcasting and sewing (Bagha Patchi), stitch sewing.

All threads should be pulled firmly, trying to keep the tension on even of a book consists of several signatures or sections. The method of sewing is adapted according to condition of the book pages, in case of new book or laminated pages of old book, sewing is done in the centre folded section of each signature which is a continuous thread is called *juse sewing/ bradel*. Generally new books are sewn with machine but in case of rebinding of an old book lypeta or over casting and sewing (Bagha Patchi) is done section wise as because pages are individual. It is a tight back binding or a hollow back. The sections are held together by sewing around the tapes or sunken cord at the head and tail by the kettle stitches. These are chain stitches. The kettle stitch is ½" down in both to head and tail of the spine.

Stitch sewing is a tight back sewing loose leaf should be perforated with soa then use awls for threading the book. It is overcasted for smoothness the spine.

Loose leaf binders of the post variety provide stronger binding but they are not flexible and plastic and wire binding are more flexible but they do not provide strength and permanency. In case of journal binding, iron becomes rusted as a result pages get damage.

In hand sewing, the thread passes out through the centre fold of the signature at intervals and locks it to the signature below. The author observed that machine sewing of laminated folded sheets and new book are very first sewing process. Juse/folded section sewing through machine takes place 4 or 8 leaves at a section. Juse (Bengali) section sewing machine is available at the Baithakana Road, Kolkata, picture is shown thorough which sewing cost involved very less than hand binding. Hand binding is required for old book preservation.

Materials Required: Tone thread, nylon thread, tape, sunken cord, Tajma (unbleached cloth/markin cloth) 2–2½ inches wide 4 inches length (according to width of book), press board, small weight, triangle, linen tape unbleached, and paper strip.

Threads are tied on with the weaver's knot. Make a loop at one end of the thread that is to be tied on by crossing the end of the thread over the longer portion, while holding the end of the thread firmly, pull it back though the loop with the thumb and forefinger of the other hand (Fig. 15.1). Place the end of the thread that is attached to the book in the second loop made, slide the loop up close to the spine, and tighten the new thread, this should bring the thread attached to the book into the first loop made (Fig. 15.2). If properly done, the knot made at the joining will remain close to the spine. The weight of thread depends on the thickness of the section and of the paper along with the size of the book and its use. In general, books made up of signatures containing up to 8 leaves can safely be sewn with a medium-weight such as no 30/2 tone thread, and signature of 12 leaves or over with a heavier thread, no. 18/2 tone thread. This tone thread is using in the National Library, Kolkata for sewing the brittle old book improper heavy thread can produce excessive swell in the spine, which creates problem in the backing of the book. The quality of thread depends on the durability of binding. The general commercial sewing is juse sewing of folded section containing 4 or 8 leaves, where tajma is used as guard. Tajma is a cloth guard 2 × 4 inches width and length, unbleached cloth/ markin cloth covered over the spine. It is placed one inch inside from the head and tail both. It is called *philadelphia patent-back guards,* also known as *Franklin guard* in some area. This method is adapted on large volume or laminated pages that must be lie flat when those are open. Each signature is sewn to a cloth guard. One kind of guard is a folded strip of cloth and another is an accordian-folded strip, known respectively as *single guards* and *continuous guards.*

Guard-sewn books are hard to forward but they are durable as well as flexible. The sections may be sewn to the guard by hand, but a more uniform job is produced if they are sewn on the signer machine. The stitches should not run close enough to the head or tail that they will be cut when the book is trimmed. The last few stitches should be doubled and the thread ends pulled through and tied inside the guard to keep the stitches from reveling. In some cheaper classes of work the tying of the thread ends is eliminated and the stitches are secured by putting a line of glue on those inside the guard, but this is not so secured as tying the stitches. More detailed juse sewing process section with picture is given in the "Preservation of Documents".

In machine sewing, the thread passes out through the center fold of the signature at intervals and locks it to the signature below. The same is true of hand sewing which can be done on tapes, or on cords which may be raised above the level of the back of the book or flush with the back. Heavy books are sewn on tapes usually, and this is the best method for blank and other flat-opening books. It leaves the back of the book smooth enough to permit the use of either a light back or hollow back. In hand sewing on either tapes or cords. The thread passed through the centre fold of the signature, out the back, around the tape or cord and back inside the signature. Sometimes the thread passes through the tape instead of around it.

Sewing on raised cords may be done on either single or double cords. If double cords are used, they are placed side by side at intervals across the back of the book, and the sewing thread passes around each cord of the pair individually before it enters the back fold again.

It is an ornamental/decorative binding when books are sewn on raised cord. Raised bands are sometimes bound in canvas, but it is unfit for ornamental/decorative binding when books are sewn on raised cord. Raised bonds are sometimes bound in canvas, but it is unfit for ornamental large volume. Leather is only fit for ornamental raised band binding. The dressing material must be stretched to fit over the bands and it is easy to stretch leather but rather difficult to stretch any canvas covering material.

Sewing on Tapes: This type of sewing is suitable for case of Bradel bindings and for tight back, etc. when a smooth-spine is desired. Three tapes are sufficient for most 2 to 4 inches large volumes. For larger book, a good rule of thumb is to space the tapes about 1½–2 inches apart. These direction are for sewing on 3 tapes. Jog (tapping the material as an unit lightly against a clean, flat surface to get the pages or signatures lined up evenly) the book to the head and then the spine, place it flat on the press board with the head to the left. Put the weight on the fore edge and square the head and spine up against the triangle. Fold the strip of paper in half twice, length wise.

Lay the strip of paper against the spine of the book and mark on the spine the position on the folds. The middle tape is centered on the center mark and

Fig. 15.1

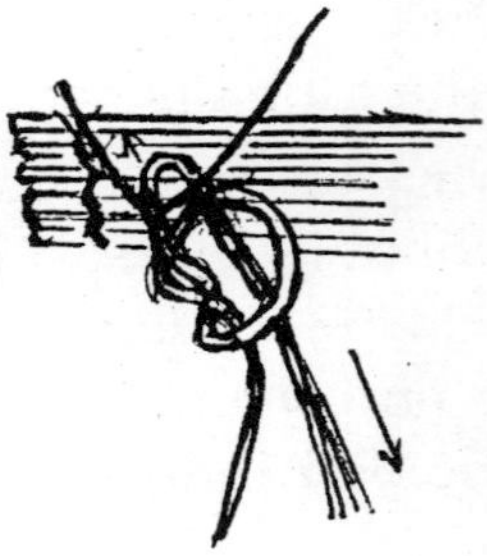

Fig. 15.2

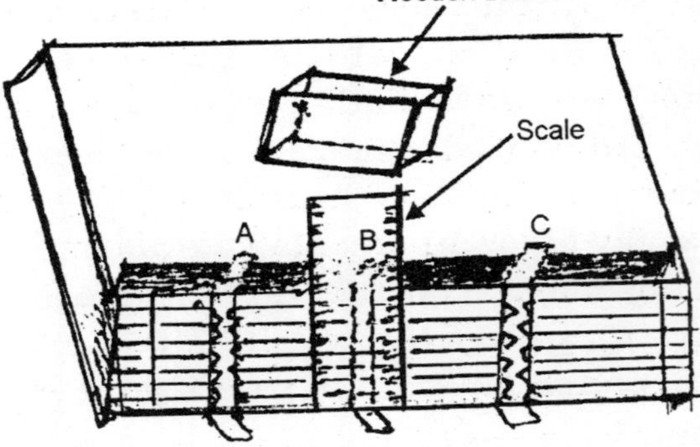

Fig. 15.3

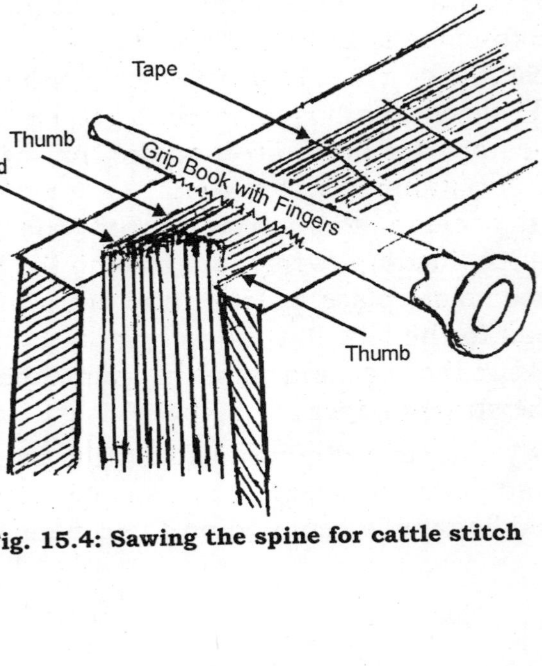

Fig. 15.4: Sawing the spine for cattle stitch

the other 2 tapes are positioned from the mark towards the head and tails, respectively. Mark the position of the tapes, making the spaces slightly wider than the width of the tape used. Draw lines across the spine at the marks using the scale/triangle to keep those straight and neat mark the kettle stitches at both head and tail in the same manner. These are generally marked about 1/4 inch inside from the head and tail, of course 1/12 inch trimming will be required from head and tail in case of old book, that they will not be endangered in the trimming (Fig. 15.3).

Sewing on Cords: The style of sewing most commonly used is on sunken, cords, which leaves the back of the book smooth. It is easier than sewing on raised bond or tapes, although it is considered to be not so strong. Sewing on sunken cords involves cutting grooves in the back of the book to allow the cords to set flush with the back and permits the use of a hollow back. Sometimes this style of binding is very stiff because of poor workmanship, such as saw cute (Fig. 15.4) that are so deep as to allow glue to enter between the leaves, the use of hard glue on the back of the book, and lining the book too stiffy.

Five cords or bands are the traditional number for large books and 4 bands are for octavos and smaller books. Five bands will divide the spine into 6 panels, and 4 bands will produce 5 panels. Before deciding on the number of bands, check the length of the title and author's name to be sure that the size of the planned panels will accommodate them. If title and name are too long to fit comfortably into the planed planes, reduce the number of raised bands or sew the book on tapes.

With a view to ascertain for 5 cords, cut a strip of paper the width of the spine and 1/2 inch longer than the book. The mark should be done after trimming the edges of the book. Mark 1/4 inch off at each end of the strip of the paper. The space between these marks indicates the length of the book. Divide the length of this strip into 6.

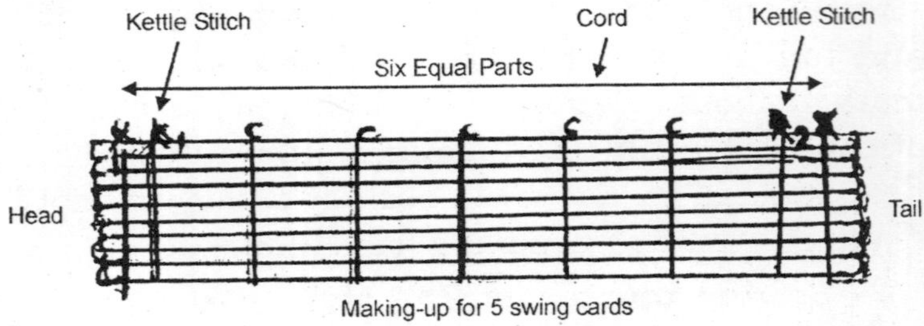

Fig. 15.5

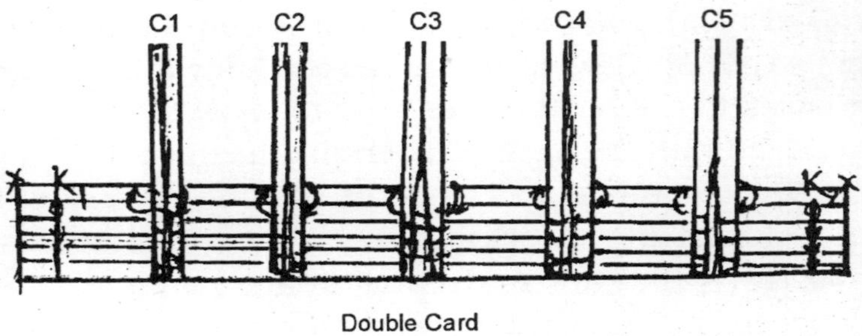

Fig. 15.6

Fig. 15.7

If the strip is 12 inches long, the gap between the bands will be approximately 2 inches, the gap between the last band and the tail of the book is, however, slightly larger than the space between the other bands.

Jog the book to the head and spine, square it up against one inch wide scale or triangle and place a weight on the fore edge to prevent shifting. It is

Fig. 15.8: Board setting on tape binding

especially important in this type of sewing that the head is evenly lined up and straight.

Lay the strip of paper against the spine of the book, allowing it to extend 1/4 inch beyond the book at each end. Lightly mark the position of the cords and the kettle stitches, using a scale, draw 1 line across the pine at each mark (Fig. 15.5). Alternately, these marks of cord placement can be done simply with the graduated scale within a short time.

Sewing on Double Cords: This style of sewing is adapted for a tight back binding. It is used in the case of larger volume bound with a tight back. The choice of cord depends on the size of the book and the effect wanted.

Start the sewing at one of the kettle stitches. Bring the needle out between the 2 cords: circle the near cord by bringing the thread back towards the kettle stitch: carry the thread between the cords and the outside of the signature to the far side of the second cord: circle this and take the thread back into the centre of the signature through the same hole between the cords (Figs. 15.6 and 15.7) and continue in this manner around the other cords, add the next signature and so on.

In an ordinary sewing where the stitches pass down the centre fold of the signature, two kinds of stitches are used. One is known as *all-along sewing*, in which the thread passes the full length of the centre fold of each signature and leaves the fold only to pass around the cord or tapes.

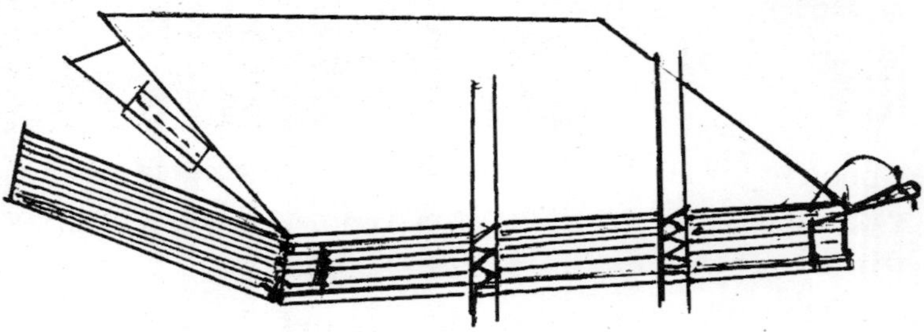

Fig. 15.9: Cord binding

Fig. 15.10: Tape Binding

Fig. 15.11: Cord binding

The other kind is known as *two-on sewing* which is used to reduce the sewing swell. In case where a book is made up of thin section—2 or 4 leaves—or when laminated or guarding of the folds has been extensive, it is often reduce the thread by using this method of sewing, in order to minimise the swell in the spine. It is not strong as "all along" sewing, but most cases it is preferable to avoid excessive swell. This same sewing technique is used in both cases. This method of sewing can be done on either tapes or raised cords. The first and last 5 or more signatures should be sewn all-along. In two-on, the first signature to be treated in this way are laid in position. The needle goes through at the kettle stitch, out on the near side of the first tape, the next signature is added, opened at the centre, and the needle inserted on the far side of the first tape, brought out on the near side of the second tape, carried down to the first of the 2 signatures and inserted on the far side of the second tape, brought out on the near side of the third tape, carried up to the second signature, and inserted on the far side of the third tape, and out of the kettle stitch (Fig. 15.8). The thread comes out at the kettle stitch mark on only one of these signatures, so the kettle stitch is made by going down to the last one made at each end. Since the sewing is alternating between 2 signatures and the centre of each has to be found several times.

Stitch Sewing a Single Signature Book: Two processes are given—one for individual a few sheets and other for a heavier signature. A piece of 18/2 tone thread is taken about 4 times length of the book.

In this case, instant endsheet section is prepared. The fly leaves and end papers are prepared of folded sheets. These are required for a hard cover canvas binding. 1 folded flyleaf, 1 folded endpaper, 1 folded unbleached cloth hinge, and 2 protection sheets. Cut all materials should be cut according to the size of the document as previous discussed. Hand-made paper should be used for endleaves.

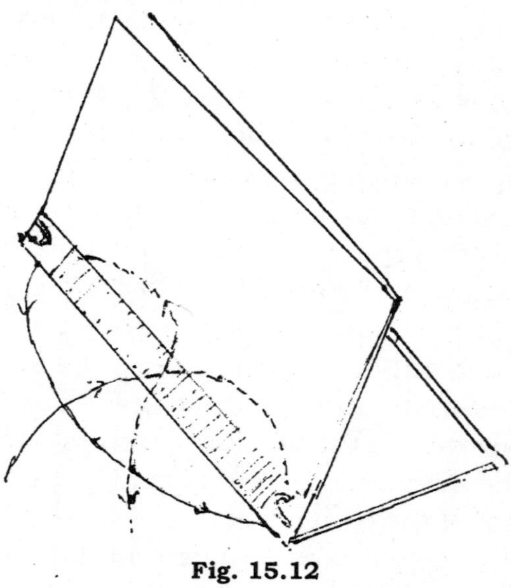

Fig. 15.12

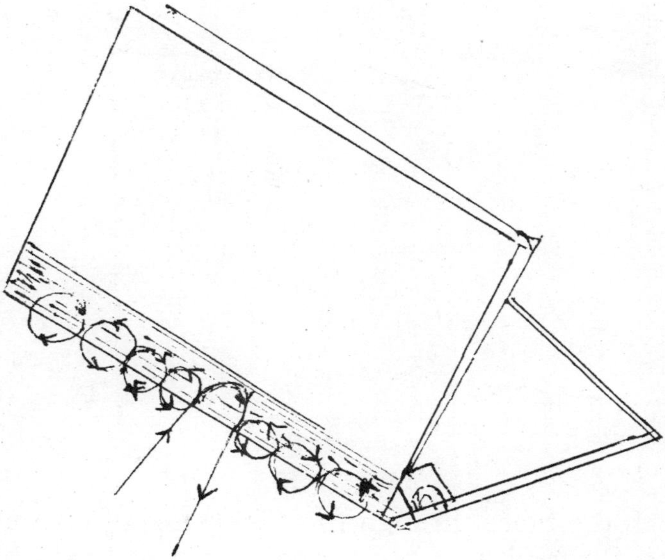

Fig. 15.13

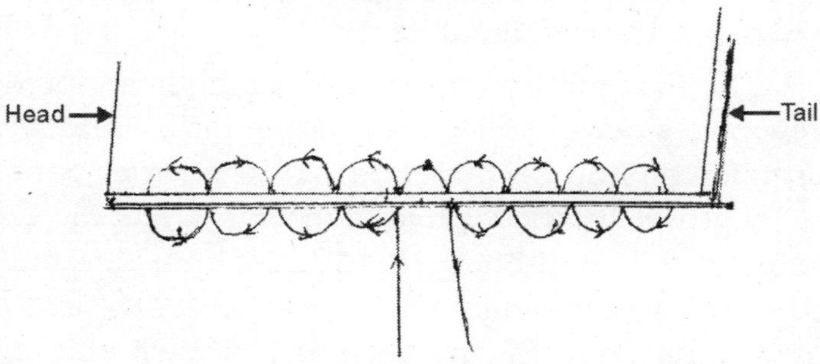

Fig. 15.14

The protection sheets are attached after the book is sewn, set up the other materials in position on the book and jog it to the head and spine open the book at the center by a folded strip of paper over the edges if one-half of the book at both head and tail, and secure with paper clips. It is required to prepunch the holes for sewing from inside of the centre fold. Asertain the location of the holes, after opening the book partially.

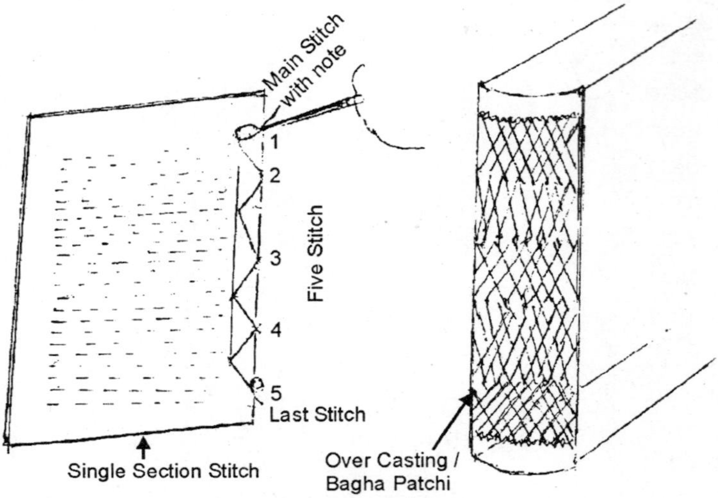

Fig. 15.15

Punch the holes through the centre fold of the entire book. Examine that the needle comes out exactly in the fold. This is important in a thicker book as it is easy to get the needle at centre.

The first method, butterfly sewing is adapted for a few pages sewings. Determine the location at which the holes should be punched, cut a strip of paper of the length of the book, fold it in half lengthwise, and make mark on it at both ends 1/2 inch inside from the end. Lay this strip against the inside centre fold and punch 3 holes, at the center and 1 at each end at the point where the strip was marked off. Start sewing on the outside at the center hole (Fig. 15.9). Bring the thread through to the inside center fold, leaving a free tail of thread about 3 inches long at this point. Carry the thread on the inside to the head of the book and take it out through the hole, carry it on the outside from the head to the tail. Go back into the inside of the book at the tail, back to the middle and out at the centre hole where the sewing was started. Tie the tail left at the beginning and the remaining thread together with a square knot after checking and to be sure that the thread is pulled tight all along. Cut the surplus threads back to about 1 inch in length. Trim the fore edges of the fly leaves and end leaves even with the book pages. Insert the protection sheets between the cloth hinge and the end leaf on both front and back of the book, and secure in position with tabs of marking tape.

A book only having a paper cover, the selected cover paper is cut and folded as fly leaf, wrapped arround the book, and sewn on along with the book. In this case, start and end the sewing on the inside of the book. This will prevent the knot from showing on the outside and also protect it from wire by rubbing. The significant thing is that the 2 threads to be securely tied together..

The second method, for a heavier book, differs from the first above only more holes are punched and used in the sewing. Cut a strip of paper the length of the book, mark it at both ends 1/2 inch in, mark off the space between these 2 points in part of about 1 inch. Lay the strip against the inside center fold and punch the holes as indicated by the marks. Start the sewing on the outside at the hole nearest the centre of the spine in length, being the thread into the inside, leaving a 3 inches tail, take it out at the next hole, moving in the direction of the head of the book, and back in at the next hole, and so on until the head of the book, it is reached (Fig. 15.10). Retrace the stitches, using the same holes, proceed to the tail of the book and return to the centre in the same manner. The last stitch made from the inside out probably will not come out on the spine at the point where the sewing was started, but 1 space away. Tie the 2 threads together and cut off the surplus.

Stitch Sewing of Single Page: Prepare the endsheet section as earlier. These directions are for a book or pages with sufficient margins so that these can be trimmed on the head, tail and fore edges after the book is sewn.

This method differs as follow cut 2 pieces of clean straw board according to size of the book pages. Place one on the top and one on the bottom. Jog the pages to head and spine, and weight down. Glue the spine lightly and set aside until the glue is dry.

If the book is maximum 3/4 inches thick. It can be sewn as a whole (*i.e.*, one section). If the book is more than the above thickness, it is required to sew into several sections and then sew these to tapes as earlier.

In case of this book, after the glue is dry, draw a line 1/8 to 1/4 inch in from the spine edge from head to tail along on both first and last pages of the book. The line is to be considered according to gutter margin of pages. One spring clamp can be fixed at the middle where awl (soa) will not operate the hole. Use an awl whose head will be pointed as well as needle's diameter. The drill holed with awl and hammer about 1¼ inches apart along the line. Prepare the last hole at both head and tail 3/4 inches in from the edge. The awl (must drive vertically so that it comes out on the opposite side on the line down. This drill can be done on wooden block, who will work setting on floor. Secondly to keep the surface of the table in order. Lay the area where the holes are to be made on several thickness of the heavy straw board.

18/2 tone thread, cut a piece about 4 times the length of the book. Start the sewing in the centre, length wise, and leave a 3 inches tail of thread. Carry the thread in a running stitch, using the prepunched holes, to the head of the book. Retrace the stitches, proceed to the tail, and back to the centre (Fig. 15.11). Tie the 2 threads together and cut off the surplus.

Sewing on Endsheet Section: Cut 2 tapes 3 inches longer than the thickness of the book. Number and space of tapes depend upon the thickness and length of the book, glued the spine of the book and set up the tapes. Do not glued the tapes. Prepunch the holes in the endsheet section to conform to the position of the tapes. Prepare the point of the cattle stitches which is fall in line with the outermost thread at both head and tail. Open the book 8 or 10 pages from the front sew through this in and out arround the tapes as if it has a folded signature. Place the endsheet section in proper place and sew it on in the usual manner.

Leave the usual 4 inches tail of thread at the beginning point, and when the endsheet section is sewn on, tie the 2 threads together. Then whole book is turned and repeat this step with the back end section. The endsheet sections are now attached directly to the first and last pages of the book. Open the front endsheet section; place a strip of paper on the fore edge side of the sewing; apply a small line of adhesive to this area, so that adhesive does not spread beyond the thread. Withdraw the strip and close the book.

Repeat this step to the back endsheet section: then weight the book down until dry. It is done to prevent the stitches from showing when the book is opened. Now the book is ready for cutting.

In case of thicken book, the above procedure is same, till the point of sewing. After the glue is dry, measure the thickness of the book and separate it into section of equal thickness 3/4 inches to 1/2 inch. Each section is then sewn as described above for a thin book.

These sections, alongwith the endsheet sections, are now sewn with tapes. The general procedure for sewing on tapes are followed with these exceptions. Sew each section to tapes about 3 or 4 times by roughly dividing the section into equal parts. The sections are attached to each other as the sewing progresses. Several paper strips and mixture will be needed. Lay a strip of paper on the fore edge side of the original sewing. Apply adhesive a thin line to this area covering the threads. Remove the paper and lay the next section in place, lining it up properly with the edge of the one just sewn. The endsheet sections are attached with mixture directly to the first and last pages of the book as described earlier for a thin book. Weight pressure down and when dry, reglue the spine. When this is dry, the book is ready to have the edges cut. Those pages are not wide enough, extend those with a guard strip. Attach these to the pages with about 1/4 inch tip-on, using adhesive.

Error Correction: If the thread tear, tie on a new thread, after remove the sewing back to the nearest tape, cord or kettle-stitch.

If kettle-stitches have been missed and came to know this before the sewing has progressed more than a few sections from the missed point. Sew the thread downward along the kettle-stitch to the spot and add the missing kettle-stitch. If the missing stitch is not detected until the sewing is completed, tie a piece of thread to the nearest existing tail and catch the sections together, then secure the thread by making a couple of additional kettle-stitches.

If you find that a signature is disorder or upside down, cut the threads in the centre of the affected signature, pull the threads out at the kettle-stitches. Freeing the signatures, and correct the error. Tie a new thread to one of the pieces that was pulled out, resew the signature or signatures and secure all loose threads on the spine by making additional kettle stitches or tying them to an existing thread.

If the centre of a folded section is missed and there are a few loose pages, then tie a thread on at one of the kettle-stitches and resew the section.

Now and then the book and a long loop of thread is found later on. Pull this out at one of the tapes on the spine, cut it in 2, and tie the 2 pieces together.

Examine the sewing in the endsheet sections. If any thread is visible between the hinge and the endleaf or between the endleaf and the first fly leaf, the section has been pressure on incorrectly. Remove the section by cutting the thread at the centre tape and pulling it out of the section at the kettle-stitches. Tie on a sew thread and resew the section correctly through the folded fly leaves, just off the fold on the fly leaf next to the book.

QUESTIONS FOR DISCUSSION

1. What is the purpose of sewing?
2. What is meant by kettle stitch, weaver's knot?
3. Describe the method of hand sewing on tape or cord?
4. What is the special characteristic of all-along sewing?
5. What is the purpose of two-long machine?
6. Describe the method of sewing on Tajma/Philadelphia patent back guard?
7. What is meant by overcasting? How is it done?
8. For what classes of work is overcasting suitable?
9. What is the first step in sewing procedure?
10. Describe the sewing method which involves both overcasting and sewing?
11. What is signature? How are the signatures sewn to each other?

16

Rounding

Rounding of a book after sewing, cutting and gluing is a natural phenomena. A book becomes convex back and concave fore edge systematically due to prolong use. Rounding gets rid of a certain amount of the swelling in the back caused by the presence of the sewing threads in each section and this swell is given a more even distribution. Even though a book tends to have a flat back, it should be rounded very slightly to prevent the fore edge 'flying out'. Flat book certainly open better than round back, but it would be a mistake to allow the fact over rule the necessity for a little rounding. Rounding of a book depends on a few criteria such as swell caused by sewing thread, number of guards used and purpose of the book for preservation. A book of thick sections has very little thread in the back and will therefore tends to have a flat back, where as a book of thin section will have a larger quality of thread, and so develop a much rounder back.

MATERIALS REQUIRED

- Small headed hammer
- Shaken jar
- Wooden (chawki) or charano tool (Bengali)

In order to carry out the rounding, place the book upon hard wooden chawki. Its fore edge is towards the binder and glue is not yet complete dry. Place the left hand index finger on the book forward gently and at the same time place the thumb along the fore edge, and press against that edge to balance the drawing motion of the fingers. Tap this book with a backing hammer very lightly down the back edge of the end paper through out its whole length. Turn the book over and repeat the operation on the other side in the same manner. By pulling with finger and pushing with the thread, the hammer is brought down along the books of the sections in the upper half of the book. These will begin to slide slightly over each other, and this produced the rounding. Turn the book over and repeat, and continue turning over in this way until a fully rounded back is achieved, making sure that both sides are evenly balanced.

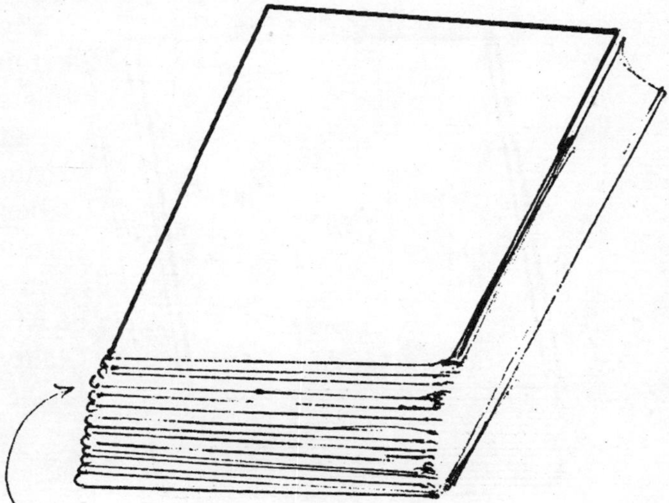

Fig. 16.1: Hammer Stroke

Fig. 16.2: Rounding completed

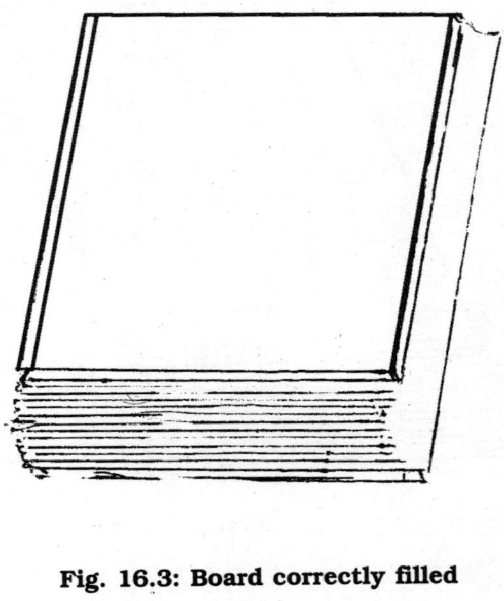

Fig. 16.3: Board correctly filled

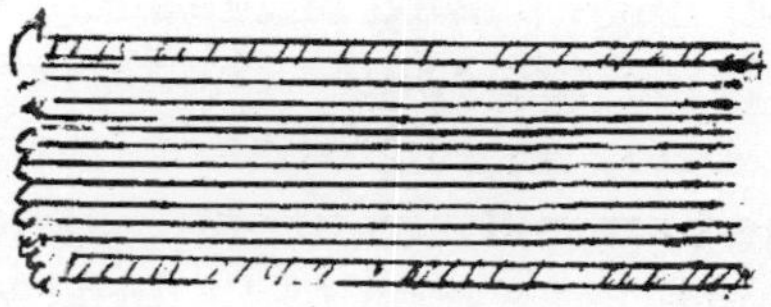

Fig. 16.4: Board too thin or groove too deep

Fig. 16.5: Rounding of brittle book

Great force must never be used, on to some extent brittle book. Heavy hammer strokes can be damaged brittle book. In dealing with a book sewn flexibly on raised cords the hammer must not fall on these cords and it is necessary to use a much smaller headed hammer.

Core should be taken in case of rebinding different condition of frazile brittle documents. A few books are not in a position to rounding. Those are needed to straight binding and covering. Those are little bit brittle or tissue laminated, the book can be backing only with small hammer holding the fore edge by the left hand thumb and other fingers. Next strike slightly with small-headed hammer on the spine. The strike of hammer will fall on the back very lightly not exert very heavy force. When the hammer strike on the back, left hand will displace down, as a result full force will not exert on the spine (Fig. 16.5). There will be no chance of damage the spine. During operation two binding boards are placed both sides which are little bit below the spine edge of the book.

BACKING

From the long experience of restoration work, it is observed that backing is an important segment of whole operation to binding work. Failure in backing spells, failure in the whole binding work. One should realise what she is doing and why she is doing it.

During the sewing of the book, every time a fresh section is added these, is also added another thickness if the sewing thread to the total thickness of the book. When the sewing is completed, it will be obvious that the book will be thicker at the back, by the number of threads in the sections, than it is at the fore edge. This extra thickness must be disposed of by backing. In a sense to set the rounding and distribute the reminder to the swell, and simultaneously, providing shoulders to accommodate the thickness of the boards to be used in making cover. The operation of backing a book' indicates the method by which the back of the sections are bent over from the centre towards the right and the left until a groove is formed into which the boards will fit comfortably. This groove also acts as a hinge for the boards where opening or shutting the book; unnecessary strain is removed from the joint, preventing the latter breaking away, and its presence gives an assurance that the back will return to its proper shape every time it has been opened.

The proper thickness of the board should be selected before starting the backing. There are three categories of weighted board such as 2 lbs, 2½ lbs and 3 lbs. A larger heavy book will need heavier board, and therefore, a deeper groove, whereas a small book, having thinner boards will have a correspondingly smaller groove/kakri.

There are two alternatives, either the boards are chosen first, and the groove made to fit them, or the groove may be made first, and boards chosen to fit the groove. If the boards are selected first, it is wise to draw a line on each side of the book indicating the thickness of the boards. This measurement can be marked by standing the board on its edge, as shown in the diagram, and then a line drawn through this point parallel to the back edge of the endpaper. It will

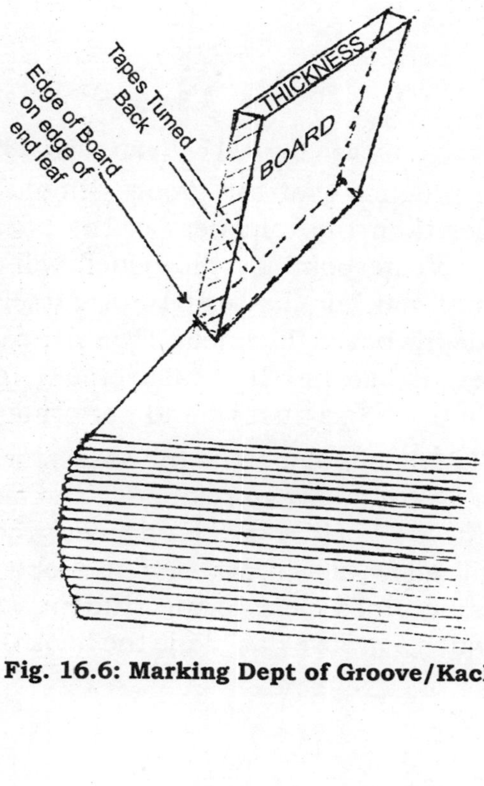

Fig. 16.6: Marking Dept of Groove/Kacki

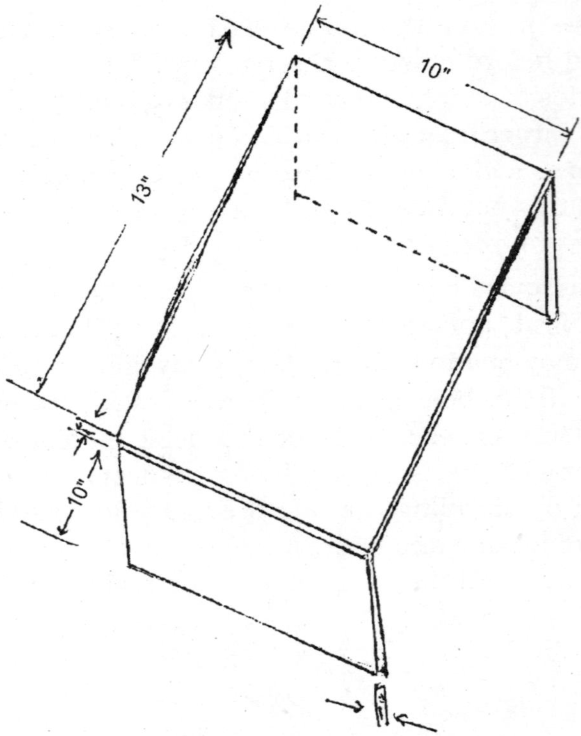

Fig. 16.7: Wooden Chawki or Takti (Bengali)

be found in practice that the groove should be very slightly larger than the thickness of the boards, but the marking of the point by the pencil will give the necessary addition, for the pencil mark itself will be slightly inside the board thickness. Experienced binder need not require so much measurement, only eye estimation is better productive and performance.

The second point concerns the assessment of the depth of the Kakri/groove in relation to the amount of swell present. If a book is given a deeper groove than the swell will allow, it will never shut properly when bound. This becomes clear to the student when it is raised that such a groove has made the book thickness

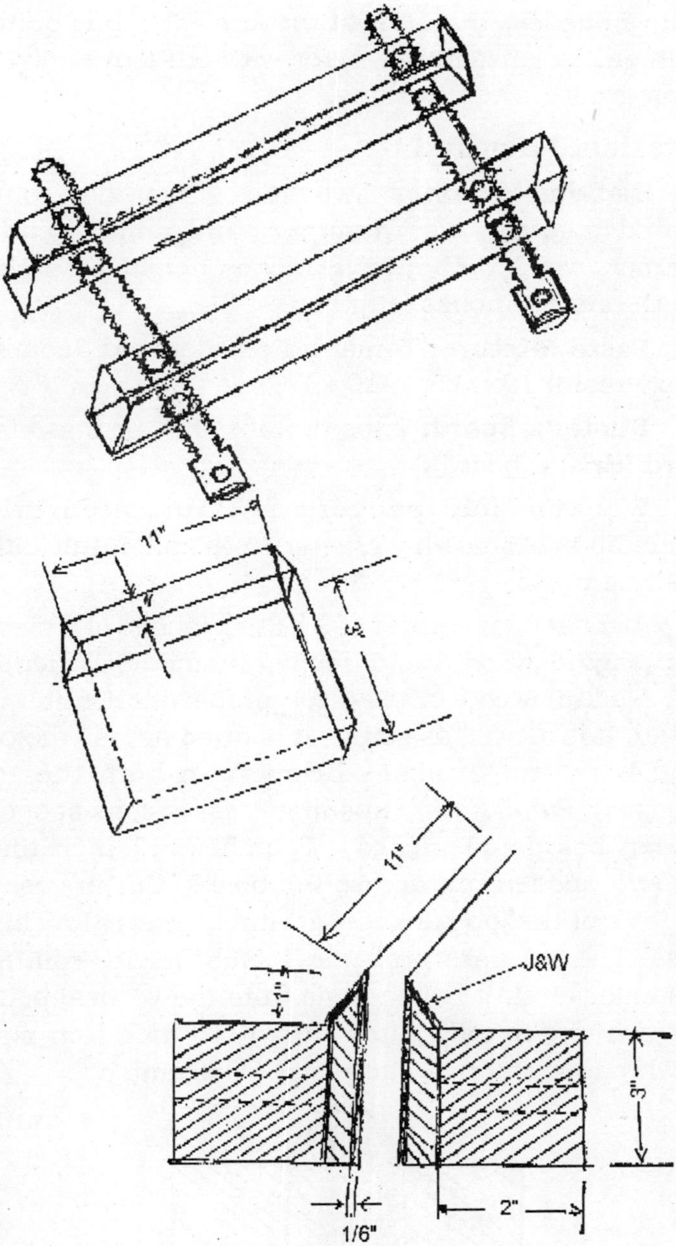

Fig. 16.8: Section of job backer

at the spine less than it is at the fore edge. It is quite a common, but disastrous, error with student to give to much groove when backing.

Materials Required

Backing Hammer: Two types of hammer, round headed medium size hammer, and small headed hammer, wooden chawki: 8 inches height 10 inches breath and 13 inches length.

Paste Mixture: Tamarind powder and Jebanjor (epoxy resin) 10 : 0.5 to 10 : 1

Binder's Board: 2 lbs to 3 lbs D.B. or masonate board (Bristol board).

Wooden job backer, is fabricated with combination of shaken jar/lying press and putuli kath/ finishing press.

A shaken jar consist of 2 × 3 × 2 inches of 2 pieces teak (sagun) wood and 2 inches diameter 1ft length teak (sagun) wood is used for preparation nut with thread. It is as well as screw. It is fitted across the two wood bars and 2 inches below from both the end (diagram). *Putuli Kath*/ Finishing Press is consist of two wooden boards 11 inches × 3 inches × 1 inch thick and two wooden nut across the board. But in case of two jaws of the job backer are without nut of finishing press. The jaws are protrude 1 inch height from the shakenjar level. It is 30° angle from the vertical point. The jaws are to tally gilted with 1/16 inch iron plate for which hammering can resist (diagram).

Fig. 16.9: Appropriate position in press.

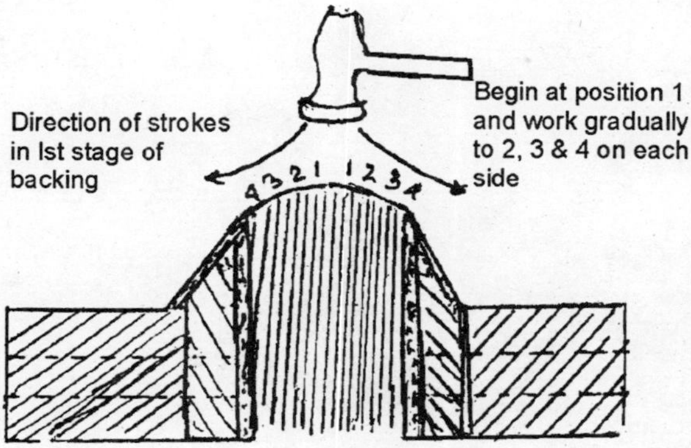

Fig. 16.10

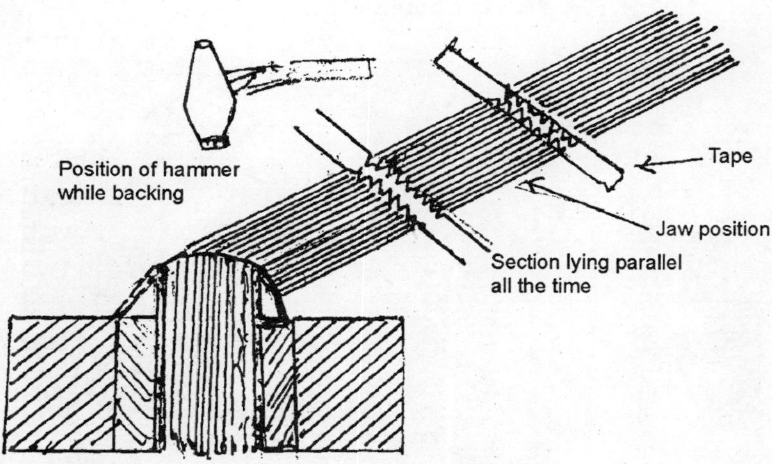

Fig. 16.11

Place the book flat on the wooden chawki as diagram set up a binding board at 90° angle at the spine edge of the book that may be 2 lbs or 3 lbs board according to thickness of the book. Draw a pencil line on the both front and back of the book, 2/16 or 3/16 inches from the spine edge. This line gives an added advantage in that any slipping of the board is immediately detected.

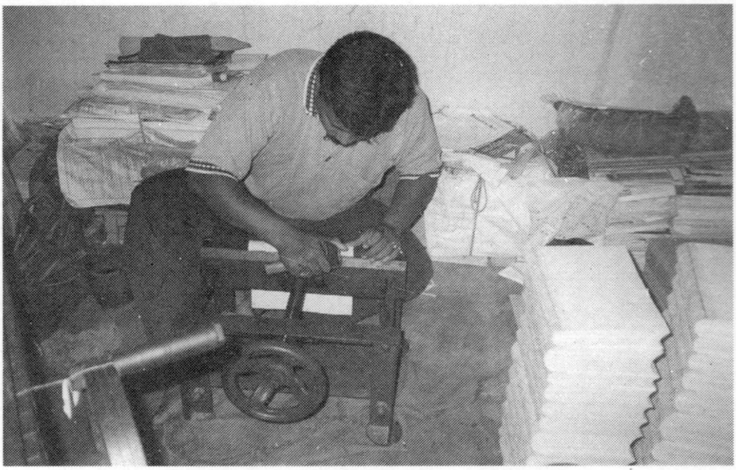

Fig. 16.12: Charano tool (working)

Fig. 16.13: Charano tool

Nipped very slightly for a few minutes the backing wood boards will have adhered to the book. Tapes or slips should remain outside the round state. Adjust the book so that the pencil lines are just visible above the jaws of the backer. Check the head and tail of the

Fig. 16.14: Shakenjar on the wooden chawki

book to make sure that those have retained there roundness and that the rounding is systematical. If adjustment is necessary, catch the book on the fore edge, hold it shut with the thumb and 3 fingers on opposite sides of the book, and with index finger push it up in the centre, while holding it firmly in position on the lines with the other hand. Check it again to be sure that the edges of the jaws are on the line, and check the evenness of the rounding by placing a small piece of board on one end and drawing the shape of the end of the book on it. Place this drawing again the other end of the book and repeat. With the shape of the two ends drawn one on top of the other, any difference in shape can readily be seen. If there is a marked difference in shape, try to get those uniform before proceding.

Screw up the press very tightly, and commence to back the book with a backing hammer. The hammer strokes should not fall directly upon the backs of the sections, but a glancing blow is used. The hammer should fall first at the points marked 1, and gradually work down both sides of the back as shown by 2, 3 and 4 until the backing jaw are reached, and the book takes on the appearance shown.

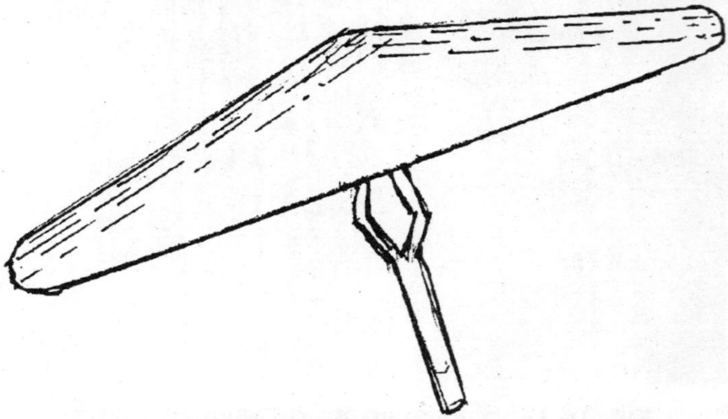

Fig. 16.15: Backing hammer for brittle book of and raised band

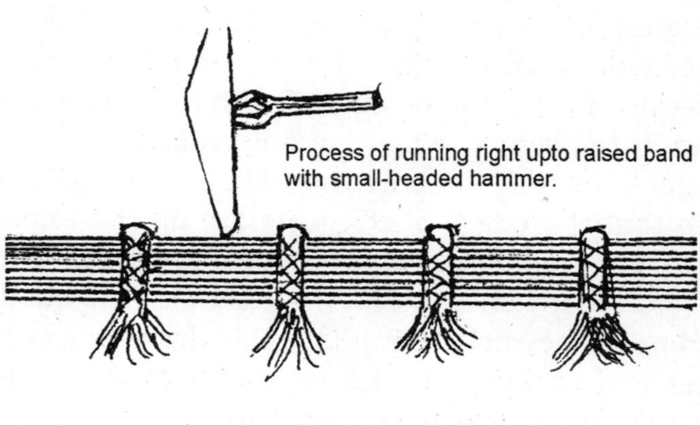

Fig. 16.16: Book fix in job backer

The sections should tie straight and parallel as those are before the backing is commenced. It will be found that when the hammering is done, there will still be a small space between the edge of the end

Fig. 16.17: Rounding and backing method

papers and the backing jaw. *To leave it in condition is to remain the backing in complete.* The hammer must be used in a different way. A direct blow must be employed along the whole length of the endpaper until this small aperature is closed, and outer sections lie snugly on the backing boards. This last process is one which is often neglected, but it makes all the difference between an indifferent piece of work and that done in a craftman like fashion. Realisation of this reason will prevent its omission.

It is observed that when a book is backed with glancing blow only and simultaneously taken out from the job backer, the *kakri*/groove spring back a little as a natural phenomena. Next the boards will not fit properly into such *kakri*/groove, a little bit gaps are evolved. If a book is finished off with direct blows of that points, then only the boards will fit properly into the groove. Another error often committed lies improper heavy blows with the hammer. This blow crushes the sections and spoils the shape of the book. This blows should be light and proper when backing begins, and should be increasing a little in weight according to condition of the paper. If a binder drives the hammer wrong, next operation will difficult to perform.

Nowadays the raised band has become obsolete generally raise cord band by the leather is ornamental and decorative binding. When the book is sewn on raised cords, use a hammer with a head small enough to get between the cords. Precaution should be taken to avoid hitting on the cords. Check the cords to be sure that they are parallel with the head and tail of the book. Begin the backing in the usual way from the centre outwards, carefully avoiding the bands. It will be found that the hammer will go right up to the band immediately under its head, but not right up to the band above its head. It is necessary to reverse one's position frequently, first standing at one end of the book and then at the other. This will keep the section parallel. The finishing-off process with the direct blows must be gently and carefully done. Above all, the backing of any book must never be hurried, and specially is this the case with flexible bindings. It is also observed that small headed hammer is required for brittle manuscript binding which is discussed in this chapter. The hand is quite near the head, and the handle always lies over the back of the book parallel to the sections, i.e. from head to tail or tail to head.

All backing can be done satisfactorily in either a lying press or wooden job backer. Problem evolved in the backing process is the book riding up out of the top backer when the backer is tightened firmly. This is generally due to unavoidable excessive swell, which can be remedied by placing a piece of scrap board on each side of the book from the fore edge to the drawn line. In course of backing adjustment, if you observe the jaw of the backer is deviated from the drawn line and the backen was not tight enough, release the pressure, make the necessary adjustments and start for backing.

BOARD

Material Required: Straw board, gray board, blackboard, masonate board, bristol board and distribution board.

Nowadays various kinds of boards are available in the Baithakana Road, Kolkata. Inferior and superior quality of board are required for commercial binding and preservation of old brittle document respectively. Gray and black boards are inferior quality of straw board. Masonate, D.B. boards and bristol board (available in photo material shop) are superior quality which are used for conservation of antique, though it is costlier. It is observed that insect attacked on the straw board profusely for which from the conservation point of view straw boards have been discarded. Because for conservation of antique need good quality durable board to enhance the logevity of the document. Gray board can be used for cased books and cut flush work but only black board should be used for the ordinary bindings.

The boards should be cut so that the square or projection is consist of cut with the style of binding. The square refers to the projection of the binding beyond the trimmed edge of the book. A large volume usually has a larger projection than a small book. If the book is to have french joints, allowance must be made for this as the boards must be narrower by the width of the joint than those for tight joints. The usual amount of projection for an octavo book is 1/8 inch at head and tail and from 1/8 inch to 3/16 inches on the fore edge. A 14-inch account book usually has 1/4 inch at head and tail and ½ inch on the fore edge.

The usual process of marking the board is to lay the book on a piece of board so that the back edge is properly located. A pair of dividers is set to the width of the square and is used to mark the board projection. The board is cut on the board shears, a cutting machine consists of a metal table with a knife hinged to one edge with a shearing action against that edge. It is equipped with several gauges to measure and square boards and a clamp to hold the boards immovable while they are being cut. In case of small binder who have no above equipments, he can cut the board with large scissors about 12 inches size, shown in diagram.

Board thickness is indicated by weight and number, No. 20 and No. 30 are used in most binding. These numbers indicate the number of boards in a 50 pound bundle, so 20 is thicker and heavier than 30. According to thickness and size of the volume board is required. In case of blank book two layers are glued together. These layers usually are of different thickness, and the thin layer is placed next to the book because the board generally warps toward the thin layer. A little warp towards the book is not noticeable but even the slightest warp away from it is very pronounced. Line the boards with paper to prevent outward warping on leather-bound books or books with cover material pasted on the boards.

The appearance of books bound with very heavy boards can be improved by tapering the edges to eliminate the blunt appearance. A slight amount is tapered also from the two inside corners to compensate for the thickness of the turn in at the joint. Blank book boards should have the fore edge corners slightly rounded.

The process of attaching boards varies for different kinds of bindings. A book is bound with tight back, the boards are fastened to the book so that groove height is against the backing ridge, which is the same height is the thickness of the boards. If the book is sewn on cords, the boards are laced on. Since any uneveness will show through the covering material. It is important that the lacing on of the boards be done neatly.

The boards are laid inplace, a mark is made opposite each of the cords, and the boards are removed from the book. An awl is used to punch holes through the boards from the outside even with each cord and about 3/8 inches from the edge other holes are punched from the inside about 1/4 inch below each of those punched from outside. Grooves are cut from the edge of the board to the first holes just deep enough so that the cords will be flush with the surface of the board when these lie in the grooves. If the grooves are too deep these will cause hollow in the cover, and if these are not deep enough these will cause hump. The cords are frayed out, pasted and laced through the holes. The surplus cord is cut off, the holes hammered shut, and the cords pounded flat. The boards of the cut flush work are made the same length as the book and the same width, minus the width of the hinge. This work is not rounded or backed and the width of the hinge should be such that the board will open freely. There is no waste sheet and the boards are glued to the board sheet. The back strip is glued and rubbed down on the back, in the joints, and on to the boards.

The siling material is glued on to overlap the backstrip. When cut flush work is trimmed, it is available to build up under the hinge of the book to keep the pressure of the knife from breaking the paper. Cut-flush work should not be trimmed untill it is perfect by dry or the back strip may be forced loose.

QUESTIONS FOR DISCUSSION

1. What is the purpose of rounding books?
2. How are books prepared for process of rounding?
3. What should be the consisteney of the glue applied to the back?
4. Describe the process of rounding a brittle book.
5. What is the purpose of backing a book?
6. Discuss the process of backing books which have been sewn on tapes or cords.
7. What precautious should be taken when backing books sewn on raised cords?
8. What is meant by the Square or Protrude of a book cover?
9. How is the thickness of boards indicated?
10. Why are boards sometimes tapped?
11. How are boards for cut flush work made and applied?

17

Spine Reinforcements

Three applying processes for spine lining reinforcement are known to book binders since long back. These are first head and tail band second lawn/ unbleached cloth lining between the cattle stitches and third paper cylinder/spring back, besides tape and glue. This composition is required to strengthen and smoothen the back of the book. The saw cuts made for the cords on sunken cord sewing shown through any cover material applied directly to the back, so even tight back books need back lining. Similarly, tapes would show through consequently, the back of all books are lined except those sewn on raised bands. The cover material of those sewn on raised bands provides the reinforcement and the bands are supposed to show through as part of the decorative design. The first step in back lining procedure is to attach the head and tail band. Modern work uses machine made headbands glued to the ends of the spine. They served the purpose of strengthening the binding, especially at the head where there is always a strain on the binding when a book is parallel from the shelf.

Prepared headbands are suitable for case and bradel bindings and sewn ones for tight book and tube binding. The use of leather is limited to twentieth century volumes. The rare and valuable manuscripts are preserved through leather binding. Cloth headbands prepared by hand or machine shatin clothes are used. But book cloth is not suitable for headbands because of its stiffness and commercially woven ones, which can be purchesed by the yard and are not considered in good taste by most hand book binders.

LEATHER HEADBANDS

Material Needed: Leather strip 1½ inches wide, slightly longer than twice width of spine.

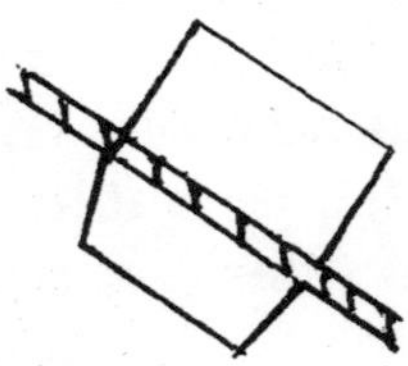

Fig. 17.1

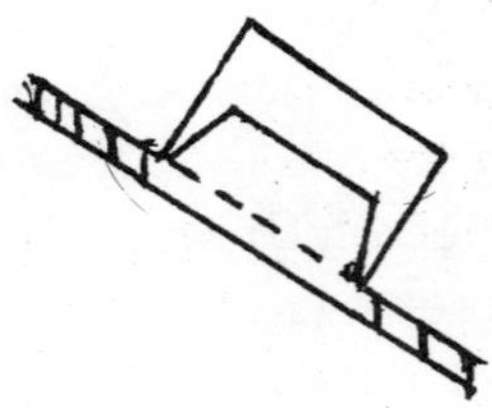

Fig. 17.2

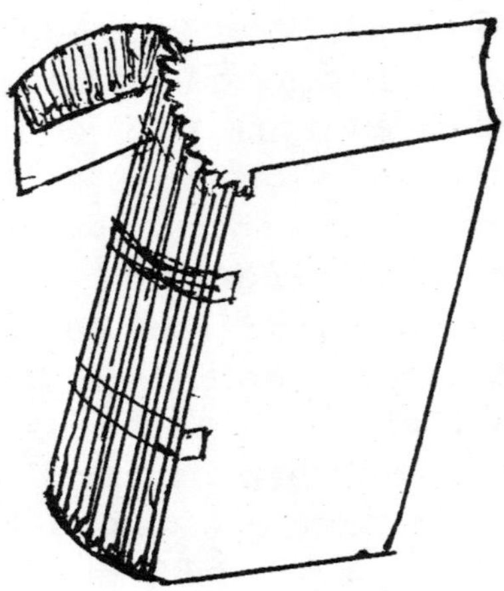

Fig. 17.3

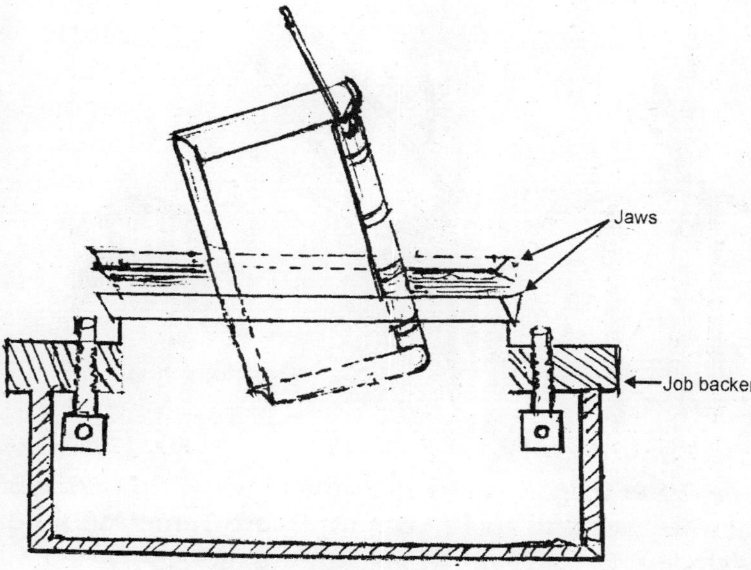

Fig. 17.4

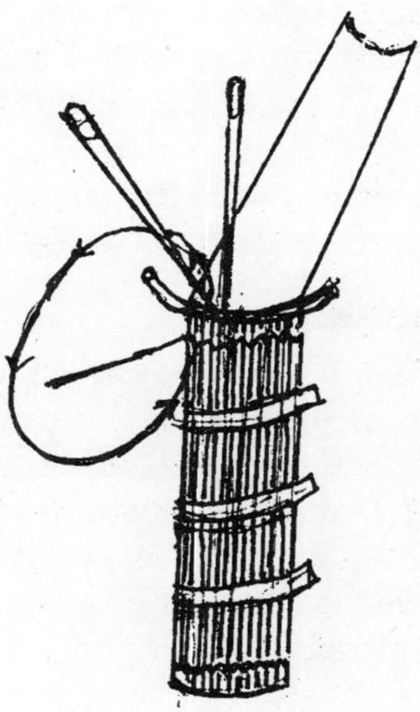

Fig. 17.5

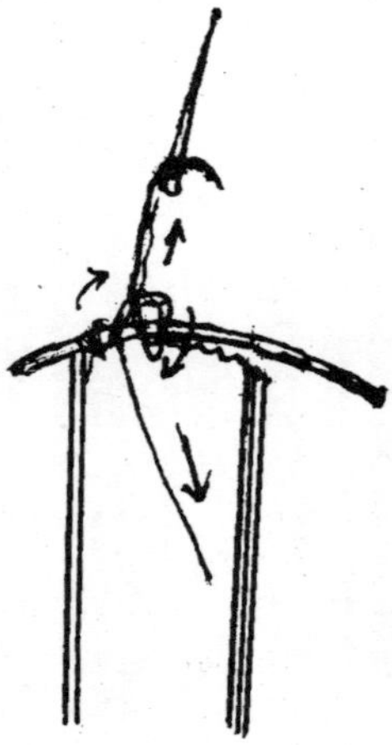

Fig. 17.6

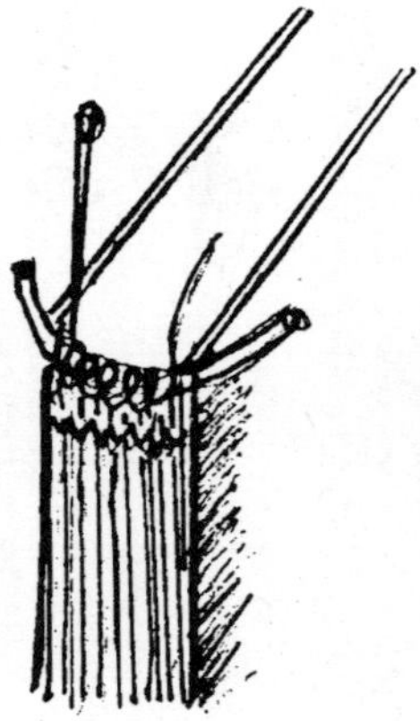

Fig. 17.7

Fig. 17.8

Tone thread, 1/16 inch diameter, 1 inch longer than leather and waste paper mixture Tamarind seed paste and Epoxyresin adhesive (Jebanjor)10 : 1 to 0.5, Pare the leather as earlier instruction unit it is uniform thin and palpable, and leather both edges in its entire length. Lay the leather strip face down on the wastepaper and apply adhesive to the entire surface, place the strings on the leather about 1/2 inch from 1 edge [Diagrams (17.1, 17.2 and 17.3)] and turn the 1/2 inch of leather over the string and with a bonefolder, push the leather firmly against the string.

CLOTH HEADBANDS

These are made in the same fashion as leather headbands. Any medium weight woven material can be used. In general, striped shating is used. The material for both leather and cloth headbands should be selected along with the other materials for a particular book so that the over all effect in the finished product will be pleasing.

SEWN HEADBANDS/SAREJA (LOCAL NAME)

These are worked directly on the head and tail of the book, customarily done after the board are attached to the book. It should be rememberred that cloth lining (Tajma) between cattle stitches is set up inside the boards. Four styles or types are described here. They are all usually sewn with a twisted silk thread, frequently using 2 colours, or on older volumes with unbleached linen sewing thread either in its natural colour as dyed. The colour or colours chosen should go well with the leather and the end leaves if coloured or decorated. If 2 colours are used choose 1 light and 1 dark one, if those are the same intensity in tone and those tend to blend together.

The thickness of the thread and the diameter of the core on which the band is worked should be chosen with some regard to both the size of the book and the square on the board.

SINGLE CORE HEADBANDS/SAREJA

Materials Required: Sunken cord, 1/16 inch diameter, 6 inches length. Needles 2, two tone silk headbands, 12 inches of 1 colour, 18 inches of the other westeboard, 2 clean pieces as large as book covers. Nepalese hand-made paper 1 strip twice as wide as spine. Tamarind seed paste and Jebanjor mixture 10 : 1 to 0.5.

Rub the cord with paste and lay aside to dry. Place the book protected by the scrap boards, in the finishing press (or job backer) fore edge facing out (or facing the binder) and tail up (Fig. 17.4). Tie the 2 silks together at one end and thread one needle with the longer piece. Secure the needle by sewing through the thread about 2 inches from the end just put through the needle.

This is done simply by sticking the point of the needle through the thread and putting the thread tight.

The sewing can start from either the outside or the inside of the book. If the knot made by joining the 2 threads will be unsightly on the inside of the book start on the outside. Cut the core material in half shape 1 piece with the fingers to confirm to the rounding of the spine. Fix its position by sticking the second needle through it and sticking the needle in the edge of the waste board.

Example, let us take the colours are red and white, the needle is threaded with red (The longer of the 2 threads), and the sewing will start on the out side of the book. Starting at one edge of the spine, just below the kettle-stitch, take the red thread up through the end sheet section, bring it down across the core, and take it up again in the same hole. This will make a loop or circle and secure the core at its first point (Fig. 17.5). Now take the red it up and white down. Bring white up, wrap it completely around the core once, then bring it up over the core, hold firmly and cross it with red. Wrap red completely around the core once, bring it up over the core, hold firmly, and cross it with white and continue in this sequence (Fig. 17.6). As the work progresses, the crossing of the threads on the tail of the book produces the desired bead (Figs. 17.7 and 17.8). About every 1/2 inch or third time in handling red, take it down into the book and bring the needle and thread out below the kettle-stitch.

When the other side has been reached, take red down through the book and out, bring white down on the outside of the spine, and tie the 2 threads together with a square knot. Paste a narrow strip of Napalese hand-made paper over the threads on the spine after cutting the surplus silk back to about 1 inch letting it extend just enough above the tail of the book to catch the edge of the headband. Shape the headband against the tissue and cut off the extra core material on both sides. Turn the book around and repeat at the head. This method produces a headbands that has 2 red, 2 white, and 2 red and so on alternating threads.

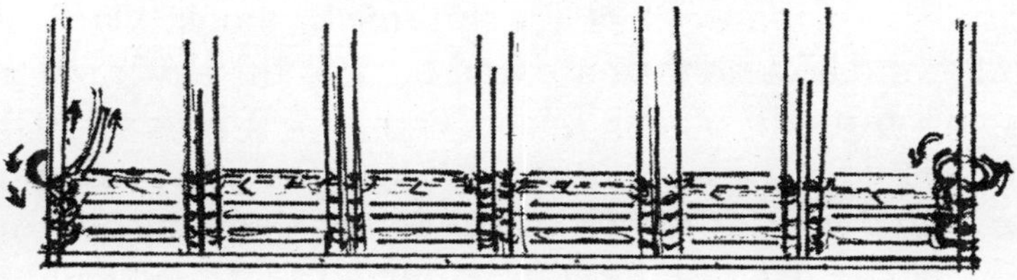

Fig. 17.9

Fig. 17.10

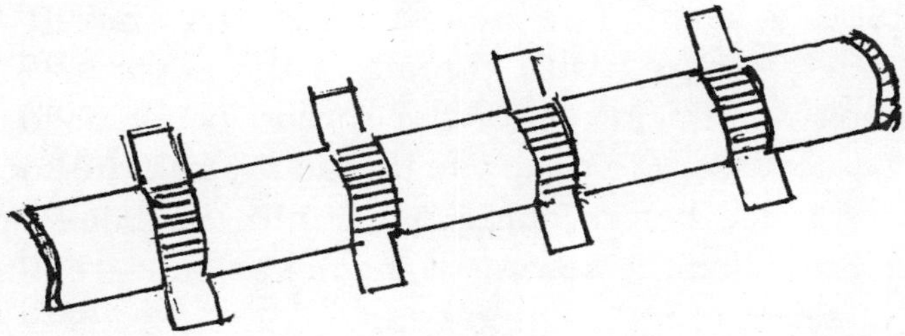

Fig. 17.11

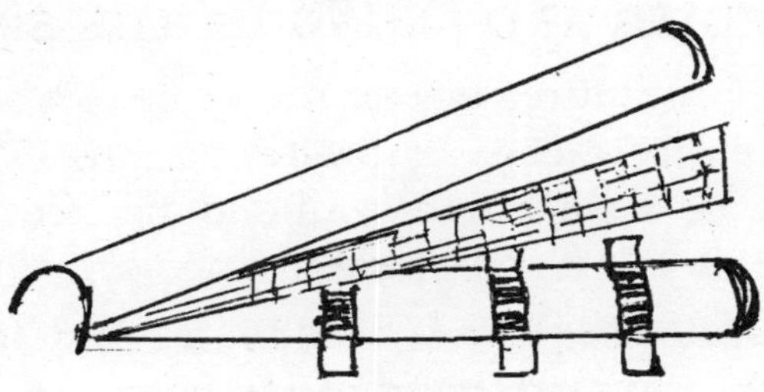

Fig. 17.12

SARAJA/HEADBANDS WORKED WITH SEWING OF BOOK

In case of a single cord at both head and tail is shown above, start the sewing as usual on the outside at the tail kettle-stitch go into the centre of the signature, but instead of proceeding to the first cord, bring the thread out at the tail of the book. Carry it under and around the cord and back to the kettle stitch on the outside of the book (Figs. 17.9 and 17.10). Proceed with the sewing in the usual fashion until one reaches the kettle-stitch at the head. Come out of the book at the head kettle-stitch; carry the thread on the outside of the spine on the head of the book, under and around the cord, back into the book at the head, and out at the kettle-stitch. Add the next signature, go in at the kettle-stitch, out at the head of the book, under and around the cord, back to the kettle stitch on the outside, and back into the book. This is repeated at both ends with each thread until the book is completely sewn. The headband cores should be completely covered with thread. If the signatures of the book are thicker than the thread being used, it may be necessary to wrap the thread around the cores once or twice before going back into the book and proceeding with the sewing of the next signature. This type of sewing produces no bead.

HEADBANDING AND LINING UP THE SPINE

These procedures are for the spine of a book that is to have either a case or bradel binding. The book should now be sewn, glued, rounded, backed, and the edges treated. Put it in a finishing press.

Materials Required: Headband and tailband, spring back: Napalese hand-made paper as width of spine and length of the book, lawn cloth/unbleached cloth; acid free white hand-made paper, bond paper, waste paper, mixture of tamarind seed.

Paste: Epoxyresin adhesive (Jebanjor) 10 : 1 to 0.5.

1st Step: Attach the head and tail bands first. Fabrication of it is shown in the previous chapter. Cut those to exact width of the spine. Apply mixture to the ends of the book, lay the head bands in position with the string area resting on the head and tail, not on the spine. Rub strongly and shape with the fingers. These take shape more easily if attached immediately after being made and not left to dry in a straight or flattened condition.

2nd Step: The thin hand-made paper is attached with tamarind seed paste. It is acid free, strong, soft, local made is used to fill in the areas on the spine between the headband and the first tape, between the first and second tape, and so on (Fig. 17.11). The strip is equal width of the spine; cut this into pieces to fit the spaces, apply paste to the spine, and set up the pieces in position. The mixture is fairly thick. Rub uniformly with the knife's handle. Let it dry completely before proceeding. The drying time depends on the quantily of mixture used, and its consistancy, general atmospheric conditions.

3rd Step: Jaconet/unbleached markin cloth is added by applying mixture to the entire spine and laying it in position, centering from head to tail. If it is properly cut, it should cover the area between the strings in the 2 headbands and the entire width of the spine (Fig. 17.12). Rub this down firmly and again leave to dry thoroughly.

4th Step: Moisten spring back (Nepalese hand made paper) with water, apply a layer of thin adhesive, and set up it in position on top of the cloth (jaconet/markin). Rub with the knife's handle to remove any air bubbles or wrinkles.

If a mistake has been made in cutting any of these materials, recut those. Sufficient drying time is needed to these steps, for if the cylinder paper/spring back is added before the cloth is dry, the paper will dry first because of its exposure to the air and will tend to pull cloth away from the spine of the book. The paper cylinder is moistened because it is easier to handle if relaxed before gluing. This prevents curling up where it is glued. And in drying, it contracts a bit making for a firmar spine. After about 30 minutes, the book can be removed from the backer. It should not open until paper is properly dry.

PAPER CYLINDER/SPRING BACK

The spring back is used on large volume such as encyclopaedia of Britannica and account books. It has a clamping action on the back of the book that causes it to snap open and shut. This clamping action helps to retain the round in the back of book. Spring backs are generally prepared of thin finder's board. Thickness is to be used which depends upon the weight of the book, the heavier books requiring thicker backs: 1/2 lbs board is used as spring back when a heavier back is required. It is best to make it of two layers of Nepalese hand-made paper, or cartridge paper, etc.

The spring back should be the same length as the boards of the book and extend around the back and over onto the sides about 1/8 inch. The spring back should be made to confirm to the round of the back. It can be shaped by hand or machine. If done by hand, one side of the board is moistened and the other side heated and it is bent over a pipe with the dry side against the pipe. It is then placed in the hollow of the back forming mold and rubbed down to shape. Various back forming machines are in use which produce a spring back in much less time than hand method. The basic principle is the same in all the machines. The moistened board is placed in the machine and is then formed by the pressure of heated forms. After the back is formed, it should be lined to keep it from flattening out. A piece of ledger or other strong paper is used for the lining. It should be as long as the back and three times as wide. It is glued and wrapped around the back with the double thickness coming in the hollow. This is an important operation and care should be taken to insure good adhesion between the paper and the spring back. Without this lining, the moisture of the covering material and shrinkage of the leather as it dries tends to remove the curvature of the spring back. If this occurs, the spring back ceases to perform its function of causing the book to snap open and a shut.

The cylinder paper/spring back is now ready for attachment to the book. This can be done with either paper or muslin. A strip 3 inches shorter than the back and 1 inch wider is glued into the hollow of the spring back. The back is then placed in the proper position and the projecting pieces of paper are glued to the joints.

QUESTIONS FOR DISCUSSION

1. What is the purpose of back lining or spine reinforcement?
2. How will you prepare leather head bands?
3. What is meant by the expression "hollow back"?
4. When the spring back is used? What is its purpose?
5. What is single cord head bands?
6. How are spring back/paper cylinder prepared?
7. How are the bonds usually spaced?
8. Preparation of sewn head and tail bands/saraja.

18

Binding Style

A craftman reaches the point in binding a book where specific techniques are required, the techniques will vary appreciably for different binding styles. The style also depends on the brittleness of the book. The specific techniques covered cutting material, paring leather, making case binding, a hollow back, a tight back, cord/tube binding.

CASE/JEEL BINDING

Craftsman generally called it jeel binding or case binding. Nowadays different colours *chatai* rexin are using for dressing material in place of canvas. In case of half rexin binding, both canvas and rexin have been used. Although these are not durable binding as well as leather.

Materials Required

- Masonate or D.B. board and Bristol board (neutral pH, does not attack insect) are used as binder's board 2 pieces, larger by 1 inch in both dimensions than book page, grain direction vertical with book length.
- Board strip ½ inch width, 12-15 inches long, 3 pieces.

- Masonate board 1 piece, 220 M weight, 12–15 inches length, 1/2 inch wider than twice spine width.
- Acid free bond paper/hand-made paper thin width of spine, length of boards.
- Rexin/book cloth. 1 piece, larger by about 2 inches in both dimensions than amount needed to cover entire book.
- Paper narrow strip, 5–6 inches long.
- White paper, a few sheets larger than book cloth.
- Waste paper 2 strips slightly longer than book.
- Wax paper 2 strips longer than book.
- Glue, Mixture of Tamarind seed paste and Epoxyresin (Jebanjor) 10 : 1 and 0.15% of 16 cc lime water.

Cutting Materials

On the masonate board, D.B. Board, bond paper, hand-made paper rexin cloth, cut a straight edge, than a second edge at a right angle to the first. This should produce a square a right-angle corner and provide a point of departure in measuring the materials to thin proper size. Mark this corner on all materials with a little penciled crossed check mark. The boards should be 1/8 inch longer at both head and tail of the book.

Lay the squared corner of 1 board at the head of the book, with the vertical straight edge of the board resting along the joint, extend the board 1/8 inch beyond the top edge of the book, and at the tail, mark the board at the point where it extends 1/8 inch beyond the edge. Cut both boards to the size indicated by the mark and at a right angle to the previously cut straight edge.

In width, the boards are measured from the base

of the joint and should extend 3/16 inches beyond the fore edge of the book. Lay one of the joint strips along the edge of the spine on the joint, backed area of the book (Fig. 18.1). Place one of the boards against this is such a position that the fore edge of the book will be partially exposed. Mark it at the point where it extends, 3/16 inches beyond the fore edges, cut both boards as indicated by this mark at right angles with the top and bottom of the boards.

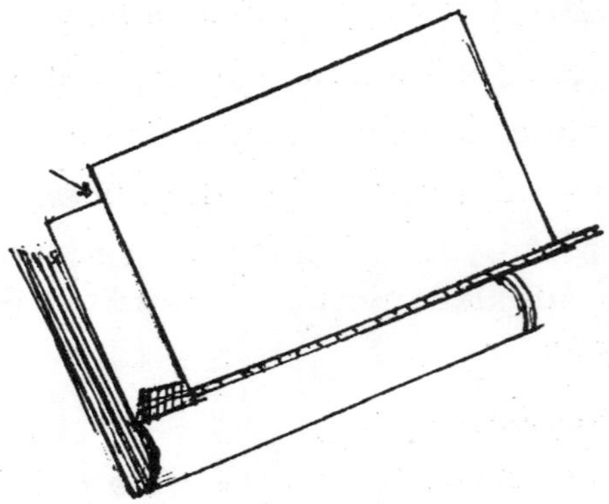

Fig. 18.1

SPINE STRIP

Lay the narrow strip of paper or bristol board (moisture barrior) across the spine, over one of the headbands (Fig. 18.2); pull it taut and mark it on both sides at the points where it crosses the edges of the spine. Check this over the other head band to be sure that the spine is the same width at both head and tail. Lay the outside one of the pencil marks on the straight edge of the D.B. board and mark on the D.B. board the position of the other pencil mark—also its outside. Cut 2 strips of D.B. board and 1 of bond/hand-made paper this width. One strip of D.B. board serves as the spine of the case; the other is used to create the depression for the indented leather title label.

CLOTH

Starting at the right angle corner previously cut draw a line on both edges 3/4 inches in towards the corner of the cloth. Lay one of the boards in this right-angle corner and weight it down. Place one of the joint strips next to the inside edge of the board, then the stiff spine strip, the second joint strip, and finally the second board (Fig. 18.3). Mark the position of the boards on the cloth at the top, bottom, and both outside edges. The cloth extends 3/4 inches beyond the 2 edges of the board laid down in the right-angle corner. On the 2 other edges of the cloth, make a mark 3/4 inches

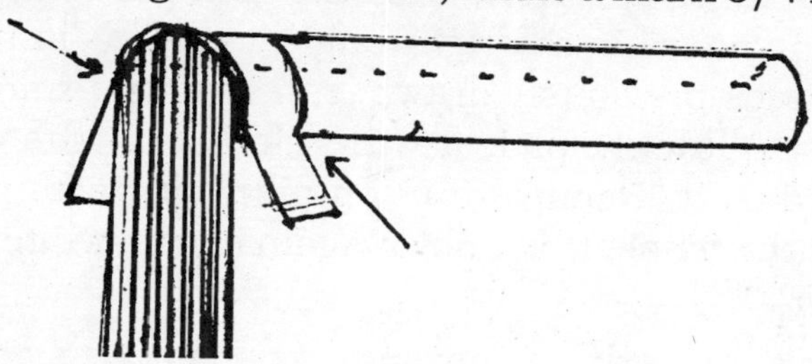

Fig. 18.2

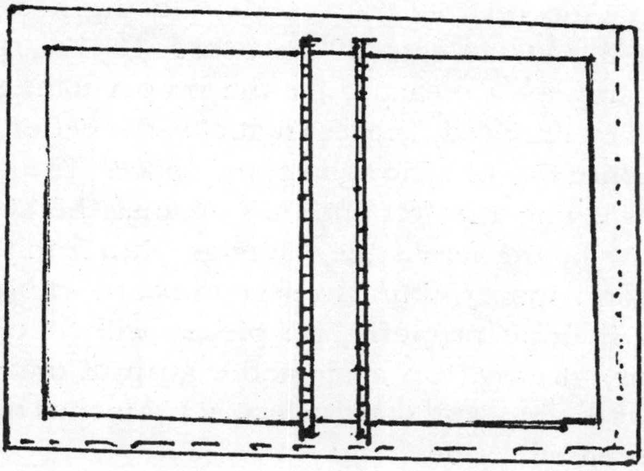

Fig. 18.3

outward from the edges of the board, and cut the cloth at these points. This should give a margin of 3/4 inches on all 4 edges of cloth, with all 4 corners right angles.

All labelling can be done with lettering sticker or direct gold lettering on the spine or top of the book where space accommodation is available.

Place the cloth right side facedown on the sheets of unprinted newspaper/white paper glue the entire piece of cloth—the glue should be thin—starting in the centre and working out in all directions with short, light strokes, while holding the cloth firmly in position with the finger tips. As soon as the gluing is completed, place one board in the right-angle corner as indicated by the lines previously drawn; rub it down firmly with the first. Quickly pick up the cloth and the board attached to it. Remove the top piece of waste paper, and lay the whole thing down again on the white sheet of paper.

Lay the strip of masonite board across the top edge of the attached board and weight in position. This serves only as a guide in lining the materials evenly at the top. Add on the joint strips, placing it exactly against the inside edge of the board. Do not rub, it serves only as a measure for the proper joint space and will be removed. The less it sticks, the better place the prepared spine strip against the spacer. The indent facedown, and the top lined up against the strip of masonite board across the top edge. Rub firmly, add the second spacer, than the second board, rubbing it firmly. If done properly, all pieces will fit closely together, all lined up against the strip of masonate board at the top, and there will be a 3/4 inches margin of cloth on all 4 sides.

Remove the strip of board across the top and the 2 joint strips or spacers. Turn the case over and check to be sure that the cloth is well stuck to the boards and free of wrinkles. Draw the point of a small bone folder along both top and bottom edges of the indentation made for the title. Turn the case over again to a clean paper.

CUTTING THE CORNERS

To make real corners, some of the materials at these points is cut away (Fig. 18.4). The cut is slightly curved, and it is important to leave the board. When all 4 corners are cut, reglue the edges lightly with a small brush. Do one edge at a time in this sequence bottom, top, and then the sides. To avoid getting glue on the work surface slip a narrow strip of paper under the edge to see glued, glue the edge, and immediately remove the strip and apply the glue.

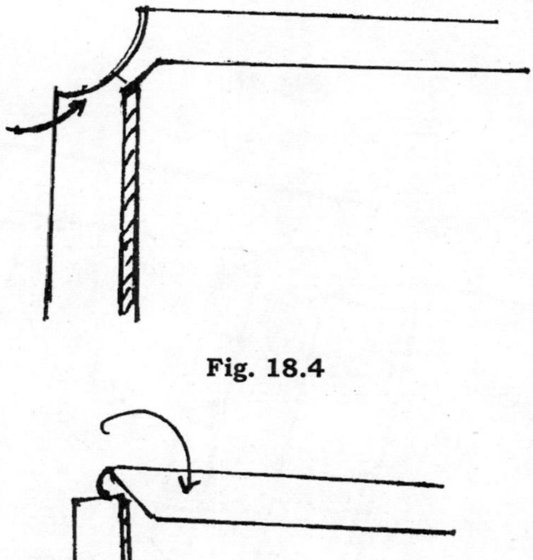

Fig. 18.4

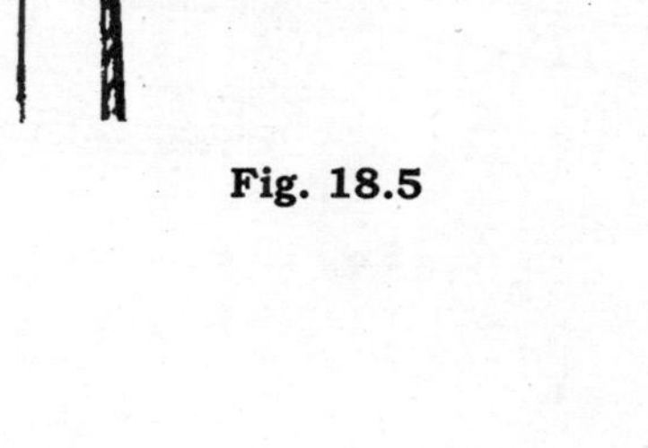

Fig. 18.5

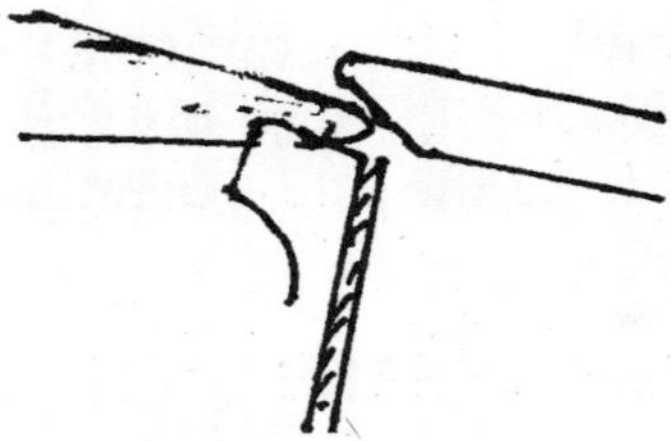

Fig. 18.6

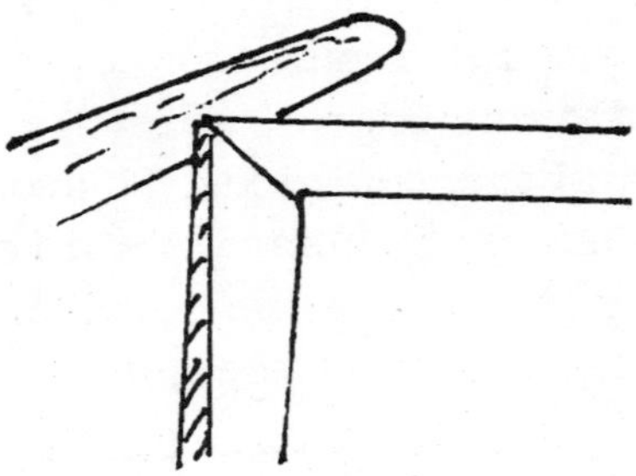

Fig. 18.7

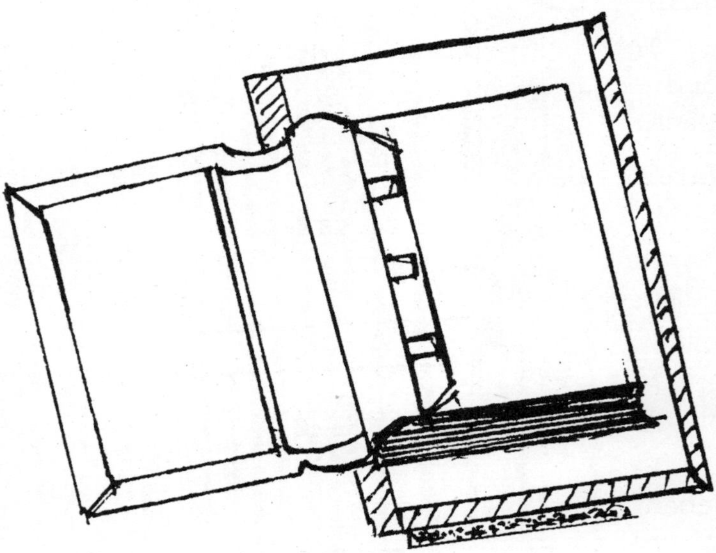

Fig. 18.8

Turn the ¾ inches of glued cloth on the board, pulling it tight and firm against the edge of the board. This can best be accomplished by running a knife handle or bone folder on the outside of the cloth and pushing it up against the board before buying the cloth on the board. Quite a bit of thumb pressure is required to get the cloth to fit lying closed against the edge and to be wrinkle-free on the board. When the bottom is turned, tuck the surplus material at the corners against the edges of the boards with a knife handle or thumb nail. Turn the top edge in the same way, then the other sides.

The case is now complete and ready to be attached to the book. Before proceeding, line the inside of the spine strip with the piece of bond paper. This cut to the proper width, in length it should fit in the area between the turned edges of the cloth. Apply glue to the paper and lay in position.

CASING-IN

The inside of the spine strip has been lined with bond paper, and now you are ready for casing-in or attaching the completed case to the book.

Materials Required

- One pair, longer than case wooden board one inch thick press boards pair small enough to fit inside wooden board.
- Waste paper strips longer than book.
- Hard board/masonite 2 pieces slightly larger than book.

Paste: It is a mixture of tamarind seed paste and (Jebanjor) 10 : 1 to 0.5, and 15% of lime water.

First, check the fit of the case by folding it around the book, centering the book in it from head to tail and pushing the book firmly against the spine of the case. While holding it firmly in this position, pinch the case in at the joints. If the square on the books seems to be 1/8 inch at head and tail 1/4 inch is on the fore edge, proceed with the casing-in.

The book is first "hung in" to prevent shipping during the process of permanently attaching the case to the book.

Lay one of the wooden board on a press board (Fig. 18.8). Paste the joints of the case up to the turn of the cloth at both ends. The joints are the 1/4 inch areas of cloth exposed on both sides of the spine strip. Lay the joint of the back cover of the case along the brass edge and press in place. Be sure that the wooden board edge is resting in the joint and that the inside of the cover board is not to the wooden edge in its entire length.

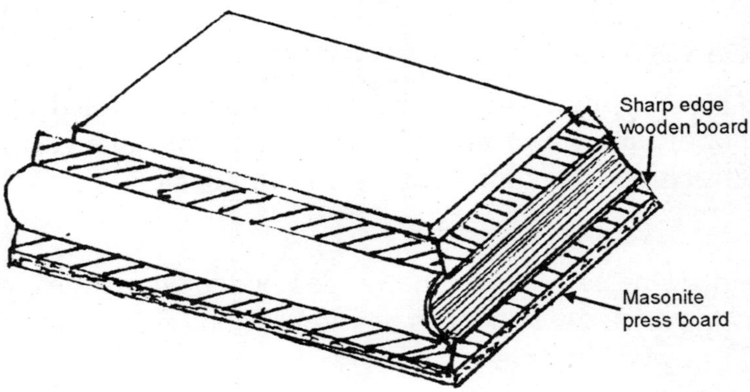

Fig. 18.9

Hold the book tightly in position with one hand, and with the other hand, bring the case lying closed around the spine of the book and into the joint, putting pressure on it at this point. Remove hand from the book and let the front cover (the other half of the case)

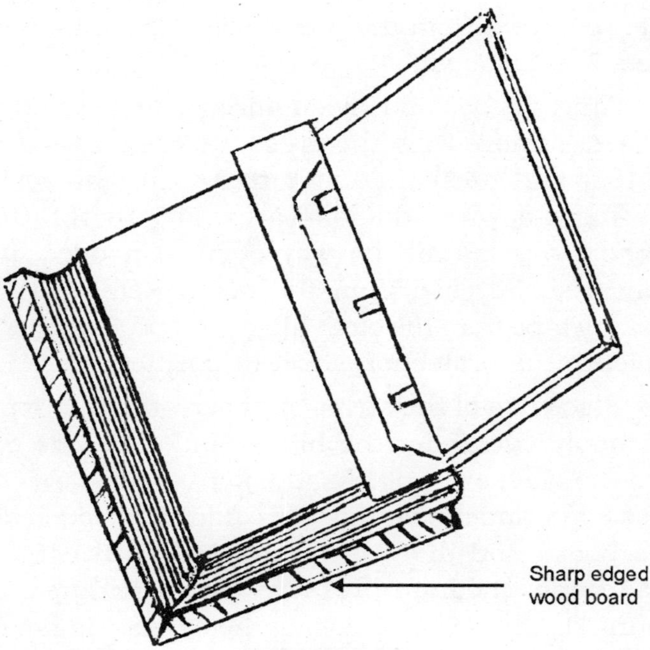

Fig. 18.10

fall into place. Hold the front cover in position and place the wooden board edge on the second board in the joint area, add the second press board. Keep a firm grip on both ends of the press boards and put the whole "package" in the press so that the centre of the book is approximately under the spindle of the press, and with the spine of the book exposed at the front of the press (Fig. 18.9). Tighten the press, check to make sure that the spine of the case is firmly against the spine of the book. This is done by pressing on it at the ends over the headbands. The headbands increase the width of the spine slightly in these areas, so if the spine of the case is fitting tightly at these points, it should be all right. Also check to see if the square on the boards is even on all 3 edges. If all is well, leave in the press for 10 or more minutes, if the book has slipped in the case, remove it from the press, free the joints, regular these, and try again.

After the book has been hung in successfully and pressed, remove from the press, take the 2 boards off the top, and open the cover to an upright position, pressing it down in the joint area (Fig. 18.10). Do not let the cover fall all the way open. If it does, it will likely free the case from the book. Remove tabs of masking tape from the cloth hinge and protection sheet, but leave the protection sheet in position.

Place one of the strips of paper—the waste paper previously cut under the hinge, and close the cover. Turn the book over, placing the joint of the case on the brass edge, and repeat this step. Add the wooden sharp edge board and the pressboard and return it to the press under medium pressure for 20 minutes. After pasting the hinges and closing the covers, do not open these until the book has been pressed. Binders often have a desire to peek to see if all is well. Curiosity, can result in wrinkled hinges.

The binding is now ready for the board papers. These should now be located and cut to size. First, get a square corner on each. In length those should be cut slightly shorter (1/16 inch) than the fly leaves to allow for possible stretching. In width those should be 3/16 inches from the fore edge of the board and about 1/8 inch from the spine, again make allowance for stretching. Generally speaking, those will stretch more in width than in length, although the amount of stretching depends on. The type of paper, the size of the sheet and the amount of moisture absorbed from the paste. No portion of the board papers should show on the edges or squares on the boards when the covers are closed.

Open the back cover all the way and support it with pressboards equivalent in height to the thickness of the book (Fig. 18.11). Paste the wrong side of the board paper (the paste should be thin enough to spread easily) hold it tightly and continue to brush it without adding more paste, until the paper creases to curl. Pick it up position evenly on the fore edge, and centre it from the head to tail. Lay it down, gradually smoothing it out at the same time. When in position, lay a clean piece of paper over it and rub gently but tightly. Insert a piece of hard board between the board paper and endleaf and close the cover. Repeat on the front cover. Return to the press between the wooden board. Screw the press down tightly. In about 3 minutes remove it from the press and check to be sure that no paste has oozed beyond the edges of the board papers. If all is well, with the board in place, return to the press, this time screw the press down just enough to hold the covers flat. Leave several hours or overnight. If paste has oozed. Wipe the surplus away, free any stuck area with a knife handle, replace the hard board with fresh one, and return to the press and repeat when the board papers are attached, the boards are very likely to wrap outward. This is a normal reaction and nothing to be alarmed about, when the board papers have dried in a flattened state under light pressure. These will balance the pull set up by the cloth on the outside of the boards and the covers should remain flat.

HOLLOW BACK

Bradel Binding is one of the hollow back binding. The book is now sewn, glued, rounding, backed, edges treated, headbanded, spine line up, and tapes attached to the protection sheets. It is now ready for the cover. Read the instruction in making the case for a case binding before undertaking the bradel binding.

The following instruction are for a 1-colour book cloth cover, with cloth hings and indented leather label. Many of the various remedies for problems discussed in the next sections.

Materials Needed

- Divider, boards pair, sharp edged wooden board.
- Press boards, pair small enough to fit inside wooden board.
- Masonite/D.B. board 2 pieces, weight determined at time book was backed, ½ inch larger in both dimensions than book.
- Photo cartridge paper thick 1 piece, width of spine plus 4 inches length of cartridge, 1 piece slightly wides than spine, length of cartridges, 1 narrow strip.
- Bond paper 1 piece slightly wider than spine, length of boards, books cloth, canvas one colour one piece longer than 3 inches.
- Leather, lens tissue paper (imported), hand-made paper, few strips white paper, wax paper.
- *Paste*: Mixture of Tamarind seed powder, Synthetic adhesive Jebanjor 10 : 0.5 and 10 cc lime water.
- Get one square corner on all of the materials that make up the binding and mark it.

First, make the cartridge 1 bristol board or bonnet. Find the centre of the largest piece of cartridge, mark it at both ends, and draw a line at this point from top to bottom. Measure with a strip of paper, over a headband, the exact width of the spine of the book, examine this against the other end to be sure that those are the same width. Mark the width of the spine, half on one side and half on the other of the line just drawn at both ends of the photo cartridge. This can be done with divider of a folded strip of paper (Fig. 18.12). Place a straight edge on the marks on one side, and with a knife's handle fold the cartridge paper, repeat on other side. Sharpen the folds by running a knife's handle along the folded edge. Mark the depth of the joint — which should be 1/4 inch on the outside of the cartridge, measuring from the folds just made. In the manner just described, fold both sides of the cartridge paper again. The first fold will be inward, the second outward. In other words, these are reverse folds. Measure and mark off 1½ inches from the second fold toward the edge of the cartridge paper/bristol on both sides and cut away any excess.

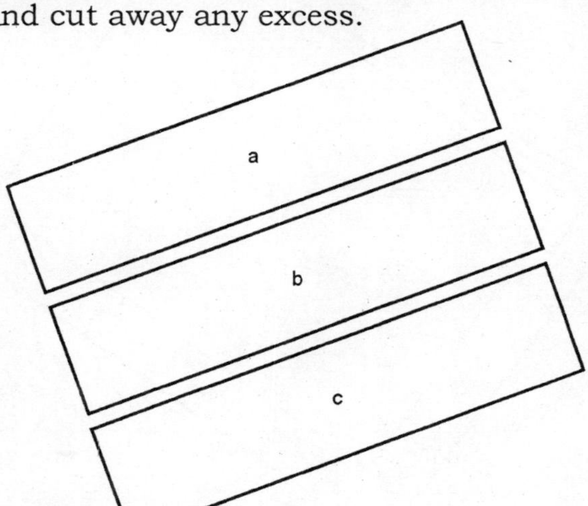

Fig. 18.11

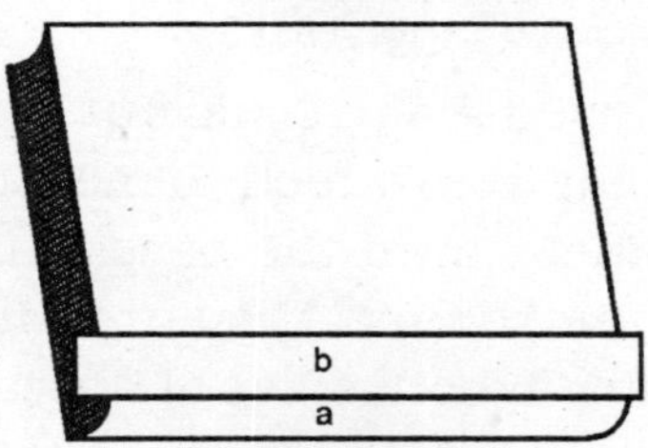

Fig. 18.12

Lay the folded cartridge paper/bristol, in position over the spine and check it for size, it should fit tightly against the spine of the book, and the joint areas—the spaces created by the second folds—should not rest on the backed area of the book (Fig. 18.13). Sand or pare to a feather edge both outside edges of the cartridge paper/bristol. This is the side to which the boards will be attached, and it describes that the joining of the 2 materials be as smooth as possible, not an abrupt step down.

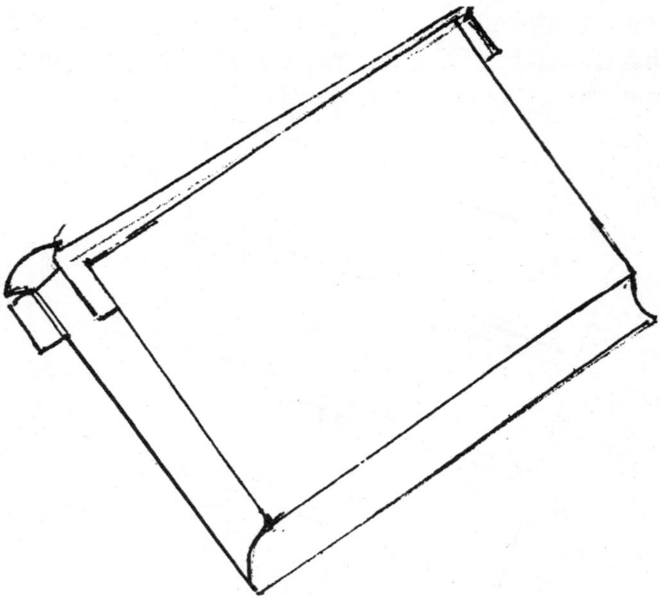

Fig. 18.13

The measured boards is cut with 10 inches scissors. The point from which to measure their width is a board thickness from the base of the joint or the second fold on the bonnet. Measure this off and draw a line at this point on both sides of the cartridge paper/ bristol. This will provide a guideline for attaching the boards. This additional space is desirable so that the boards will open freely. After cutting the boards, check those against the book to be sure that these are the proper size and that 1/8 inch square has been provided for on all 3 edges — head, tail, and fore edge. If these are correct, continue, if not remedy the trouble.

Attaching the Boards: Apply glue to about 2 inches of 1 board, from one edge in towards the centre and along the entire length, lay this in position along the line just drawn on the photo cartridge/bristol at the base of the joint taking care that the square on the board is even at head, tail and fore edge. The position of the board from head to tail can be marked on the bonnet before gluing the board, if this seems helpful. The glued area of the board should cover the cartridge paper/bristol and extend slightly to the protection sheet.

Turn the book over and place it on a level surface glue the second board and place it in position in the same way. With a triangle (Fig. 18.14), check all 3 edges to be sure that they are lined up evenly with the edges of the first board. When both boards are attached, put the book between press boards. With one edge of each press board lined up with the spine edge of the Masonate board. Put in the press, under firm pressure, for 1 hour.

Take the book out of the press after the specified time and cut the bonnet at both head and tail flush with the edges of the boards. Do this by laying a narrow strip of cartridge paper/bristol along the edge of 1 board. Carry it across the spine, and line it up with the edge of the other board. Draw a line along the edge of the bristol and cut with scissors along this line, repeat at the other end.

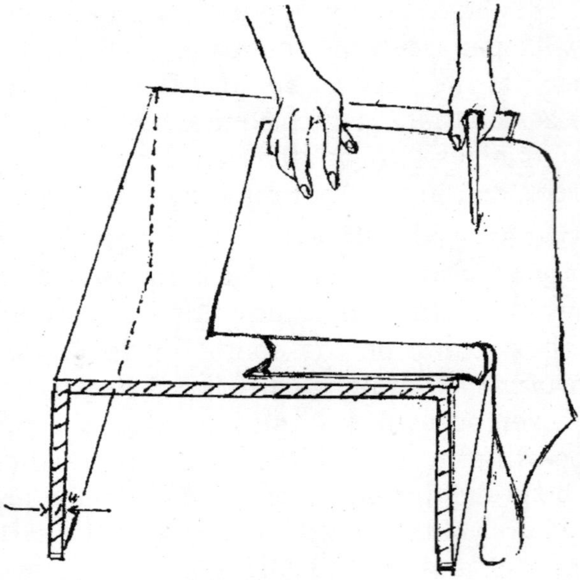

Fig. 18.14

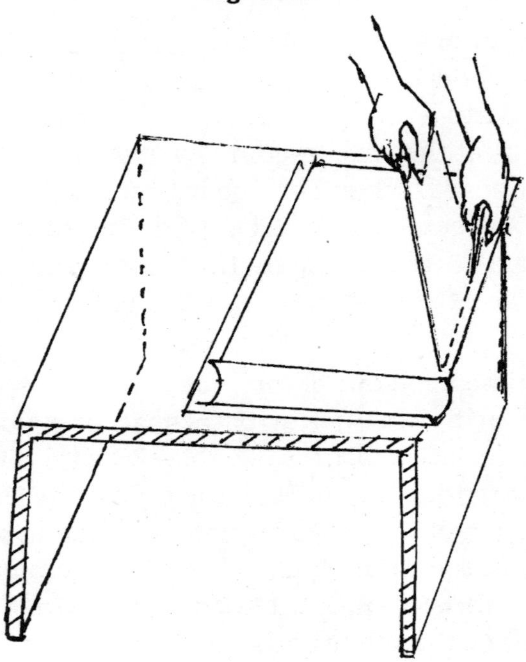

Fig. 18.15

Open the book, one side and then the other, and tear away the portion of the protection sheets that is free—that is, not glued to either the cartridge paper/ bristol bonnet or the masonate board. At both head and tail front and back; still the protection sheets with a small knife handle at the point that they wrap around the end sheet sections or along the edge of the spine. These slits should be about 1 inch long enough to permit the covering material to be turned into the bristol bonnet. Insert new protection sheets between the hinges and the end leaving. These should be cut the exact size of the book pages.

Covering: At the right-angle corner cut on the cloth, mark off a right angle corner 3/4 inches or one inch in from both edges and carry the lines the width and length of the material. Lay the cloth face, or right side, down on a smooth clean surface: place the book in this 90° corner so that the fore edge of 1 board and the head are resting on the lines just drawn. Mark a cutting points at the tail allowing a ¾ inches to 1 inch turn in, turn the book over carefully on the spine along the line at the top of the cloth so that the second board is resting on the cloth, and mark the cutting point for the other edge, again allowing the usual one inch margin, or turn in.

Shift the cloth to a sheet of board/white paper and glue it in its entirely. Place the book in position in the marks off corner. Pick up both the book and cloth, turn them over and lay the book down on the edge of the wooden *chawki* (platform) with the spine extending beyond the edge allow the cloth to hang free (Fig. 18.15). Rub the cloth down on the board to which it is attached. With a knife's handle rub the cloth into joint the point; then pull the cloth firmly over the spine and rub it down well. Turn the book over again and while holding the cloth free of the book, rub it into the other joint (Fig. 18.16). Then lay the cloth down gradually on the other (bottom) board, rubbing it down smooth and evenly in the process. With a knife's handle, mark the edge of the indention on the spine provided for the level.

Cut all corners at right-angle, reglue the edges one at a time and turn than in the following order tail, head and fore edge. On the tail and head, the cloth must be turned into the bonnet or hollow spine area. Turn the edges on both boards from fore edge to spine, then work the material into the bonnet. This is best, or more easily, done with the book standing up and open.

More space for turning the material into the bonnet is provided if the book is open, for it arches away from the spine of the covers. If the book is thick and heavy, support its fore edge during the process. A few scraps of low graded straw board can be slipped under it.

After the material is turned into bonnet, lay the book open on the table and rub the turned area with a knife's holder to ensure its sticking and to smooth out any small wrinkles, give special attention to the joint areas. Repeat at the head, then turn the fore edges in the usual manner.

Place the book between sharp edge wooden boards, the edges of the wooden board resting in the joints. Put in the press under medium pressure for an hour. Remember to protect the sharp edge of wooden board on the other sides of the boards with press boards. If the sharp wooden board is not available, lay a clean piece of waste paper over the joint areas. The point where the masonate board is attached to the bonnet and rub with the side of a knife holder. Put the book to press between pressboards, taking care to line up the edges of this boards with the spine edges of the masonate boards.

Remove from the press, open one cover to an upright position, slip a piece of waste paper under the cloth hinge, and glue it in the entirely. Replace the waste paper with a strip of wax paper and close the cover. Repeat on the other side, and return the book to the press for half an hour, cut the board papers to size and attach as described earlier under case binding.

STITCH/TIGHT BACK/CORD BINDING

Many of the steps and techniques applied in producing these styles of binding are same. The basic difference is that one has tight back, as its name implies and other has a hollow band. Where techniques differ, these will be discussed separately: otherwise, assume that these instructions apply to both styles of binding. At this point the book is sewn, end leave preparation and attached, glued, rounded, backed and edges treated.

Materials Required

- Masonate board 2 pieces, one inch larger than both dimensions of book.
- Bond paper 2 pieces acid free, 3 inches wide length of boards.
- Bristal board heavy, 2 strips or other board the thickness of leather to be used on binding, same width and length as boards.
- Sand paper 120 No.
- Paste: As described previously.
- Press board, wax paper.
- Hammer.

The first 2 steps are to prepare and attach the board. The thickness or weight of the board to be used have been determined during the book was backed.

Preparing the boards leave 1/8 inch square on all 3 edges, except that the boards fit into the right-angle joints produced in the backing and are not offset. If uncertain about width, make those slightly wider. Those can easily be cut to the proper width after those are attached.

Draw a line on both boards about 1½ inches from one edge, fold the strips of the paper in half lengthwise and attach one strip to each board. Glue the paper lay the fold along one edge of the board and attach half the paper to one side of the board. Pull it tight around the edge of the board and lay the other half on the other side of the board rubbing it down firmly on the edge and both sides of the board. This prevents possible splitting of the board by the **"Pull"** created when the covering leather and the leather hinge are in position. The edge, thus, treated is the spine edge of the board. When the paper is dry, pare up sand the edge to a feather edge, and sand away any surplus paper at head and tail.

Back Cornering: Both corners on the spine edge of each board are now back cornered on one side. It is done by cutting the corners of the boards off at a level, starting about 1/4 inch from corner (Fig. 18.17).

The thinning of corners at these points gives a bit more space for the opening of the boards at the turns of the leather in the spine are where it is double thickness and aids in shaping the headcaps.

Glue the narrow strips of hardboard and attach these to the edges of the boards on top of the bond paper. These may be slightly narrower than the thickness of the board, but should not be wider. These prevent the boards from being pulled too close in the joints in the contraction of the leather when drying. The boards are now ready to be attached to the book.

Attaching the Boards: There are several methods of attaching the boards. The traditional way, and the one still thought by some binders to be strongest, is the technique of laciniaty the cords into the boards. The point of wear on the cords, however, is in the joint and not where these are attached to the board.

One Acceptable: Theory for the development of this early technique is that it saved boards and time when these were scarce and tedious to make and cut boards were—and still are—needed to protect the joints when the book was screwed up in a press preparatory to ploughing the edges, and if one pair could be cut to the proper size for the covers, and loosely attached so those could be shifted up or down, this eliminated the necessity of additional boards for this purpose. The two most common methods are used today for attaching cords and one for attaching tapes to the boards will be given here.

***Laciniating* in the Cords:** These directions are for a book that was sewn on raised cords and the cords are intact, in other words not wear off by rubbing. Draw a line on both boards 3/8 inches from the spine edge —the line will be on the bond paper attached earlier. Lay one board in position on the book. Check the eveness of the squares; and mark the diameter of each cord from the edge of the board to the line, pulling those tight and straight across the board. Turn the book over with this board still in position. Put the other board on the book and with a stringle line up the edges of it with those of the first board, and mark the location of the cords in the same way. It is safer to mark off the position of the cords on both boards and not mark the second board by the first. The cords do not always fall in exactly the same position on front and back boards, although ideally these should mark the boards by simply putting an "F" on the front board.

Remove the boards from the book and at the points where the cords crossed the drawn lines, bore a hole, use a gimlet or a hand drill with a bit the approximate diameter of the cord. Draw a second line on both boards about 1/4 inch from the first and parallel to it toward the fore edge (Fig. 18.18). Bore another series of holes along the second time about 1/4 inch below the holes already made, in the direction of the tail of the book. Notch the boards at the edges where the cords cross it, and cut a V-shaped groove between the notches and the first series of holes. It is assumed that the boards are heavy enough to permit the cutting of these grooves sufficiently deep to accommodate the cord without wear off by rubbing it. This should be just deep enough for the cords to fit lying closed **snugly** into it. If too deep, a depression will be evident after the book is covered, and if not deep enough, a bump will show. Work on one until the cord seems to tie flat, then proceed with the others. Next turn the boards over and cut similar grooves from the first holes to the second. Put a bit of paste on the end of each cord and twist it to a point, let dry for a few minutes. Lace all cords in to the first series of holes from the outside, on the inside of the board, carry those from the first holes to the second ones and bring those out to the outside surface of the board. If the edges of the book are to be cut “in boards” with a machine, the cutting is done at this point before the cords are permanently attached to the boards.

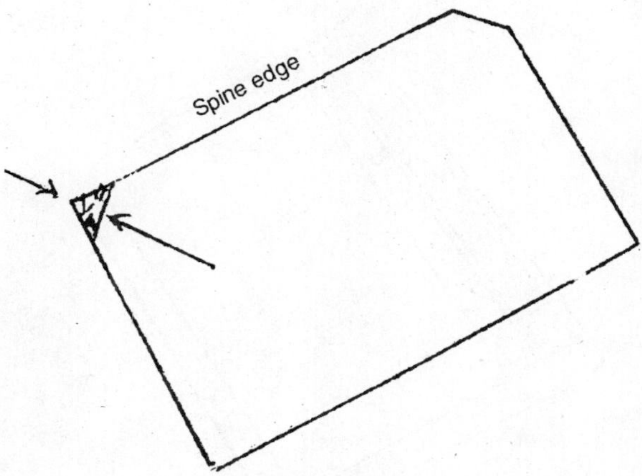

Fig. 18.16

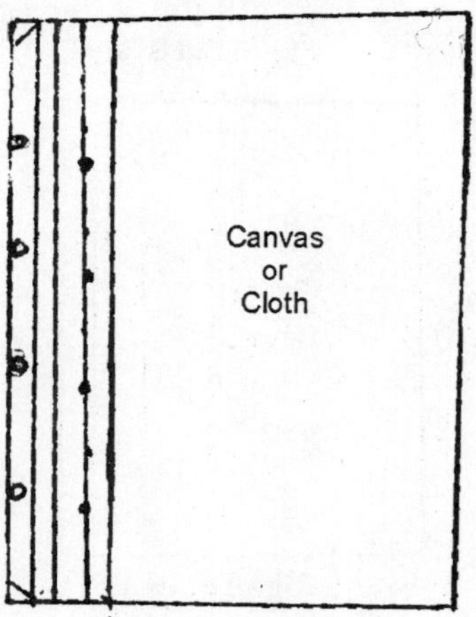

Fig. 18.17

Setting the Boards and Securing the Cords: First one board is loosen the cords, then the other. Now apply paste to all the cords and where those fit into the notched edges. Hold the board in a vertical position and pull the cords tight (Fig. 18.19). Lay the board down on the book. If the board seems to ride up excess on the fore edge, loosen the cords a bit until the board lies flat. After both boards have been so attached, check the evenness of the squares with a

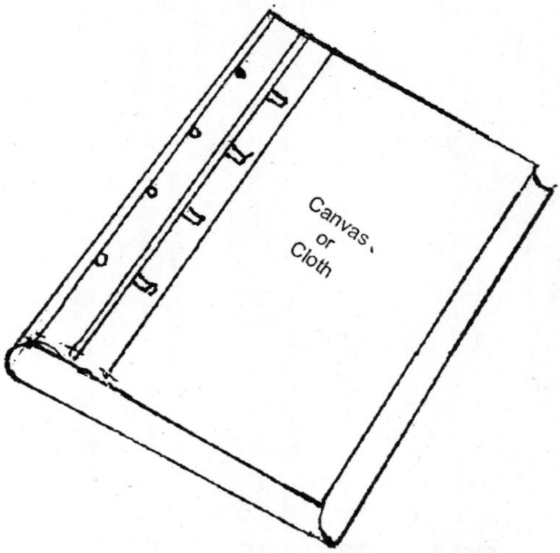

Fig. 18.18

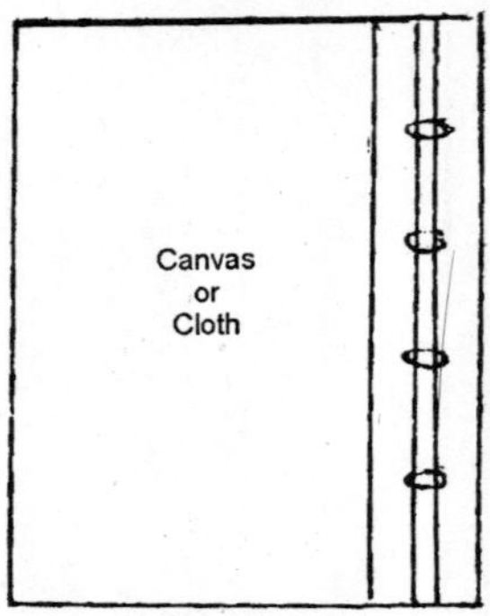

Fig. 18.19

triangle and make any necessary adjustment while the paste is still moist.

Cut off the surplus ends of the cords flush with the surface of the board. Lay wax paper over the pasted areas, and put the book between press boards and weight down until dry. When dry, if the cords are higher than the surface of the boards moisten the exposed part both inside and out side with paste. Open the cover and lay it on a firm surface. Put a scrap of hard board even the cords and hammer then flat. If the cords

Fig. 18.20

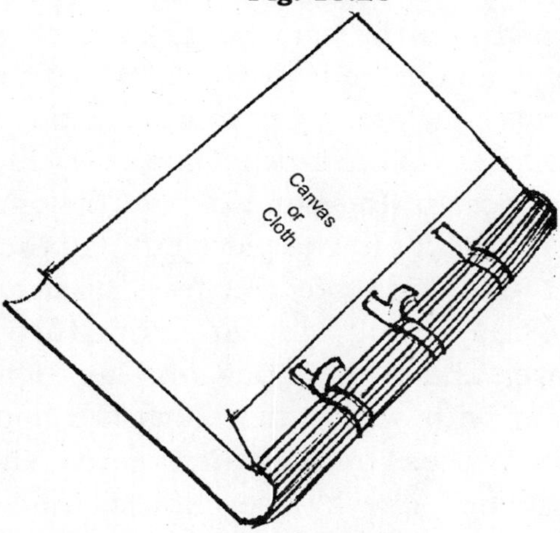

Fig. 18.21

are depressed as a result of the grooves having been cut too deep. Fill these in with strands of cord to which paste has been applied.

The second method of attaching the cords is to cut these approximately one inch long. Lay the boards in there proper position and mark the location of the cords on the edge of the boards. Notch the edge of the boards at these points to accommodate the thickness of the cord in its unfrayed state: lay the cord in the V-shaped groove and fray the reminder of it. Untwist it and separate the fibres by combing with a needle. Apply mixture to the cords, lay these on the positioned boards in a fanlike fashion (Fig. 18.20). Combing out the fibres to make these lie as flat as possible. Attach one board, lay a strip of wax paper over the frayed cords turn the book over, and repeat. Take care to check the evenness of the squares: adjust it necessary and weight the book down between pressboards until dry.

Attaching the boards in a book that has been sewn. Cut all tapes one inch long with a straight end. Lay the boards in the book and check the squares. When properly set up, pull the tapes, one at a time, tight and straight on the board, mark the exact width and length of each on the boards. Using a small metal edge as a guide, cut along the marks as deep as the estimated thickness of the tapes. This is very little more than the thickness of the bond paper. Try one before cutting the others lift out the piece cut, lay the tape in the indented area, and see if it feels flush with the board (Fig. 18.21). If all right, apply mixture to both the cut-out area and to the tapes, and lay the tapes in position. Cover with wax paper, turn the book over and repeat the process on the other board. When both boards are attached, check the evenness of the squares and weight down.

LIMP AND FLEXIBLE BINDING

During the discussion of end papers, mention was made of a divinity circuit binding which is a limp binding. Limp and flexible bindings are both made off the book. The book is either rounded not backed, or it is rounded and then given the smallest possible amount of backing.

For a flexible cover there are no boards but instead two pieces of flexible paper such as rag backing or Nepalese hand-made paper are cut to the board size. These are lightly tipped in position on the book by a spot of paste at the back edge. Another spot of paste is put on the back edge of each piece of paper, and the leather which has been cut to size and pared is fitted around the book. The papers are pulled loose from the book and left sticking to the leather, and the edge of the leather is pasted and turned in on the paper.

A limp cover consists of a piece of leather with the edges turned in upon itself and a cloth or leather board sheet pasted down only around the edge. The divinity circuit binding overlaps the book edges sufficiently to cover those. The leather lining, which corresponds to the board sheet, is cut from a piece of this leather.

It is as large as the completed cover. An opening is cut the centre of this piece of leather to accommodate the back of the book. It should be so cut that there will be two flaps to paste against the fly leaves. The cover material is cut to size and pared, pasted and turned in over the edge of the lining.

QUESTIONS FOR DISCUSSION

1. What is case binding?
2. What is the difference between light back and hollow back?
3. How will you prepare Spine and Cloth Strip?
4. Discuss about cord binding.
5. What is lacinating in the cards?
6. Discuss about *alfach* the board on the book.
7. What is board paper?
8. Define about spring lining, end banks.
9. Discuss the cutting of the Vellum Cover.
10. What is back corner?
11. Define fore-edge, ribbon ties and leather thong-ties.

19
Conservation Binding

ENDPAPERS

The endpapers are made up from a single sheet of paper with a cloth backing. This sheet which will become the "Board Paper" is guarded around a blank section and is sewn on as part of the book block. In addition, the first section of the text and the last section of the text have a guard of Nepalese hand-made paper tipped on as shown in Fig. 19.1.

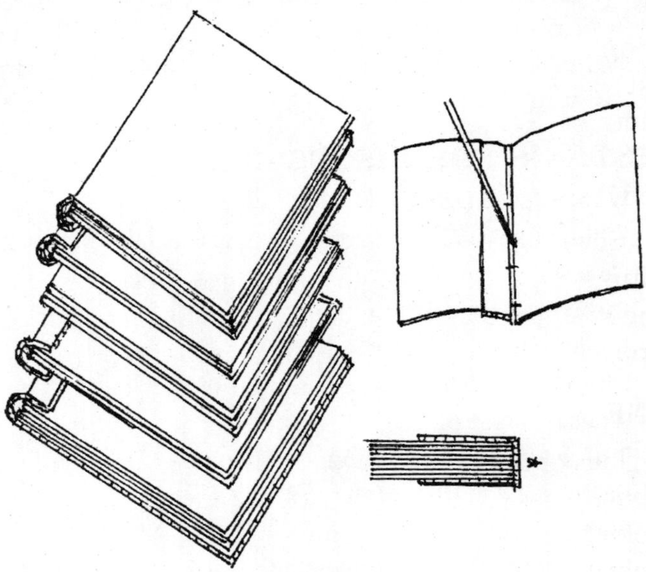

Fig. 19.1

SEWING SUPPORTS

The sewing supports are 4–5 mm wide throngs of alum-tawed sheep goat or pigskin. There should be long enough to be able to reach half way across the text block on each side.

The number of supports depends on the size and thickness of the book. (as well as on the binder's personal preferance) as a round guide: A book that is 15 cm would require no more than 3 supports. Books taller than 20 cm, would need 4 to 5 supports. Once the number of supports are determined, the sections are either punched of slit for sewing. The kettle stitches are 1.5 cm to 2 cm from the head and tail.

SEWING

A sewing frame is necessary to ensure the supports which are held upright and under tension.

The choice of sewing thread will be determined by the number of sections. The thickness of these sections and the quality of the paper and the thread must be thick enough to ensure adequate strength without inducing any spine swell. Limp-vellum binding which is not rounded or backed, so a said swell is not noted.

Sewing is "All Along" with "Packing" around the sewing supports. When joining threads make the join at the kettle-stitch or tucked tightly against the sewing support.

SPINE LINING

Limp binding styles parely have any lining should the book be large or very thick it might be advisable to attach a thin paper lining in the spaces between sewing supports.

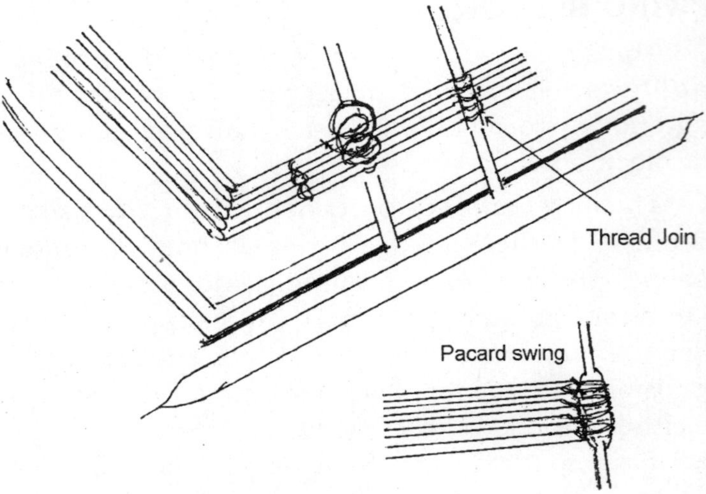

Fig. 19.2

ENDBANDS

The endbands are an important part of the structure, strength of this type of binding. These can be sewn on to supports similar to similar. The sewing support, or these could also be sewn on to few vellum tawed are then laced through the covering materials. This type of endband will be described in the leather on vellum cover.

When using tawed strip, the endband core can be twisted into a rounded core, or if its flexible leather it will round itself if the sewing is tight the strip damp and then held under weights until fully dry. If the strip is thick and stiff levelling one edge of the strip will produce a more rounded core.

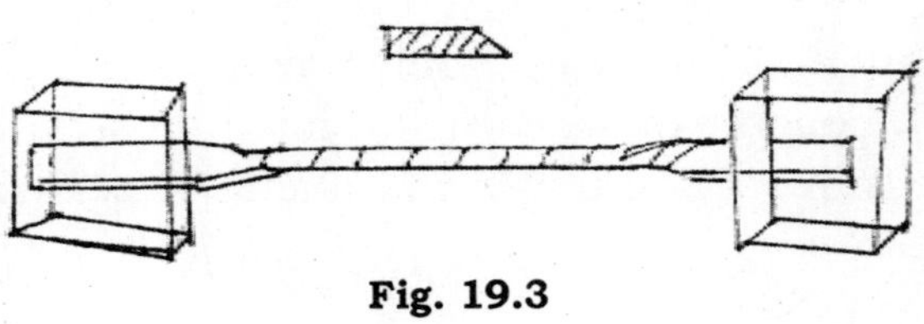

Fig. 19.3

One of the easiest way to do the end banding is to hold the book block in a finishing press in the manner shown in Fig. 19.4.

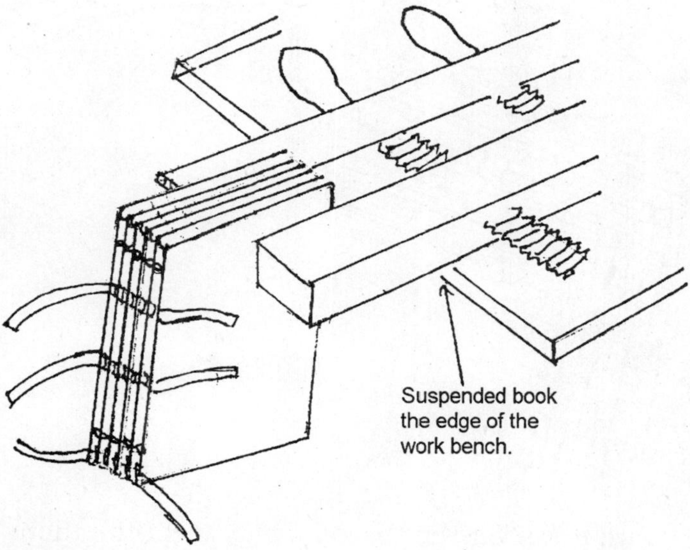

Fig. 19.4

The loose end of the sewing supports can be taped on to the sides of the text block to avoid **entanglement** of the thread used for the endboard. The thread should be the same as used for sewing of the sections. It is also a good idea to mark the centre of each section with a thin slip of paper. There are a great many different ways to sew single core endbands each binder varying the detail a little. The following method is as good as any.

Tie the free end of the thread to the thong and then push the needle down through the centre of the first section (at the extreme left of the book) and also the needle in around side the slip of paper that marks the centre of the section so as to avoid damage to the pages of the book. The needle must emerge below the kettle stitch.

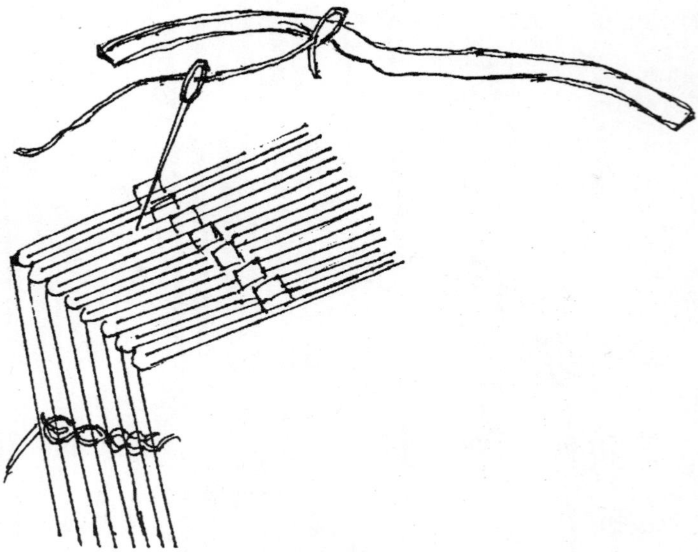

Fig. 19.5

Pull down on the thread firmly until the thong is sitting on the edge of the book. If the book is large and heavy enough to warrant the use of Spine Linings then a paper lining should be placed over the tie-downs of the endband and it should reach half way up the end band itself.

CUTTING OUT THE VELLUM COVER

Before cutting out the vellum one should decide if the cover will have a fore-edge *Yapp,* then use one of the patterns that shown in Figs. 19.6 and 19.7.

LINING THE VELLUM

If one wishes to line the vellum with paper, the binder should use an acid free paper not more than 100 G.S.M. (Preferably bond paper or thin hand-made paper). The lining can be attached using either paste

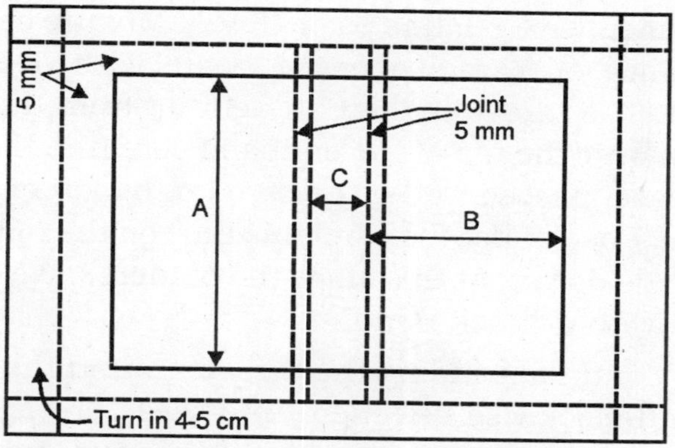

Fig. 19.6: Books without *Yapp*

Lines shown dotted are scored with bone folder

A = Height of the book block

B = Width of book block (including sewing supports)

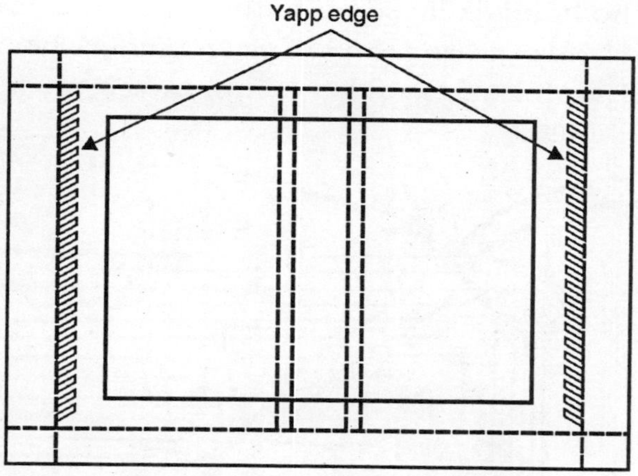

Fig. 19.7: For books with *Yapp*

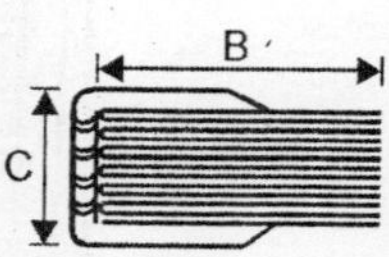

First decide on the size of the Yapp. These could be anything from 2 mm to as much as 10 mm. About 4–5 mm is quite common.

Note : Make sure that when one decides on the size if the "SQUARE" that one will allow enough at the head and tail to accommodate the endboard core as it is laced through the cover.

parchment give gelatine paste/P.V.A. Mixture or Methyl Cellulose or Tamarind seed paste with Jeebanjor 20 : 1. The thread is then brought up from the spine. Taken over the top of the endband core (the thongs in this case) passed under the core (to the left of the tie-down). Base under the care (this time on the right hand of the tie down). At this stage the binders have one tie-down with a "Back Bend".

Continue winding the thread around the core in an anti-clockwise direction until these are level with the centre of the second section. Make sure the thread is pulled firmly at every turn so that the flat thong is gradually formed into a rounded core for the endband. Push the needle down the side of the slip of paper and make another tie down, with a back bend as before. Once the lining is layed on to the back of the vellum, place it between two pieces of clean binders board and then in a press. Leave the vellum in the press for at least 4 hours.

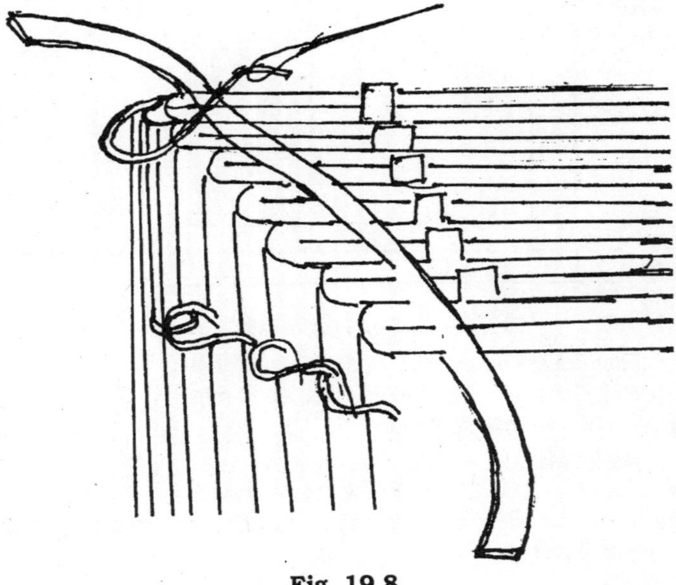

Fig. 19.8

CUTTING THE CORNERS

There are a large variety of corners used on vellum binding, many of them self-locking. The method shown is one of the simplest ways or methods of this type to make.

Begin by cutting away the excess material in the corner. Use a needle to punch the holes, place a scrap board under the corner to avoid putting a hole right through the cover.

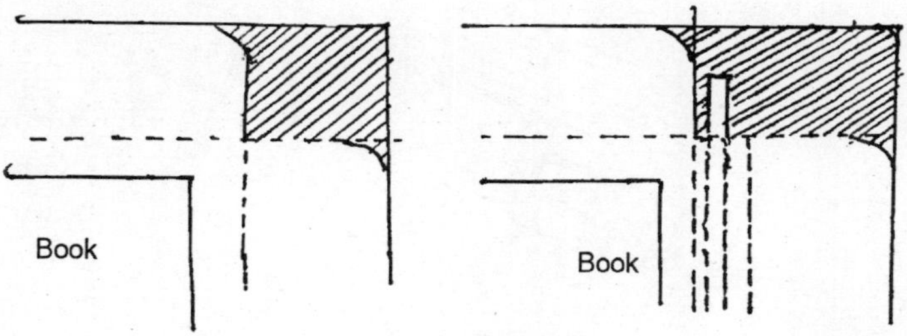

Fig. 19.9

Open up the corner again and cut the Notches and Slots.

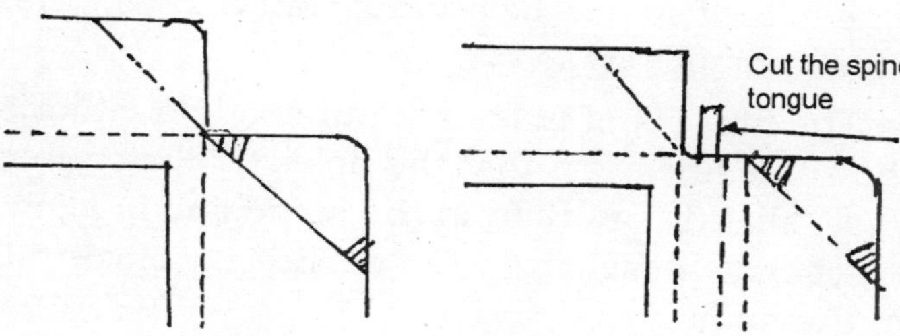

Without *Yapp* Edge **With *Yapp* Edge**

Fig. 19.10

ATTACHING THE 'CASE'

Prior to laciniating the book block to its cover, one must locate and punch the holes to pass the sewing supports through.

Begin by turning in the vellum, use a set square to accurately mark the centre of each sewing support and the endband cores.

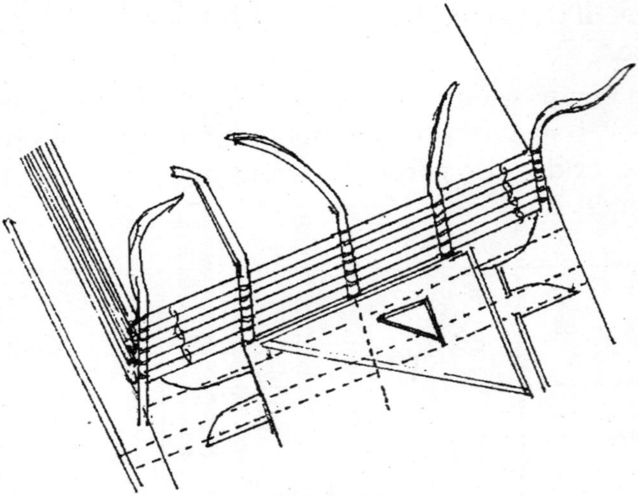

Fig. 19.11

Make sure the hole punches are kept sharp to avoid tearing, or damage to the case or the book block. The hole itself should be approximately 2/3 of the flat thongs in diameter.

The first set of holes are punched on either side of the spine line. Note that the holes for the endbands are set "slightly" away from the spine line to allow for the fact that these sit on top of the text block rather than the spine.

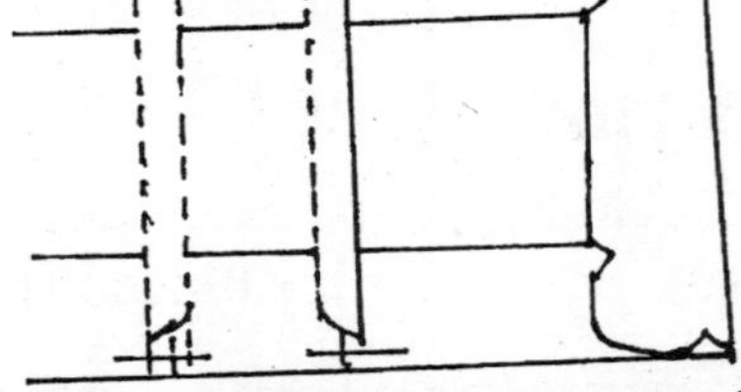

Fig. 19.12: The sewing supports can now be laced on.

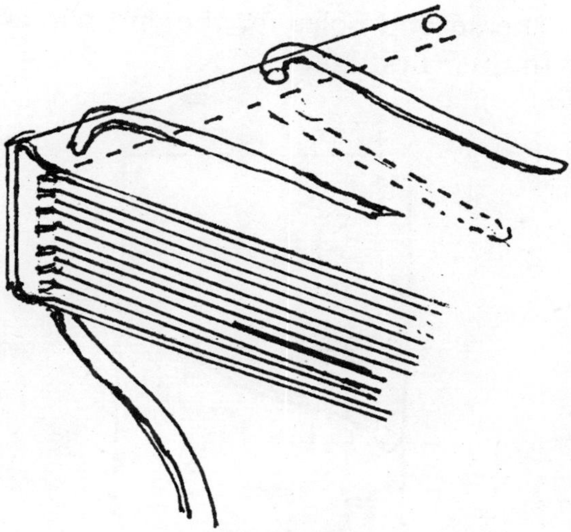

Fig. 19.13

Fig. 19.14

The second set of holes are punched lever with the first, but set about 1 cm towards the fore-edge of the case. The second holes for the end bands should be at 45° to their first holes.

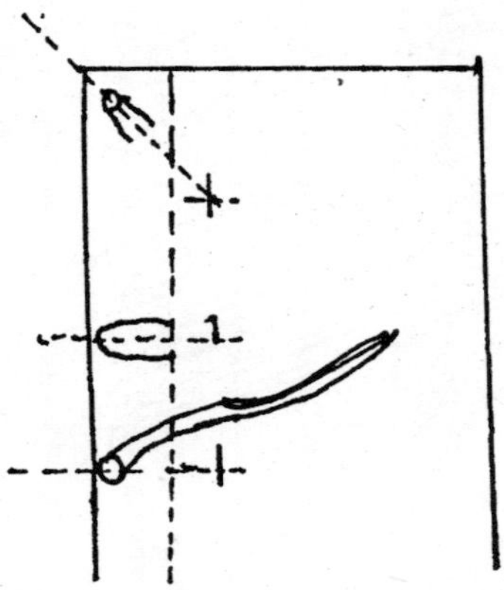

Fig. 19.15

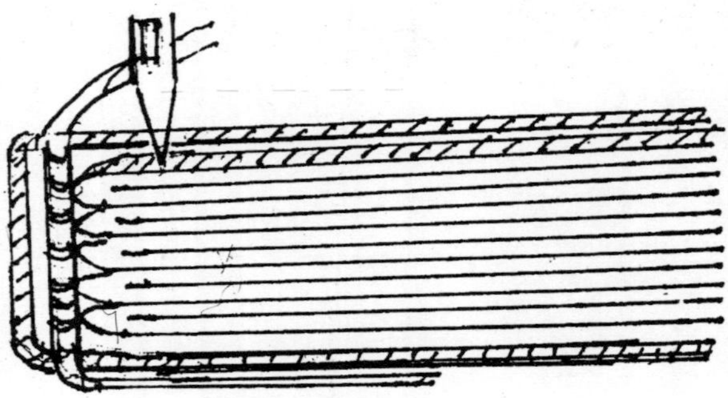

Fig. 19.16

These holes must also pass through the board papers. To avoid damage to the text block, place a piece of scrap board under the board paper.

Another set of holes is punched in line with the previous two sets of holes. A further 1 cm towards the fore edge, but this time from leave the piece of scrap board in place for protection through the board paper only. Do not punch the third set of holes for the endbands yet.

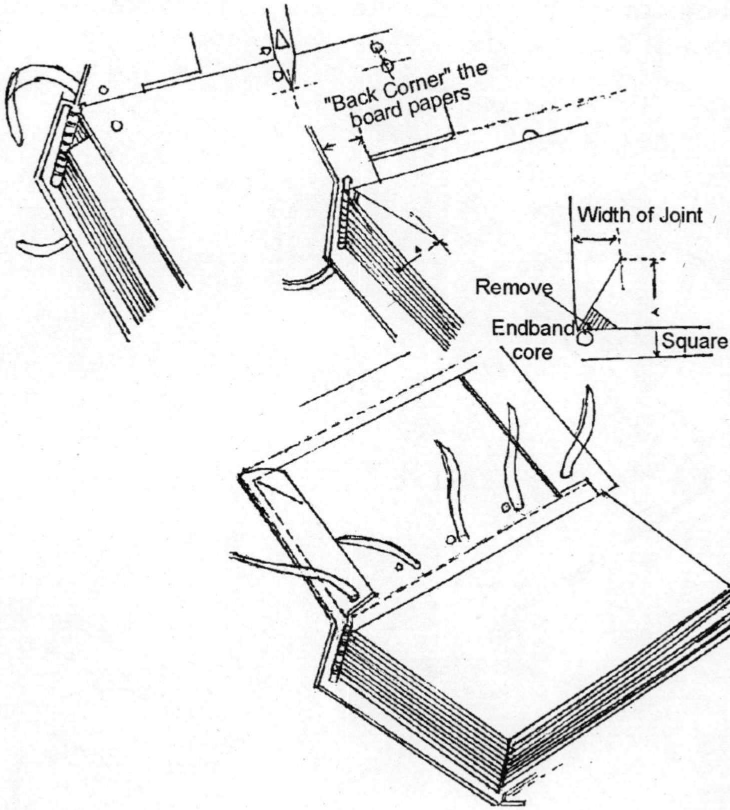

Carefully slip the board paper under the head and tail turning the **"Back Corner"** of the board paper will automatically "lock" into place. Laciniate the sewing supports through the second set of holes.

Fig. 19.17

The third hole for the endbands can now be punched.

The sewing supports are finally *laciniated* through the last hole in the board paper so that the free end are sandwiched between the board paper and the covering vellum. This operation can be of different uses, a pair of long nose piece to reach when and pull the thongs through. Turn the fore-edge in onto the board paper and "Lock" the covers.

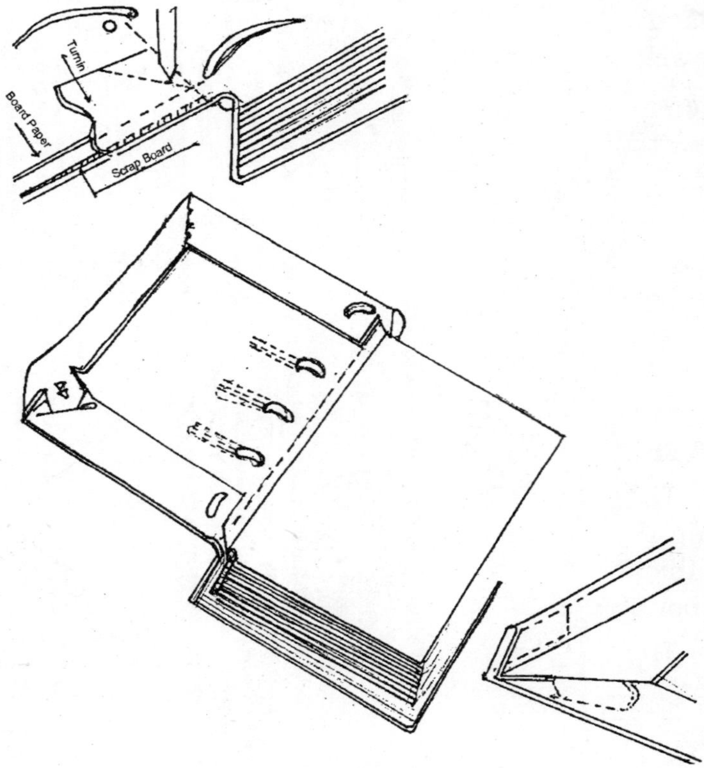

Fig. 19.18

FORE-EDGE TIES

There are several different ways to make fore-edge ties as well as various materials that can be used. In broad terms, one could classify the ties as ribbon ties, leather thong tie, button and loop ties, loop and catch tie or strap ties. The number of tie's swell as per the location which will depend mostly on the size and format of the volume being bound and the personal preference of the binder. Small format books can be bound with a single tie centred on the fore-edge.

RIBBON TIES

Any material is suitable for ribbon ties. However, "Petersham" or corded ribbon makes a strong and attractive tie. Those can be attached in either of the following ways.

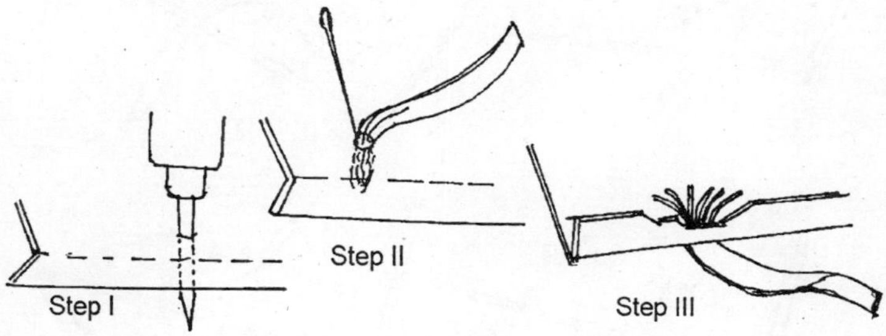

Fig. 19.19: Viewed from inside

LEATHER THONG TIES

The "Leather" used should be "Alum-Tawad", sheep skin, goat skin or pig skin. Avoid skins that are two thick [about 1 mm is acceptable] with a thong width of about 5–6 mm.

Thong attachment can be, by a "one hole" "two holes" or a three holes system.

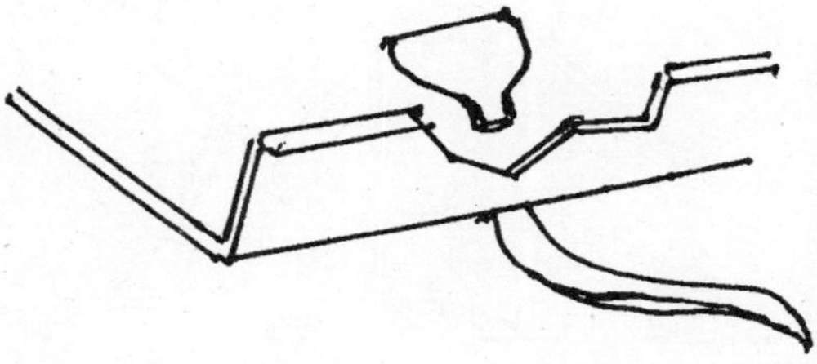

Fig. 19.20: One hole system

For most bindings, the above fore-edge ties should be sufficient to prevent the book from **"Gapping"**. The pear that this type of tie will be pulled out, is not borne out historically—it is very common to find that the thongs or ribbon has broken off on the outside, leaving the tab or paste down still in place.

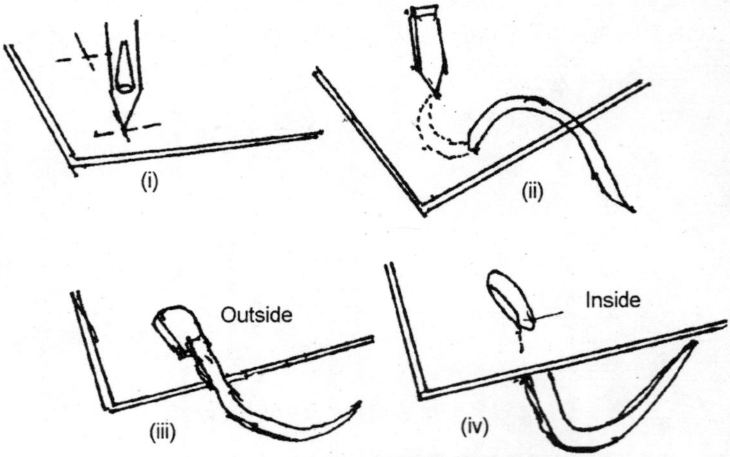

Fig. 19.21: Two Hole System

One of the most advantages of the two and three hole systems is that these are self-locking needing no adhesives to hold those in place.

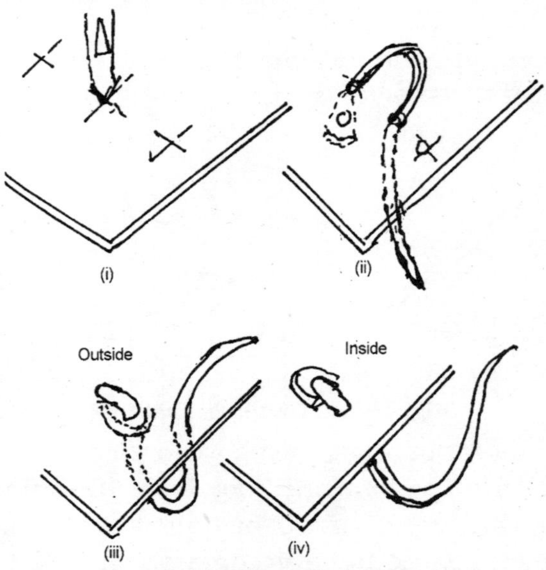

Fig. 19.22: Three hole system

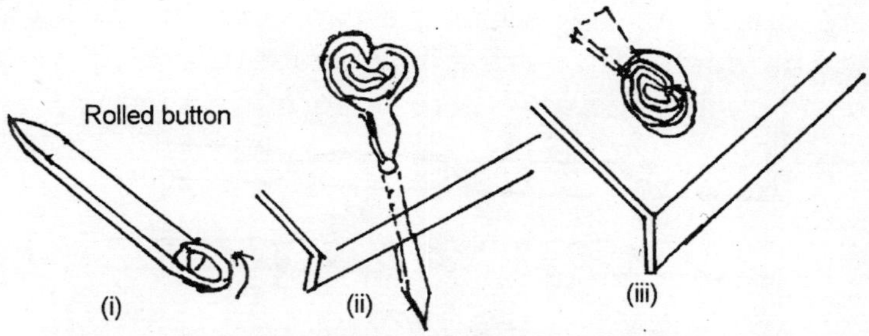

Fig. 19.23: Button and Loop Systems

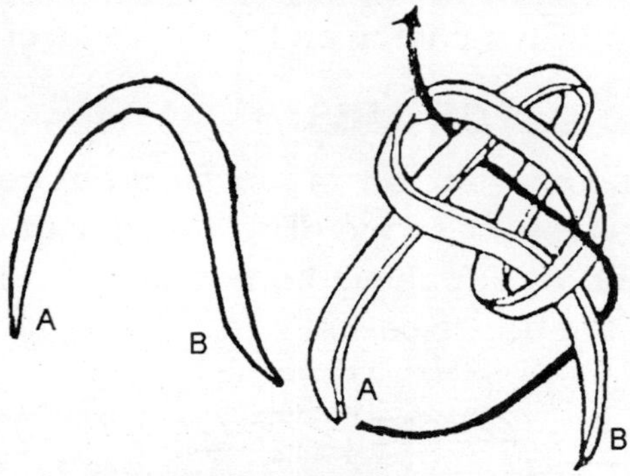

Fig. 19.24: Diamond Button

The rolled button is by far the easiest to make and will be more than advantage for most books. The diamond button is very complicated to make but no more pleasing to the eye.

At this stage the looseness is very carefully worked out, progressively tightening the thongs until a firm button is formed. It is not a bad idea to practice this button using a length of cord first (it is easier to work with a rounded cord). Only after restorar is confident with the cord restorar should try to use a flat thong. When the button is as tight as one can make it pass the two "Tails" through the cover and paste those down on the inside.

MAKING THE LOOP

A length of thong is twisted until it will take no

more turns. At that stage the two ends are brought towards each other—this will cause there to wrap around each other and there by forming a loop.

Fig. 19.25

The two free ends are passed through a hole in the cover and then pasted on to the inside of the cover.

LOOP AND CATCH TIES

The Loops can be made from ribbon leather **Thongs** or Vellum strips. The catch can be either, plastic, wood or Japanese bone toogle. The loops are located on the upper cover.

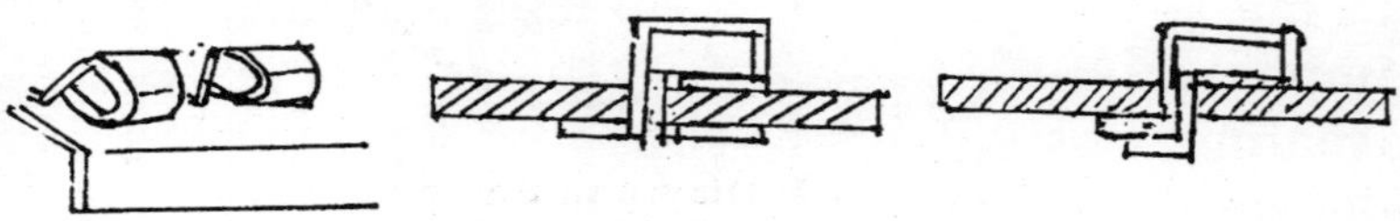

Fig. 19.26: Loops

Although not "absolutely" necessary, it is a good idea to use double loops as shown above because they will hold the **toogle** catch much better than a single loop.

The Catch: The catch can either be attached to a ribbon or leather thong. These can also be attached to vellum string but this is not too strong. The following methods are the most common ways of securing the catch to its ribbon or thong.

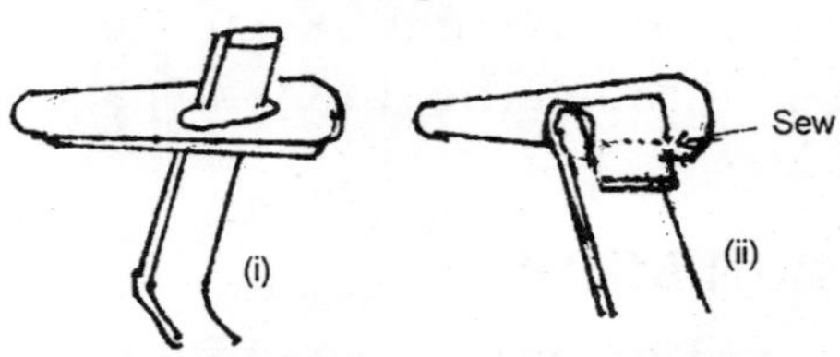

Fig. 19.27: Ribbon Attachment

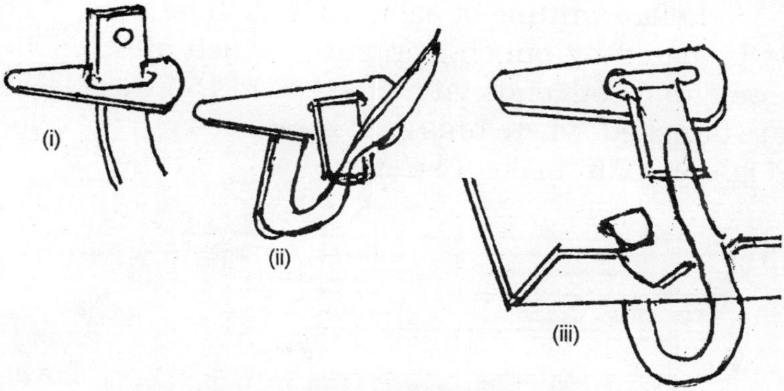

Fig. 19.28: Leather Thong Attachment

BUNDLE

Palm Leaf used as a writting material before invention of paper which is called *palm manuscript.* It is available in South India, West Bengal, Bihar which is made up of cellulose fibre. Its binding is less important than repair and lamination, Chemical treatment which is enunciated in "preparation of document". Palm leaf binding is an edge old practice which is given below.

Required Material: Wooden ply, 2 nos, brass/ steel rod 5 mm dia 2 nos, sunken cord.

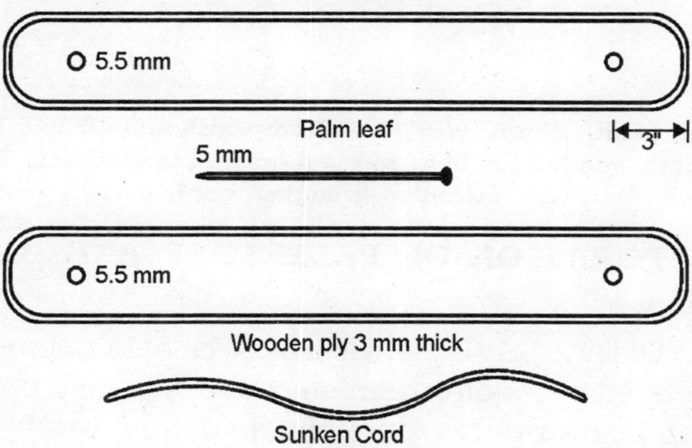

Fig. 19.29

Before writting of palm leaf hole 5 mm dia, 2 nos is prepared by punch/perforated which are 3 inches away from both ends. At a time 100 to 150 sheet leaves are punched, where brass rod is inserted top to bottom (Fig. 19.30) to make it straight.

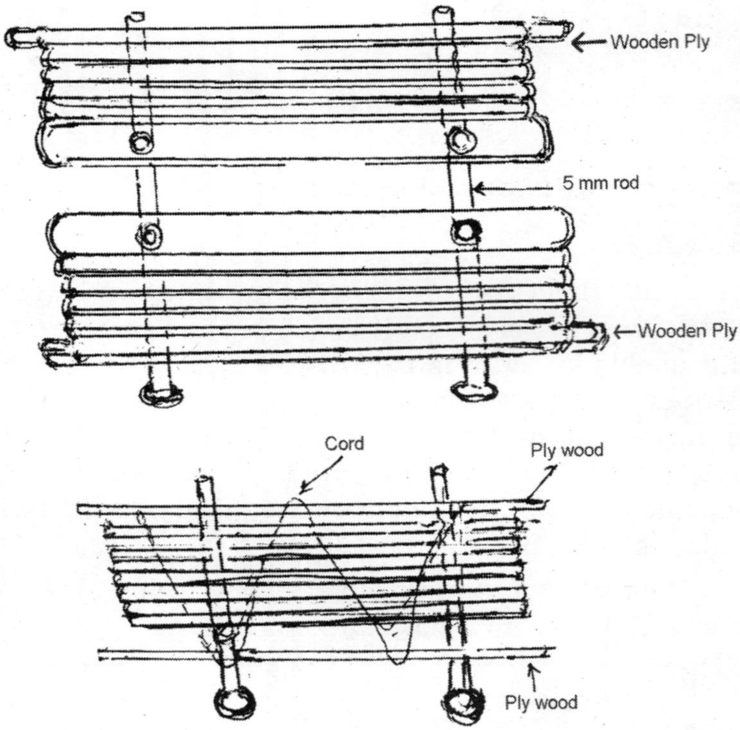

Fig. 19.30: 3 mm thick, 4 to 5 cm width and 40 to 50 cm length wooden ply both top and bottom is attached. Then fasten with sunken cord.

RESTORATION OF PALM LEAF AND BIRCH BARK

Old and brittle plam leaf or birch bark manuscript sheets often require re-inforcement for their upkeep. Dust accumulates on palm leaf and birch bark manuscripts, if kept improperly and the writting is creased there by. Manuscripts, where the ink is not washable in water could be cleaned with a solution of glycerine in water (1 : 1), while those where the ink is soluble in water could be cleaned with benzene or acetone. Palm leaf manuscript written in carbon ink, if faded, cannot be restored, while in case of those inscribed with stylus, re-inking is possible. The process of re-inking consists in rubbling graphite powder with a cotton swab.

Birch bark or palm leaf manuscripts stuck together due to exposure to rain water or storage in humid condition. Separation of the solid block of palm leaves may be done by immersion in a bath of hot (65°C) liquid paraffin.

Palm leaves which have stuck together may be separated by placing them in a humidification room or exposing them to steam. When these have become sufficient moistered, each leaf is separated carefully by means of blunt spatula.

These leaves may be separated by placing those in bath of hot water (60°C) containing 5 to 1% of glycerine. The water in bath is changed every half an hour. After absorbing for an hour, individual layers are lifted by means of a metallic Spatula.

Fig. 19.31

20

Library Binding in Leather

All voluminus books like dictionaries, encyclopaedia that are constant use and antique need very strong binding that open easily and lie flat, in order to achieve this, those can be found with leather covered spines in such a way that the leather combines the functions of back-lining and cover.

The principles involved and the variety of tools used in the pairing of leather are discussed in previous chapter. This chapter considers the details of selecting of leather, cutting of size, pairing leather, covering of with leather and sliding.

Leather is one of the few materials used by the binder that has no grain direction, so a given piece can be cut from what seems the most desirable area of the skin both from the standpoints of appearance and economy. It is wise to be as economical as possible for fine work, however, quality should come first.

The areas nearest the spine of the animal are the stronger and move durable portion of the skin. So, it is advisible to use these when cutting for a full leather binding. The National Library, Kolkata used Morocco leather for preservation of antique.The goat, sheep and culf skins are smaller in size. Therefore, accommodation should be made according to size of both book and leather. There is scope for use of small piece leather in half leather binding.

Try to centre the spine of the animal on the spine of the book. There are occasions, however, when the graining of the skin in this area—particularly near the neck—is too coarse and heavy to title satisfactorily. In such instances, it should not be used. When a skin is large enough to get a whole cover out of one side of it, in covering the book orient the leather so that the area nearest the spine is at the tail of the book.The tail is subject to more wear in taking the book in and out of a shelf than is the head. If the book, however, is to have a protective case other than a slip case, this is relatively unimportant. There are other times when it is necessary, because of the largeness of the book or the smallness of the skin, to orient the spine of the skin horizontally on the volumes. If so, try to place the spine on the book covers so that it will fit into the planned decoration and not interfere with it. Reserve the blank area, or softer part of the skin, for headband and tailbands and labels, neither of which is subject to heavy wear. The legs of a skin are of little use because of their stretchy characteristic.

PAIRING LEATHER

Book binding leather generally prepared thin by the lanner either by delibrerate splitting of very heavy skins or in the process of producing a smooth finish on the inner or flesh side of the skin. More thinning is usually desirable in the area where the leather turns over the edges of the boards, at the head and tail in the spine area, at the corners and in the joints this is usually done by sanding.

The amount of thinning is assertion by the original

thickness of the skin and size of the book and its expected use. The binding leather should be thin enough to execute the work easily and not create a bulkely appearance in the specific areas mentioned, simultaneously not thinned to the extents that its strength and durability are appreciably reduced. The leather should be fairly thin at all turning points. One solution is to use small skins, such as goat, sheep skin for small and medium size books.

But in case of large volume, pairing is essential for thick buffalow or cow skins. Now and then craftsman should be spent practicing on scraps before pairing a large piece cut out for the cover of a book. Experience can also be achieved by pairing pieces that can be used for head bands or patch labels which will be waste a little. The blade of the chesal/niskarta/ knife is kept constant motion as, it is drawn across the area to be paired. The leather should be on the smooth surface of a wooden block or Lithographic stone. The chesal/niskarta/knife should be always sharps so frequent sharpening is necessary. The fibre of dry leather is hard and the chesal becomes blunt quickly. The Indian chesal/niskarta is rounded end which is used primarily to thin a whole cover or area other than the edges. The work should begin at the edges, which can be started with an edge pairing chesal and worked back towards the centre from all 4 edges. The chesal/niskarta is held at different angles, as for edge pairing (Fig. 20.1).

SPOKESHAVE

This is a carpenter's tool can be used in thining an entire piece of leather and is considerably faster than the niskarta/chesal. The leather must be firmly attached to a smooth surface a large stone is ideal, for its weight will keep it from shifting. It must, however, be large enough to allow space for the leather to be clamped to it. Without the clamp coming in contact with the leather. Two C-clamps big enough to fit over the edge of the stone and a strip of wood will be needed. Lay a portion of the leather on the stone, place the strip of wood on it at the leather. On the stone, place the strip of wood on it at the edge of the stone and attach the clamp-1 at each end (Fig. 20.2).

The edge of the stone to which the clamps are attached must extend beyond the edge of the table on which it rests. The blade should be reversed from its usual position, so that beveled edge is down, and the corners of the blade should be rounded. Use both hands on the spokeshave and start the pairing near the edge of the piece of wood and work outward in a rapid pattern, using a slicing motion. When one area is pared, move the leather, clamp it again, and proceed.

Held the leather in position where flesh side will up. Now restorer can start to thin it. Hold the spokeshave with both hands and push it along the surface, it will cut, move easily if one side is slightly ahead of the other to give a slanting cut. Work systematically all over the surface and check frequently to be sure that there are no local thin spots and even more frequently, remove any shavings that have slipped under the leather. Restorer will find that fingers are more sensitive to thickness variations that restorer expected, and by folding the leather and running finger and thumb along the fold. Restorer will quickly notice any variations of thickness. If the end of the leather tends to catch as the spokeshave goes over it, bevel it with the pairing chesal/knife.

When the leather is thin enough lay the book on the flush side and mark the positions of the head and tail edges of the boards. Anything outside the lines will be turned in and will need pairing. Hold the leather down with three fingers of the left hand, have the chesal/knife edge at 45° to the edge to be pared, and just hold it.

Fig. 20.1

Flat: Now, get the four finger—tips of the left hand lined up with the index finger touching the back edge of the chesal/niskarta/knife press down with three and bend them the index finger remains straight, pushed the back of the chesal/knife and move it along. If any one has kept the chesal flat, nothing happens.

Start near the edge of the turn-in and bevel it about ¼ inch then work into make a wider bevel until one can reach the line. The turn-in has been pared, but one will need to be sure that the central portion: which is to be doubled over on itself and stuck to the spine, will not cause a bump to appear on the spine of

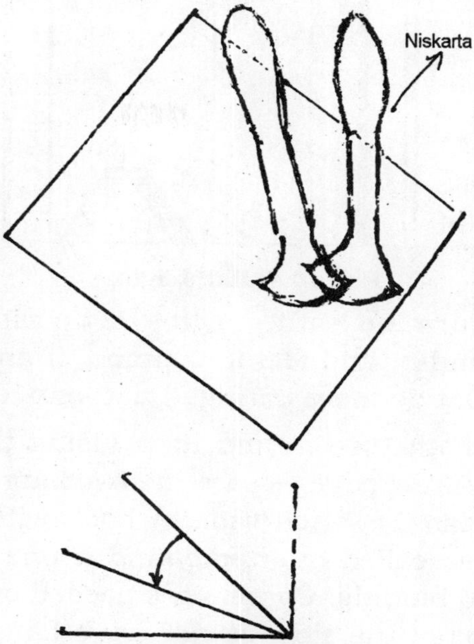

Fig. 20.2: Paring

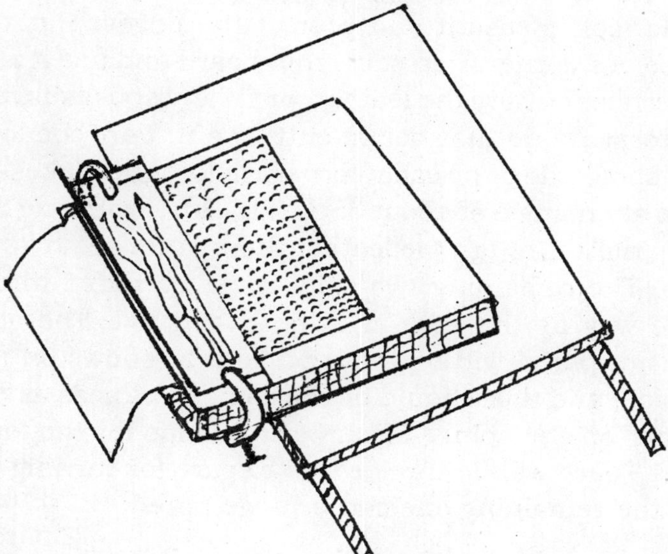

Fig. 20.3

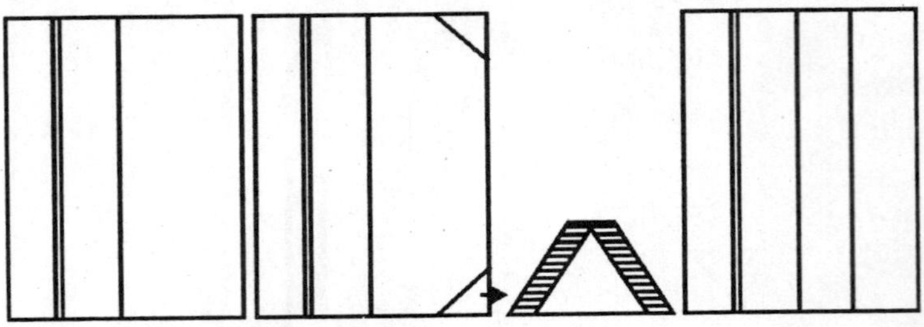

Fig. 20.4: Half binding

the book. Turn the leather right side up with the turn-in folded under, and feel for bumps. If anybody find any, he must do more paring: if not, one has won.

Pare both turn-in and then, using the point of the chesal/knife edge — pare the two long edges. But no more than 1/4 inch wide. A book with a leather back only is called quarter bound if one decides to make a half binding. Corners are needed or, if the five sided shape of the sides is not one's liking: one can have leather strips along the fore-edge of the boards— These look pleasant and protect the edges. Cut the shape of a corner from some thin board and use it as a pattern for cutting the leather, but if any spokeshaving is necessary do that before cutting out. Pare the long and short edges of each corner, holding the chesal/ knife at an angle of about 35°C (Fig. 20.1) with one cut going right through the leather there must be no fluffy edge. The remaining two sides must be pared in the same way as the turn-in at head and tail. The only part not pared will be the triangle that shows on the outside, and that should be the same thickness as the leather on the spine. When paring strips for the fore-edge. There will be three edges to pare for turning in, and the remaining one can be edge-pared.

COVER-IN WITH LEATHER

Leather binding is a time consuming procedure

for preservation. It needs several break up time with a view to drying the paste. Before leather binding of periodical, Journal should remove iron stitching. In contact with iron will make black stain on damp leather. Binder should use glove for pasting the book or the paste brush should be string-bound or aluminium ferruled.

Paste the leather corners or the fore-edge strips well but thinly and leave there with the pasted surfaces face to face to become tacky. While this is happening, make a protective "cap" for the edges of the book, a sheet of paper larger than the book, laid inside the back board and with the front board open, wrapped tightly over the head and tail and fastened over the front endpaper with tape. The width should be sufficient to overby the fore-edge by about 1/2 inch. This is to guard against getting paste on the edges of the book.

Lay the leather on the boards in correct position. Open the boards, and adjust the leather so that only the parts to be turned in are showing. Put the outside of one board down on the tape, hold it there with the book resting on one hand, and use the pointed end of a folder to lift the turn-in and set the leather against the edge of the board. Turn in one edge, tuck in the corner with a spot of paste on the trucked-in part, and then trun-in the other edge. This should make an invisible joint, if, however, there is a ridge or hollow where the edges over lap. One will find that leather will stand a lot of pushing around, so aim to get the perfect joint. If one is turning in fore-edge strips, cut off the corners is much the same way as one would with cloth, but with the point of the pairing chasel/ knife held about an angle 35° and put some paste on the cut edge before turning in.

Now for the spine, paste the leather in the same way as the covers. Then bend it over on itself without making a crease. This traps the moisture which can only get out through the skin. If one cover two books at once, paste both covers and put those face to face. Leave them for about 30 minutes. During this time, find a piece of string of the same thickness as the boards and work paste into the fibres, one only need about 4 inches if the book is not a thick one. Open up the leather and paste it once more; close it again and leave it to become tacky, if, by pressing the pasted surface with one's finger, one can pick up the leather, it is ready to put on the book. Cut two pieces of the pasted strings to put inside the turn-in at the head and tail-those should be the same length as the thickness of the book and boards. Also clean the table (glass top) on which you will work, get rid of any leather shavings, clean a pointed folder, and have a damp sponge ready for when one need it. The turn-in of the leather will go between the book and the boards. So, cut the waste sheet where it goes into the split of the boards but no further than the tape.

Paste slightly the spine, the joint an inch of the boards, to keep the **Porous surfaces** from drawing the moisture from the pasted leather, open the leather and lay it. Paste side upward on the glass table. Place the spine of the book on the leather in a middle portion and lift, if the paste has the right tacky, the leather will be adhered by the book. Stand the book on its fore-edge without stretching the leather, use the palms of one's hands to draw the cover down on the boards and, still with one palm, rub along the spine.

Lay the book on one side, lift the leather as far as the joint, press it into the groove with the bone folder/ knife's handle, and put the leather down with the side of one hand, then do the same on the other side. Well set joints ensure a good opening of the boards. Put the short pieces of string on the pasted leather, so that these lie curved along the head and tail of the book, and cover the turn-in at one end with a piece of waxed paper so that one can stand the book on that end without getting paste on its edge.

With the book on end, and its spine away from one, put an oily paste on the outside of the middle portion of the turn-in above the spine. This will help it to stick to the book when it is turned in. Open the boards, place your index and middle fingers about 2 inches down in the spine, rest the middle portion of one's palms on the edges of the boards and use one thumb to draw the turn-in over the edge of the boards and down inside. With any luck, the pieces of string will stay in position to thicken the leather over the head and tail. If when one close the book, the ride is on the spine, one must put it right at once. Stretch the leather down inside the boards with one's thumbs, turn the book over, remove the waxed paper and turn in the other end. Use a folder to set the leather in the joints again, then make a slip knot from smooth string and tie the book with the string lying in the joint and the knot at the head or tail. **Scotch tape** the end to the paper protecting the edge to keep it out of the way.

Stand the book on end again. The leather is pulled in by the slip knot, so use the point of a folder to push out the leather on each side of the string until the boards are straight and the "head Cap" as wide as the rest of the book. Hold the book firmly and rub down the leather on the spine with the palm of one's hand, turn the book over, girp it with both hands, and roll the head and tail on the glass top table to make the string lie over the book instead of causing a bump at

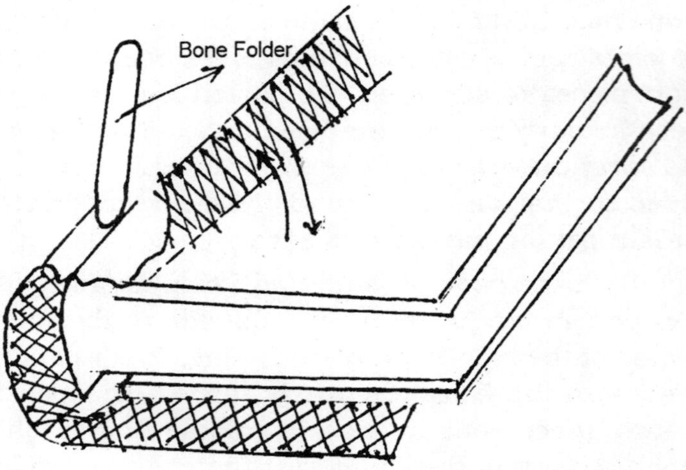

Fig. 20.5: Covering with Leather

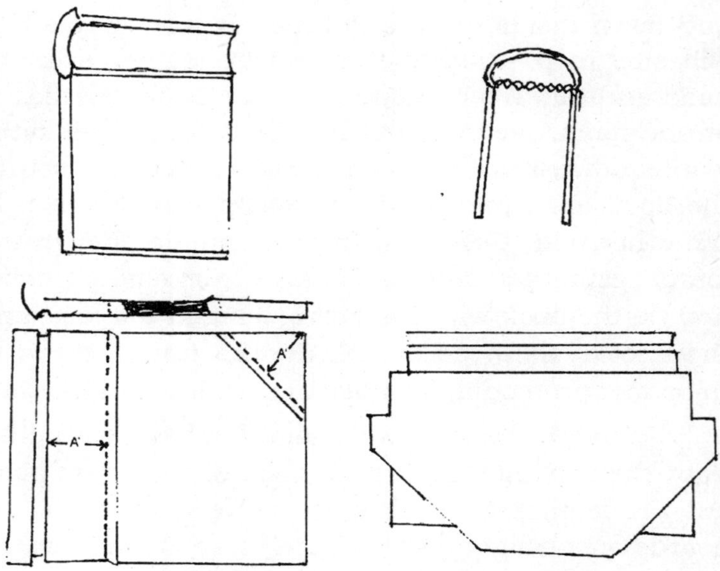

Fig. 20.6: Siding

each end. Wash off any paste marks with a damp sponge, slip a sheet of waxed paper inside each board to prevent moisture penetration, and put the book between two lean boards to dry. Before you leave it with a weight on the top board, took to see that nothing is twisted. Remove the string when the leather is dry.

SIDING

Cloth or paper sides are thinner than leather, so the level of the boards must be raised to give a neatly finish. This is called 'filling in'.

To get the position of the dotted lines in the drawing, set one's divider to a quarter of the board width and mark both ends of the spine cover; increase the setting by a half to make marks on the corners. Lay a rule to the marks, and run a pointed folder along it to make grooves.

Use a knife to bevel the leather without cutting away the line, and remove the strips. Where the corners go over the edge of the board, these should be trimmed at 45° not square. So that there will be no gap when the sides go on.

Cut a piece of ivory card to fit with its edges half-way up the bevels that one has cut, but let it hang over the edges of the boards. Glue the ivory, lay it on the board, rub down with the edge of a folder, and trim off the projecting edges with scissors.

Make cloth sides by laying the straight edge of a piece of cloth on the line marked on the spine cover, holding it in position and folding back to the lines marked on the corners. Put the cloth on the wooden block and use a knife and straight edge to cut through the folds. This should fit the side on which it was marked, so slip it inside the board while one cut the other side. Trim the turn-in of the cloth to about 3/4 inches glue the side, lay it to the marks on the leather, and turn in.

Mark an even margin on the inside of each board with one's dividers, and trim it round with a sharp knife held at an angle to produce a bevel. After removing the off cuts paste down the endpapers and give the book light nip in press before opening it. Remove the paper cap, put in pressing tins with paper folded over these, and leave the book in press to dry with pressing boards laid to the groove.

VARIATIONS

A case binding can be fabricated in a variety of materials or combinations. As in decoration of a full leather binding, there is almost no limit to the number of pleasing and attractive possibilities. A few are full leather, half leather with cloth or paper sides, with or without leather corners, two-tone cloth, cloth spine, paper sides with or without corners, cloth spine and fore edge with a pannel of another colour cloth or decorated paper, woven fabric, other than book cloth, acid free paper.

The cutting of paper materials for any of these variations differs little from that previously described. What follows are some differences in techniques. The hings that are attached to the end sheet sections are made from the same material that covers the spine.

If a paper label is preferable to leather, an indentation on the spine strips is not necessary, so only one strip hard board needed.

When the end leaves and board papers are folded sheets, reinforced with unbleached cloth, the book is hung in the case. Then place a piece of clean waste paper, larger than the page size between the board paper and the end leaf. With the covering board (one side of case) in an upright position, paste the area of the board paper to be covered by the cloth and lay the cloth in position on it. The tapes should have been attached to the cloth earlier if not, attach these at this time. Then paste the entire board paper, including the cloth, remove the waste paper and close the cover, press on the cover for one minute; open it just enough to slip a piece of hand board larger than the book, between the board paper and the end leaf. Repeat on the other side and put the book in the press between brass bound boards.

When the care is to be either full or half leather, the leather is first pared. The spine is made from 2 pieces of Nepalese hand-made paper. One layer or piece of this paper is mounted in the center of the leather. This is done by gluing the paper, laying it in position and weighting it down until dry.

The boards are attached by using the same joint strips and strip of binders board. Work from the spine strip, first side and then other side. Taking care to get all materials lined up properly across the top and fitted closely together. Where the boards are in position and before the edges are turned, glue the second spine strip and lay it on top of the first, lining it up exactly on all 4 edges. In two-tone binding where the materials are of different weight or textures, it is customary to let the material covering the sides overlap by about 1/8 inches, which covers the spine. Where the book cloth of the same texture and weight is used, the 2 pieces can be common bounding. These difference should be taken into account when cutting the materials to proper size.

There is no set rule regarding the amount of one material in proportion to the other. This is a matter of personal preference. If, however, for instance, the sides are to be covered with a decorated paper (marble paper) one wants to use the whole board covered with the paper the material covering the spine must be brought over onto the boards about 1 inch. This means that the overlap of the 2 materials would be greater than the above-mentioned 1/8 inch. This is required for strength in construction, if only 1/8 inch of material is attached to the board, the edges will be difficult to turn and might pull away in the process of casing-in.

In any two-tone binding, the spine strip is attached first to the material selected for this part of the case. Then the boards are attached, and finally, the material to be used on the sides. At this moment, the board can be left slightly wider, the case partially made, the book cased-in, and the hings attached. The fore edge of the boards cut to the desired square, and the covering material added to the boarder, if the board paper and end leaf are a folded sheet. The book could only be hung-in the case by following this sequence of steps.

The spine materials is cut, allowing the usual 3/4 inches turn at head and tail and in width it should be the width of the spine plus 1/2 inch for the 2 joints, twice the amount of material that is to be attached to the boards and 1/4 inch for possible overlapping of the 2 materials mentioned earlier.

After cutting the material to size, find its center and draw a line on the wrong side from head to tail at this point. Do the same on the spine strip, on the side that will be visible after it is attached to the material. Apply adhesive to the material. Lay the spine strip in position, lining up the centre lines drawn on the material and the spine and centering it from head to tail. Add a joint strip on one side, then the binder's board. Lay the strip of binder's board across the top of this board and the spine and add the other board in the same manner, taking care to keep those all lined up evenly and squarely.

If the material was carefully and accurately cut and the spine strip and boards attached properly, the space from the edge of the material to the fore edge of each board should be the same.

It is desirable, of course, that the material covering the sides—both front and back—be uniform in size and parallel with both spine and fore edge of the boards. Check the distance from the fore edge to the edge of the material on front and back, at both head and tail, measuring from the fore edge of the boards. This can be done easily with a strip of scrap board. Mark on this board the distance at one of the points mentioned and compare it at other 3 points, if these distance are the same or nearly so and the material on the sides will overlap the spine material, mark off an additional 1/8 inch on the strip of board with which the measuring is done. Using this as a gauge, mark at the 4 points (head and tail of both boards) this exact width, this mark can be just a dot. Lay a straight edge between these marks—both front and back—draw a line with a bone folder this which provide a guide for laying on the covering material.

When the two covering materials are to about, make the measurements but instead of making a guide with a bonefolder, the surplus an irregular material is cut away with a mat knife against the straight edge to get a clean-cut edge on the entire length of the material, slip of a scrap of binder's board, the thickness used in constracting the case, under the overhanging material at both ends. This should give it proper support so that the cut can be made with one stroke of a sharp kinfe. Lift up the surplus and pull it away in the direction of the cut. If a bit of the surface of the board is pulled off in the process, sand the roughened area with fine sand paper, then furnish it by rubbing with a bonefolder.

The edge of the second material that is to about this cut should, of course, be a clean-cut, straight edge, and great care should be exercised in bringing the two togethers. Any overlapping or gapping of or between the two materials will produce a far from pleasing result.

Corner Size: Where corners are desired, those are made from the same material used on the spine. Those are attached to the boards before the materials is added to the sides, and the material covering the sides should overlap both the spine and corner material by about 1/8 inch. In size, corners traditionally are in proportion to the width of the spine material showing on the boards. If, for example, 1¼ inches of this material is to show, 1¼ inches plus allowance for overlapping should be marked off on both edges of the board at each corner and a diagonal line drawn between the two points. Possibly an easier and more accurate way to get all 4 corners, the same size is to make a pattern of some material stiff enough to draw against (Measure the corners through scale and penciling). Lay the pattern in position on each corner and draw a line along the diagonal. There would seem to be no logical reason why corners could not be any size that is aesthetically pleasing to the binder. In cutting the material for the corners, the usual 3/4 inches turn-in must, of course, be allowed for.

Material: For the material that will cover the sides of the boards cut 2 pieces 1¼ inches longer than the boards and ¾ inches wider than the board measured from the points on the leather in the area of the spine. Where the material will be placed, the leather should be marked with a bonefolder line and a similar line should be drawn on all 4 corners. For fabric other than book cloth, choose a medium-weight, closely woven material. Cotton such as unbleached cloth, lawn cloth, mark in cloth, jaconet and silk, etc. Other heavy, loosely woven materials producing rather unattractive bulky corners that are very subject to fraying.

Some materials will stain when they come in contact with adhesive no matter how carefully those are handled. Before attempting to cover a book in an unfamiliar material, take the time to test a sample following the techniques described below. It is very difficult to keep the lines in a striped material absolutely straight. Stay away from symmetrical or geometrical patterns unless there is some special reason why those seem particularly desirable. If used, much care must be taken in keeping the pattern straight so the end result will be pleasing, again, try. The procedures or techniques for strips or plates are somewhat different from those previously described. After the cloth is cut to size, mark off an area in the centre equivalent in weight to the width of the spine, the two joints or 1/2 inch plus an additional inch. Cut a piece of lens tissue paper. This width and the length of the material from head to tail, apply a coat of mixture to the tissue, let it dry for 1 minute or so, then lay it in position in the marked off area. Weight down with a board and brick until dry. The tissue serves a two-fold purpose: It gives body to the cloth, thus preventing the joints from being wobbly, and it serves as a barrier against the adhesive used in the casing-in from oozing through the material. The hinges attached to the endsheets should be similarly lined for the same reasons.

In making the case, the spine strip is added first in the centre of the tissue, the joint strip are laid on position, then the boards are added after the adhesive is applied to them and permitted to dry for one minute or so. The adhesive should be lacky but not runny. When the boards are attached, turn the case over, lay a clean piece of waste paper on the materials, and rub it down gently. If the material is not sticking properly, weight the case down with a board and bricks/stone for a few minutes.

The corners are cut in the usual manner, but the edges of the material are turned onto the boards and after the mixture (the estimated width of the turn) has been applied to the board allowed to dry for the usual 5 minutes. The cloth is not stuck to the actual edge of the boards. Just pulled tight over them. The casing-in and other steps follow as described earlier using mixture. The board papers should be put down with mixture instead of wheat paste.

If an all-paper cover, is desired, attempt to choose a good quality paper, preferably with hand-made paper that folds smoothly and nicely with grain direction. The paper will be folding in the joint every time the covers are opened.

Only one spine strip is needed the spine and joint area should be reinforced with a piece of lawn cloth cut width enough to cover this area and attached to both boards and the length of the paper from head to tail. The adhesive paste should be applied to the paper.

Attach the strip of lawn cloth first in the centre of the paper, weight down with a board and brick/stone until dry. Then make the case by pasting the entire piece of covering paper and laying the component parts of the case on it as described for full cloth, when casing-in between the wooden boards. The pressure should be very light where brick/stone is suitable.

COMMON PROBLEMS

Discussed a few problems most frequently encounted or created and its remedies:

(a) One of the most common mistakes is getting glue on the right side of the book cloth. If the material is sized, glue can be removed by rubbing the area lightly with moist cotton. If the material is starch-sized—as many of the better book cloths are—moisture will dissolve the sizing and remove the colour or some of it, so it should be used only as a last resort.

(b) If the layer of glue is thin, it can sometimes be flaked off after it is dry with a fingernail or the point of a knife using very little pressure. A piece of paper laid over the affected area and rubbed with a heated burnisher will sometimes pick up surplus glue.

(c) If neither of these works, moisten the area by putting or smear it with a word of damp cotton, do not rub. Lay a piece of paper over the moistened area and rub it with a bone folder. If it sums to work, repeat. If some colour comes off with the glue, moisten a scrap of the same cloth, Lay it facedown on the spot, and rub with a bonefolder/knife's handle. Or the faded spots can be touched up with water colours. When the glue is removed and the colour restored, rub the whole surface with a lightly greased rag.

(d) It is suggested to start with the simplest remedy first, and wise to assume a false appearance the trouble on a scrap of the same material and experiment with it until a satisfactory result is obtained.

(e) That the glue is unevenly applied and dries in

spots before the material adheres to the board. This can generally be made to stick by softening the glue with heat. Heat a metal burnisher to the point where a drop of water placed on it will extreme heat. Place a clean piece of paper over the area to be treated and iron it slowly with a fair amount of pressure on the burnisher. The burnisher should stay in 1 spot long enough to soften the glue. If the burnisher is not available, an ordinary iron set at a low temperature 60°C will serve the purpose. This treatment is effective only on cloth which has been glued with hot glue.

(f) If you experience the same difficulty with paper that has been pasted, dampen the area rub gently through a piece of paper. If a board paper, after moistening, returns the book to the press with a board between the dampen sheet and the book.

(g) When the cloth wrinkles slightly or the surface seems bumpy this is probably due to excess glue or glue that was too thick. Press the cover immediately between smooth wooden sheets or smooth pressboards as tight as possible. This should be done before the edges are turned so that any surplus glue will be squeezed out and can be removed from around the edges of the boards. In this operation, protect the pressboard on which the inside of the case rests with a piece of wax paper. The heated burnisher is also effective.

(h) In case where not enough care was taken in making the case and one board is unevenly lined up across the top or the joints are not even, remove the board and the spine strip as soon as one can detect the error. Some of the board will probably remain on the cloth, remove as much of this as possible by lifting up an edge with a blunt knife and pulling it off. When this is larger work, apply a light coat of thin glue to a small area at a time and then scrape it with a bone folder or knife's handle. When the cloth is clean, sand the board smooth and try again. Both the cloth and the board can generally be saved, but it is a tedious and time consuming process-except as a warning to exercise more care in the future, it probably is more practical to start over-unless it happens to be the only piece of cloth of the desired colour available. Even then the cutting of a new board and spine would be advisable.

(i) Where the boards have not been placed in the paper position on the cloth and the material to be turned in against the inside of the board is uneven, it makes for a neater job if this inside turn is trimmed to an even and uniform width. This is best done before the edges are turned. Set the divider to the width of the narrowest edge—if there is sufficient material at this point to make the turn adequately—and transfer this measurement to all edges. Cut them against a straight edge. If one area is dangerously narrow, but will make the turn, even the other edges, allowing a 3/4 inches turn and after all edges are turned in glue a strip of material going in the same direction and target it carefully along the narrow edge. when dry, cut it even with the rest of the edges.

(j) If you cut a corner too close, leaving the board exposed after edged are turned, find the piece that was cut away, fit it into the exposed gap, and cut off the surplus. Then glue and lay in position. If the piece cannot be found, lay a piece of material larger than the area over it and cut through both this and the material on the board. This should produce a patch the exact size and shape needed, remove the surplus from the board (the cut edges), glue the patch, and put it in place.

(k) If after the case is completed, one can see that the boards are to narrow and the square on the fore-edge is insufficient, there is little to do but make a new case, or live with the mistake, which is not recommended. On the other hand, if the boards are too wide and the square is larger than desired, lift the turned edge of the material on the fore edge and a short distance at head and tail, turn the material book, freeing the edge of the board and cut off the excess. Reglue the cloth and press the board immediately, screwing the press as tight as possible, first one side then the other, recent the corners and turn the edges again. This repair is less likely to show if one can avoid creasing the cloths.

(l) The square on the fore edge is controlled by several factors other than the width of the boards. If either the spine or the joints are too narrow, the boards will be pulled back, thus, reducing the size of the square. If either of these is too wide, the boards will be pushed forward, producing more square than intended.

(m) If in checking the fit of the case, one can come to know that the head bands extend beyond the head and tail, those should be replaced with smaller headbands. This error could be caused by using a cord or a piece of leather that was too heavy or by having cut the boards too short. Moisten with paste the paper and lawn used to line up the spine in the area of the headbands, life these up just enough to free the headbands. Remove these, make new and smaller ones, attach in the usual manner and replace the lawn and paper.

QUESTIONS FOR DISCUSSION

1. Discuss different types of binding.
2. What is different between section binding and juse binding?
3. "Juse sewing is very fast process with machine than hand sewing" justify.
4. What is spine strip and discuss cutting the corners?
5. What is difference between hollow back and light back binding?
6. What is the purpose of back lining or spine?
7. What is the spring back used? What is its purpose?
8. Describe raise band.
9. Name the different kinds of cover material used for books.
10. Why is leather usually worked with paste?
11. Describe the cutting of material for the covers of full-bound book.
12. How should the back piece be cut for half-bound work?
13. Define filling in and the two methods, followed in cutting siding material.
14. Discuss the process of applying cover material to a hollow-back book.
15. What procedure is followed to make flexible covers?
16. Describe a limp cover.

21

Process of Completion Technique

Binding is an Art: Completion of all the operations involved in the ornamental decoration and titling of book cover including gold tooling. Most of the binders are applying the titles to bound book. In early days of gold finishing, each letter of the alphabet was engraved upon a separate hand tool, as a result process of titling required a separate impression for each letter. This process of titling is obsolete and titling is done by means of movable type. Actually gold finisher's type is a made of brass which is more costlier than lead. This lead type can be purchased for the cost of a few characters of brass type. Although brass type is much harder than lead, it can be damaged easily.

Gold finisher cannot provide a wide variety of type to choose from as the printer's have, because of its high cost. As usual gold finisher's type is characterised in two, the American gothie (1, 2, 3, 4, etc.) and Roman type (i, ii, iii, iv, etc.). The American gothie have, no serif, but they are tiny dashes that finish the ends of the strokes of letters. The Roman faces have serifs. Both are available in different faces by variations in the thickness of the strokes of the letters. These may be large or small.

Type size is estimated by the thickness of the body or base of the type. A point is a unit of measurement equal to 0.01384 inch. The face size of different type of the same point size may be entirely different. Too large type face books hazy and too small type face is difficult to go through. An experience gold finisher can use appropriate type face for book ornamentation. A line of type can be beautify by spacing the letters. This is known as *lettering.*

Title: To place in order of title different factors are considered for the book. Conventionally six panels can be made on the spine and the title is lettered in the second panel. In order to beautify the title of large size book is tooled 24 point type size and in case of medium size back is tooled 18 point type size. Normal both size is tooled 14 and 12 point, of course size of type depends upon the choice of gold finisher.

If space is available author's name also is placed in the second panel separate from the title by a small dash or ornament. The author's name can be placed in the third or fourth panel. Gazette, Journal and periodical holding volume number, publication year that should be placed in the second, third or fourth panel. Sometimes the year of publication of a document is kept in the small panel at the tail. The name of publisher of book or place of publication may be kept in the bottom panel where 12 point type size is used.

It is a rule to space the type in the panel slightly above centre. Unless there is more space below the type than above it, it will have the appearance of being placed below the centre. All the main words of the title should be set in the same size of type words of minor importance such at the, and, of, for, etc. may be in smaller type. A title can be beautiful, if it can be arranged in alternate long and short lines of types. Sometimes this can be achieved by changing the spacing between letters. It is well to avoid having several times of type of identical in length.

Author: The author's name should be placed in type smaller than the title. The length of author's name should be smaller, than the length line of the title. Volume and year number will be same size type as the title. In the periodical volume month should be same type size of the title.

The publisher's name should be much smoother than any of the other size type. The mix type faces on the spine of the book looks odd. Roman and gothie types should not mix, large and small faces may be mixed but these are of the same type face.

Decoration of Spine: Each panel is outlining with gold lines. There are two ways of laying out these panels, one is the mitered back and the other is run-up back. In the mitered back each panel is laid out as a separate rectangle with the corners carefully mitered. In the run-up back, the side lines are continuous from head to tail of the back of the book and the cross lines run into the side lines. The run-up back is used with a smooth back or with false bands. In this case, the false bands are made a very short to allow the side lines to enter the end of the band.

The run-up back is a cheap way of producing a panelled back, but it is sloppy in appearance compared to the mitered back.

Full-gilt Spine: Along with the panel lines, the panel has not been lettered but tooled decorative design. This design may be only a simple ornament placed in the centre of each panel. It may be an involved tooling job which is available portion of the leather with gold finishing without panel lines contain lettering should have but little ornamentation.

Half Bound: The sides of the book can be tooled simply or elaborately, but without full gilt of spine sides can never be tooled elaborately. The sides of half bound books have little ornamentation. Half-bound books are usually finished with a single or double gold lines along the edges of the siding. A style of ornamentation known as *tied bands* is sometimes used on half binding in which lines run from both sides of each band to a point part away across the side where each pair is joined and finished off with the impression of a small floral design. Tied bands are usually blind tooled.

Full Bound Book: On the tap side of full bound book, the gold finisher can display his skill unlimited amount of decoration that can be placed on a full binding, but the design should be according to content of the book. For example, an intricate floral design should not be decorated on a scientific nature document. These should have a geometric design.

Kind of Decoration: The simplest kind of decoration is a border, which can be mitered or made of stopped lines.

Stopped Lines: Stopped lines run to the corner without any attempt at mitering, and the back of mitering is hided by impressing a small ornamention the corner. Instead of straight lines for these borders gilding rolles engraved with designs may be used to roll on the borders. A rolled border looks best if it is enclosed in straight lines.

Cornerpieces: They may be patterns made of one tool or built up by impressing many tools in a certain definite design centre ornaments of a design similar to the corner ornaments. Rest of the portion of the cover is fitted in with repeated constantly or **spot patterns**, other process of decorating the both sides involve the use of interlaced bands or similar geometric forms. The Guther's Faust published in the year 1874, the text of which is in German in Gothie scripts is a large book, about half meter long, bound in **Morocco** with raised title in gilt corner metallions and the illustrations of Faust. The preacher, an edition of the Bible published in 1809, is yet another example of a very rare binding and illuminated work. The cover is delicately carved on black wood, each single page has different, unique gold illuminated designs.

Skill gold finisher should follow illustration of old hand-tooled binding which have in the National Library. These may get new idea for the execution of gold tooling.

Edge of the Boards: Not only cover is gold tooled but also edge of the boards are finished with fine gold line and a series of lines is used on the both sides of heads.

Inside Cover: The board is usually cut a little bit small to allow a border to be placed upon the turn-in of the leather. Frequently, this border is kept within the limits of the square of books so that it is not visible until the book cover is opened. Sometimes, it may extend to the edge of the board and squares of the book may be made larger than usual to enhance the decorative effect of this tooling. The inside of the board is sometimes lined with leather and usually this leather lining or doublure is tooled. If the outside of the cover is tooled, the tooling of the doublure should follow the same general pattern. Now and then the outside is left plain and the tooling is confined entirely to the doublure.

Inlaid Work: In this process, small pieces of leather of varieties colours are used for ornamental design. Now and then floral patterns are tooled and the petals of the flowers are inlaid with bright coloured leather. The space inside the lines of a border are sometimes inlaid with leather of contrasting colour.

Gold Lettering: Material required

1. Compose stiker
2. Type: Gothie and Roman
3. Shakenjar
4. Chakki/Hatel (borders lining)
5. Sutlee (cross lining)
6. Kerosin stove
7. Gold foil (pure/immetation)
8. Egg white or albumin
9. Viniger, alcohol, etc.
10. Shellac
11. 1/8 inch breath board slip/bathi

Nowadays conventional gold lettering is done on cloth, rexin and leather binding with imitation gold leaf. It may be silver or golden in colour according to customer choice. Pure gold lettering is done in case of manuscripts, antique where librarian feels need, because it is a costlier affairs. Imitation gold leaf cost involved as per market price ₹ 800 for 25 leaves 8" × 8" size which is gold lettering accommodated 70-80 books.

Gold tooling on the spine of a book is important to beautify the shelves restoration. In open access reading room reader can avail the desired book easily from the shalves. It has some limitation such as below 1/2 inch width book, cannot be space accommodated long tittle and author's name on the spine. On the other hand, add surface on the spine cannot be done gold lettering. For this reason back spine should be pasted for filling up the join. Next fix both boards with tape or unbleached cloth (Tajma). Prepare smooth spine to some extent hand by cementing paste. Then thick cylinder paper is used at the spine [Fig. 21.1(a) and (b)]. In case of ornamental decoration 5 board strips (batti) at equal distance is placed on the spine. Each (batti) board strip 1/8 inch wide and 1–4 inches long is placed acorss the width of the spine, of course, according to width of the book. Last of all leather or rexin cover is placed for finishing of building. Out of six panels 3–4 panels are decorated with bicolour boarder lines of four edges, *i.e.*, between gap of raised band or separate three gold tooled leather or cloth strips can be used in the panel brittle, author, publisher, etc.

The gold stiker should not be high temperature, if it is rexin or leather binding will melt away. If the binding of the lettering is too deep, the gold will have to stretch too much and may break. If this happens, lay on another layer of gold with no preparation. It will usually stick, but if one breaths on the book before doing it, there will be no doubt about it.

In order to maintain low temperature at the type face, Kerosin stove is best. Traditional test for a hot tool is to touch it with a licked finger, if it remains wet the tool is net hot yet, if it evaporates immediately, it is too hot and may burn the leather; if a spot of moisture generally boils away, it should be about right—but one would better try for oneself on a piece of leather stuck to some board.

A quick, firm, but not heavy, impression of the tool should be one's aim, the fingers of his hand around

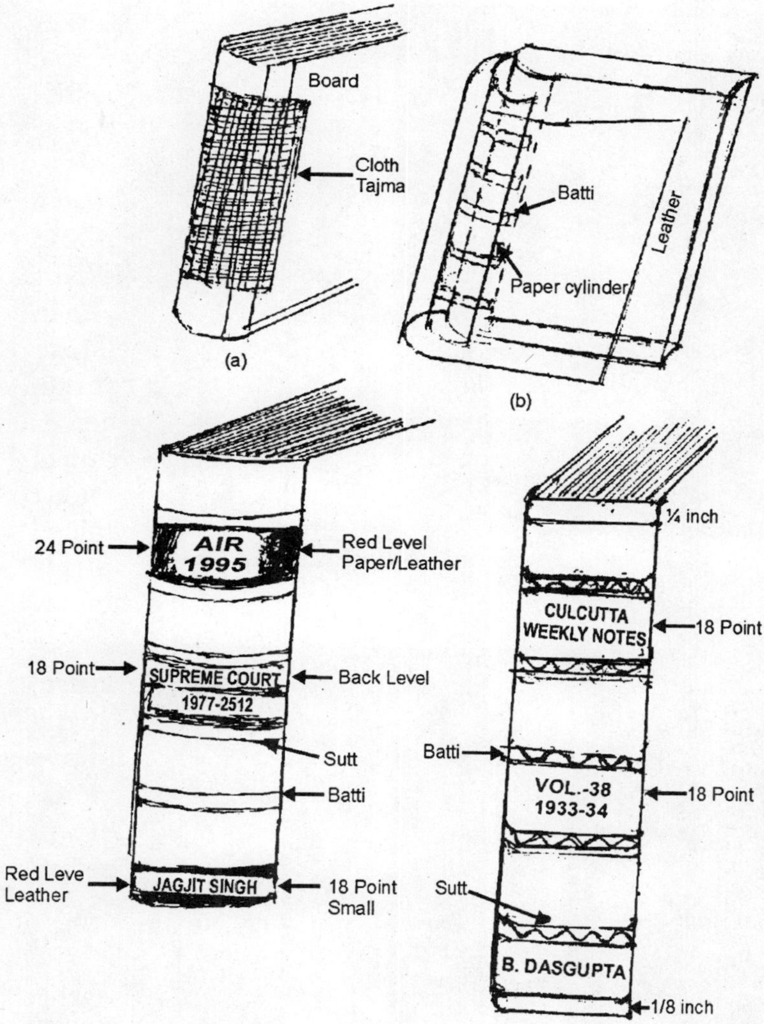

Fig. 21.1

the tool-hands, the thumb on top, and the thumb-nail of the other hand to steady the hot end as some one strike the tool.

Before gold tooling of the spine tool a blind line on each sides of the raised, caused by the tapes, but be sure that those are all the same width and equally

Fig. 21.2: Ornamental binding Bible

Fig. 21.3: Equipments of gold lettering

Fig. 21.4: Gold lettering

Fig. 21.5: Guther's Faust decorative setup

spaced by marking those with divider if the lettering is to run down the spine, one must ignore the tapes and leave the spine free for lettering.

Several materials have been used on the leather for washing, filling, glair, finishing powder. These substances should not use acidic nature which deteriorate the valuable leather.

Some glair or sizing materials hold the gold leaf impart such a varnished coating that these permanently seal the leather. This prevent any later addition of **Preservatives**.

A certain amount of moisture is required for gold tooling. Conventional method of gold finisher, uses title bit water with cloth. Some leather are so greasy that water does not decompose the grease. Next organic solvent alcohol, acetone, etc. should be used. All leathers are porous and the pores should be filled. Calf, goat, sheep skin requires the most filling. Where cowhide is less, soot with is used as filler. It may be coated with sprayer and roller is used for smooth on flesh side of the leather, is black colour and let it dry for sometime. Some binders get it done own workshop with cotton swab. Just enough black colour should be applied so that the pores are filled without leaving a coating on the surface.

Binding Medium: Glair or size must be used to bind the gold to the surface of leather canvas and cloth, but not on the cover of rexin surface. It is **thermofixed** *procedure*. Glair will melt by heat but will set again immediately upon the withdraw of the heat. Thus, the impression of a heated stiker will melt the **glair** so that it holds the gold firmly when the heated tool is removed. The glair consist mainly white portion of an egg and albumin mixed with water. Shellac size also is a good binding medium for gold leaf. The shellac size can be prepared by reducing commercial liquid white shellac with alcohol only tooling portion on the surface of the cover is coated with glair. One egg albumin can be accommodated 50 books coating. If any body desires to retain the natural appearance of the leather, the design and lettering should be tooled in blind and the glair coated to the blind impression with a small brush.

The velvet, silk and **ooze** leather, will not permit gold lettering with a liquid glair because of its discolouring effect, only finishing powder will fit for tooling in place egg albumin which is available in the market. Finishing powder does not give the solidity to gold leaf that is obtainable with liquid size. Layout the design on the spine or top is first step in the finishing process. In case of simple design, it may be laid out directly upon the leather dividing the spine or top with the divider. Gold tooling of title author, publisher will be certain distance from the top of the book. Marks are made to indicate the location of the various tools and lines that go to make up the design.

Paper Pattern: In case of complicated design it is required work out paper first upon a piece of paper large enough to turn over the edges of the board and top in place. The stiker to be used on the design are heated low temperature and impressed in their proper places on the paper pattern. The impression will go through the paper on the leather underneath.

When the entire design has been impressed, the paper is removed. Each tool is then impressed again in the marks on the leather. The tool should be warm but not hot enough to melt the size. Sometimes, it is preferable to apply the glair after the blind impression are made.

The tools used in hand finishing to tool the impression must be kept clean because dirt will keep the gold leaf from adhering. The tool can be kept clean by rubbing in face on the flesh side of a piece of leather.

Generally, dark colored leather will require more heat than light coluored, and cowhide more than calfskin. The tools are impressed exactly in the blind impressions made previously. The impression should be made firmly but quickly because the heat will destroy the size and the gold will not stick if the finishing tool remains in the impressions for any length of time.

After the impression have been tooled, the extra gold is cleaned off by rubbing the book with a gold rag. The cloth is oiled with olive oil/cester oil and will pick up practically all the excess gold.

The gold lettering is done by setting the brass to lead type in a hand sticker which clamps one line of type at a time. The sticker is heated and hatal heated line of type is then impressed across the back of the book. A gold finisher can impress the lettering in an straight line with the spacing equally divided oṅ both sides. It is best to blind in the lettering first.

Antique tooling is blind tooling that differs from that used as a preliminary for gold tooling. For this antique style the tools are heated enough to darken the colour of the leather. An attempt is made to secure uniformity in the colour of the blind tooling. No filler or glair is necessary but the leather must be dampened.

Ornamental decoration can be obtained by inlaying various colours of leather in the design. It is pared very thin, cut to the desired shape and paste in place. The inlay material is sometimes pasted face down on a piece of paper to keep in the proper place on the book and the paper backing can be washed away when those are dry. The edge of the inlay is usually cancelled by tooling which may be either gold or blind.

QUESTIONS FOR DISCUSSION

1. What is the different between types size used in title and author of the book?
2. How are types face measured?
3. What are the two general type classification used for titling?
4. In the arrangement of a title on the spine, what factors will be followed?
5. What is the simplest form of decoration for the spine of a book?
6. Discuss two methods run-up back and mitered back and their difference?
7. What is meant by a full-gilt spine?
8. What is the sides differ for half-bound books and full-bound books?
9. What is the difference between entered lines and stopped lines for borders?
10. How is inlaid work done?
11. Discuss centre ornaments, spot patterns and interlaced band or geometric forms.
12. Why leather is required moist for gold tooling?
13. What washes is necessary on the leather?
14. Why filler is used on the leather?
15. Name the two fillers which are commonly used.
16. How is glair or size applied?
17. What special treatment is given such materials as velvet, silk and ooze leather?
18. What is the first step in the actual finishing process?
19. When it is available to make a paper pattern of the design?
20. What special care should be taken in the use of tools?
21. What is meant by antique tooling?
22. Describe the process of gold lettering.

22

Modern Concept of Library Building

LIBRARY COLLECTION IS A GROWING ORGANISM

Library building is also a growing organism even at the electronic age.

The designing of a new library should not consider it only in accordance with the traditional function, but also as an old library of nearly a century, we could not seen the library without traditional service. Therefore, we should try our best to study, to understand the traditional and modern function of the cross century's library especially to understand how to transit the traditional service into modern function. The National Library India come into existance on the 8.9.1948 at the Viceroy House Belvedere. This library is enriched with the books and bound volumes about 40 lakhs besides map, manuscripts, microfilms and microfische (1992). Recently total collection is divided into Bhasha Bhawan, Aunexe Building, Prasasan Bhawan and Esplanade East News Paper Reading Room. Their area is as about two lakhs sq. ft. and main building 1,05,360 sq. ft. reader's seat is about 800. All those collections were preserved by conventional method. But at the end of 20th century a large scale air conditioned is installed as a result, **biochemical deterioration of paper** expected to slow down. The National Library is the *apes* of the library system. It is a depository library received by Delivery of Book Act, purchase, gift and exchange, Indian official document, Foreign document total 26,346 and maps 2,889, etc. altogether 28,229 in the year 1994–95. At the British Library, receives in 8,000 new items, including more than books, everyday. Their collection of printed books alone grows by more than 10 kilometers every year.

At the close of 20th century, 6 storied Bhasha Bhawan was built with total area of 40,000 sq. ft. architected by M/s M. M. Rana & Company, Delhi. All National Libraries of the major countries of the world architecturally provided with modern interior as well as with a facade which will make them one of the most beautiful buildings in the respective country. The new built National Library of the Peoples, Republic China; The new British Library Paneras in London; The National Library Franch in Parish, in Frankfort, are beautiful monument of architectural grandur. Those stand in entrance of a new edge electronic information. Those are being constructed on a very modernised scale. All these new libraries, when it is frequently claimed that the book as we know it is dying and being replaced by disc and Internet.

There are about 256 access points (LAN) in the National Library, Kolkata, where reader receives information about his desired document. Retrospective conversion (Retrocon) project work running on very fast which may available for reader service within two years. Successively, reader will receive information without coming to the library. Large number C.D. scan of rare documents have been prepared for retrieval and readers service.

In the Bhasha Bhawan each floor have special function such as basement and ground floor contain compact stack area full of dust free air conditioned. *Mazanine* floor reading room almost triangular shape one outside portion covered about 25 ft height thick blue hard glass where ultraviolet rays cannot pass. But indirect natural light coming from outside and throw sky light. Floor height of reading room is about 30 ft as well as main building where molecular friction of particle is less. Transparent roof is set up at centre of Bhasha Bhawan as well as entrance of the old main building where row of catalogues trays are situated. Floor height of building is related with rise of temperature. If height is low without air conditioned, in this situation molecular friction increases according to Brownian moment of particle in zigzag motion.

India, is a tropical country for which temperature and relative humidity is very high. Bio-chemical deterioration takes place on account of fluctuation of temperature and relative, humidity in stack area. These fluctuation of temperature and relative humidity can be controlled by construction of modern library building. Library and archival resources are of paper palm leaf, Vellum and birch bark their constituents are of alfa, beta, gama cellulose, which structure breakdown at 60°F. It is obviously proved that microfilms, microfich, CD-ROM deteriorate at above 16°C R.H. 45-60% and where paper deteriorate at 20°C ± 1 and R.H. 45–65%. Where minimum 10% R.H. remains in to survive as paper. Low relative humidity and temperature is also detriment. It helps to grow fungus which caused acidity in paper becomes brittle. Author studied temperature and relative humidity in stack area of the National Library for consecutive years. From the data it is observed that in winter season minimum temperature 13°C to 14°C and Relative humidity 40% to 50% which are ideal condition towards the cellulose materials. As a result insects become inactive and can not aggravate. But in the summer season it rises upto 30°C to 35°C temperature and relative humidity 90% to 95% which are detriment towards the paper. Besides these criteria air pollution as sulphurated hydrogen, nitric oxide, sulphur dioxide, etc. at the certain level deteriorate cellulose.

All over the world there is a need to reduce the operating costs of buildings used for archive and library purpose considering the preservation point of view. The National Library, *Asiate* Society, Town Hall Library, Metcafe Hall are all long height, historic buildings. This means primarily the costs involved in achieving through mechanical means and desirable interior climate suitable for good preservation of the collections.

Therefore, the use of local building design should be investigated in order to benefit from the contributions. These could make towards creating a better preservation environment. We need also to work hard at convincing other people that this factor of a good preservation environment is more important than that of simply creating a prestige exterior by a well known architect with an interior that perpetually causes problems for the collections. The problems of finding ways in which money could be saved is not restricted to libraries and archives. So, the maximum use should be made not only of information to be found in the conservation/preservation literature but also in related fields, such as that of building technology which is concentrated with architect. Not every one is lucky enough to be able to design and construct a new building. It is, therefore, essential that the internal environment of existing structure be throughly surveyed in order to find:

- That most climatically stable areas which could be used immediately for storage of the most unnumerable items in the collections.
- That those areas which could easily (low cost) be closed off to provide cleaner section of the building with less particulate and pollution.
- That those areas which could, at minimal cost, be converted into areas with more stable conditions. This could perhaps occasional programme of insecticides spray, soil treatment of inside or outside the building for prevention of termite attack, use of humidiffers or dehumidiffers.

It is vital that insect access to a building, through windows, doors, piping, etc. be blocked BEFORE attempts are made to control insect infestation by what ever means are available. Periodical check of the stack area should be made for early detection of reinfestation. Otherwise, it will be a non-ending and expensive struggle, use of chemical will increasingly be restricted throughout the world so the use of methods not involving toxic chemicals, such as those using nitrogen or carbon dioxide gases, in vaccum fumigation chamber can be used.

For molds, prevention is also emphasized but this is more difficult when artificial climate control is not easily achieved. It is observed that mold growth occurs when conditions are unfavourable and air stagnant. Foxing or brown spotting paper is associated at least partly with fungus growth but point out that it may also be due to the presence of iron. The organic acids secreted by the fungi in course of their metabolic processes react with the traces of iron present in paper forming the iron hydroxide and ironoxide in paper.

Investigations would need to be linked with the development of simple test equipments that could be used to check that pockets of stagnant air are not being left in the collection storage area.

It is also essential for continual surveillance of climate conditions in all areas of the collections. The mold attacks which we know in the west (Severe discolouration with red, purple, yellow, black stains and eventual degradation of the paper) do not develop to this stage over night but are the consequences of leaving materials damp for days, even weeks. The mold attacks are the result of failure to check continuously on the prevailing conditions.

As with insect damage, conventional method of non-toxic chemical use will become increasingly difficult through both national and international legislation on use hazardous chemicals. Thus, prevention is again the best approach. That is why we must try to avoid having to use chemical methods of control. But it must also be appreciated that in a large scale emergency the essential thing is to stop the attack as quickly as possible and so prevent severe damage to the collection. In such an emergency, only those materials and that technology which are immediately available in large quantities in the area of the disaster can be used because of the scale of the problem and the time factor inevitably involved in getting equipment, etc. on-site 5% thymol in methanol solvent by spray method is best to destroy at least 90% fungi.

It is observed that need for special equipment for occasional or long-term use. This has included:

- That padestal fan for ensuring continuous air movement and thus inhibiting mold development;
- That dehumidifiers for use when relative humidity remains at exceptionally high values over a period of time;
- That air conditioned for producing low temperature and relative humidity for the correct storage of photographic materials, and in particular the storage of microfilms produced from deteriorating papers or from materials kept in another respository.

The uncertainly of local electricity supplies has also been mentioned. It is of no use having equipment for improving storage condition if this cannot be used whenever it is needed.

What has not even been mentioned is the possibility of using solar-generated power for these purposes. The technology is available and if the equipment are to be installed within the archives or librarys building itself, a constant supply of electricity would be ensured. After all, those countries with most problems in arranging correct storage conditions for their libraries and archives are those with a constant supply of sunshine. The basic needs for solar-powered equipment capable of running fans, dehumdifiers and refrigerators—as a starting point at least.

BOOKSTACKS

Library is a growing organism, it becomes confusing to break up the bookstacks into irregular configurations. In using both the Dewey and Library of Congress Book Classification Systems it is easier to use bookstacks with a Continuous Sequential Numbering System without breaks for seating. For several reasons, it is also most economical to design a building with all the bookstacks in one continuous pattern.

The larger the library the greater the necessity to maintain a single consecutively numbered bookstack, for easy convenience in finding a book. Reader will spend the least amount of time in the bookstack, so consistant temperature is less important here than else where. The need to read call numbers and spine titles on the lower shelves requires careful attention to lighting fixture reflectors and *louvres* and mandates light coloured floor surfaces and shelves to get light on the bottom-shelf book. Graphics systems on end panels and shelves that clearly indicate book **sequencing** such as Dewey Break labels, will greatly help users.

Load bearing capabilities of 150 pounds per square foot live load for conventional shelving 90 inches high, and 300 pounds per square foot for high density compact stacks, require an unusually strong structural system. Top bracing structural attatched to the building 2 feet away from outside wall and a stack aisle of 40 inches also set this pattern of highly formalized space in contrast to less structural readers seating.

To orient users trying to find a particular book quickly and easily, stack-end panels and aisles should be immediately visible and clearly marked for access from the first entrance into the building.

Bookstacks size projections need to include these considerations:

(i) Present number of books shelved.

(ii) Present circulation—seasonal fluctuations in books need to be shelved.

(iii) Present configuration—aisle widths, stack height.

(iv) Book acquisition—mix of fiction, nonfiction,

references, journal, periodical, newspaper, and over sized illustrated books.

(v) Oversized book shelving procedures—integrated, bottom or middle shelf or separate section.

(vi) Networking capabilities and potentials.

(vii) Percentage of withdrawal—net annual additions.

(viii) Frequency of use objective—how many rarely used books will the library retain? For example, 15 per cent to 20 per cent that have not been issued lending or borrowing in the past 5 years.

(ix) Gift—cash and in kind.

(x) Multiple copy selection and withdrawal procedures.

(xi) Promotional activities.

(xii) Population projections for areas from which library users are most likely to come.

(xiii) Educational demographic changes, especially in the immediate neighbourhood.

(xiv) Parking access. Pedestrain access.

(xv) Nearly library resources and reader access to these resources.

(xvi) Desire of the community to support a large library.

(xvii) Stack aisles must be visible from the staff area for supervision. A bookstack area should have graphic signs and integrated lighting for access. For facility in finding a particular book as well as for good staff control the book collection should be placed in a continuous sequential one-pattern bookstack area. Books are consecutively numbered, and any break in the shelving patterns will confuse the reader.

Bookstacks design should also include these considerations:

(i) A standard section of book shelf is four to five feet long and 84 to 96 inches high.

(ii) A double faced section will have an eventual maximum capacity of normal book size four hundred fifty if all eight shelves on each side are used with space left for shelving returns.

(iii) Stacks must be braced across the top and attached two feet off from the outside walls of the building structure to prevent collapse.

(iv) A range of shelving normally of six sections long to make it possible for readers to move easily from one aside to the next. Each 18 feet double faced six sections range will hold about 2,100 books.

(v) Ranges should be spaced 65 inches apart on centres, leaving an aside 48 inches wide of 10 inches shelving is installed.

(vi) Fluorescent lights shielled by angled parawedge louvers mounted about three inches above the top of the stacks provides optimum lighting with minimum illumination. If possible, fluorescent light can be hanged from ceiling.

(vii) Seating should not be combined with stacks because this would require a wider aisle and larger, less efficient area. Carrels can be across from the end of the stock.

(viii) Gliding step stools should be kept in each aisle to facilitate reaching the top shelves.

(ix) Bookstacks, require a floor load-bearing capacity of 250 pounds per square foot.

(x) Art, Illustration, Diagram and over sized books will require 12–15 inches-wide shelves.

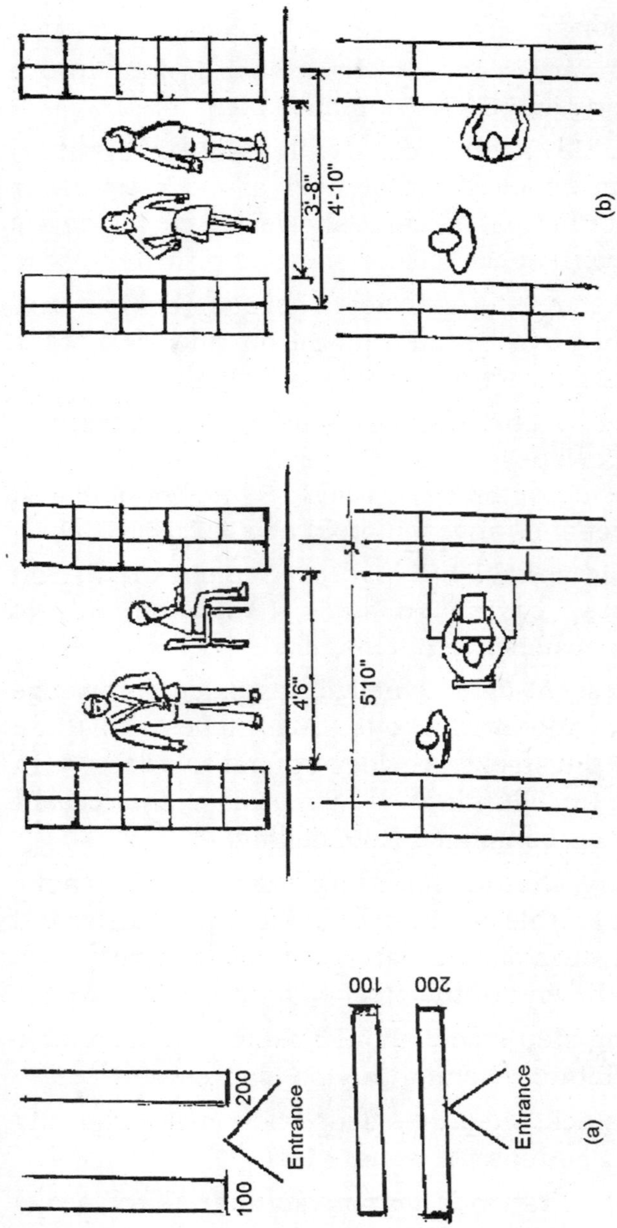

Fig. 22.1: Aisle Space in busy stacks

(xi) Bookstops should be provided to present books from being pushed back off the shelves. Non-removable thick book supports should be provided for each shelf.

(xii) Canopies are unnecessary and often create light shadows from over head lighting.

(xiii) Generally book stack capacity; adult book—ten per foot, reference books—eight per foot, bound periodicals—eight per foot and children's books—eighteen per foot, but often placed in lower stacks 54 inches or four shelves high.

Book locators such as Dewey break locators should be placed at the beginning of each major decimal section: 100, 110, 120, etc. [Fig. 22.1(a)] visible down the aisle to aid the user in finding a book.

COMPACT STACK AREA—HIGH DENSITY

Shelves can easily be moved by hand while preserving the safety of users. These require floor capable of supporting 300 pounds per square foot compared to the 200 pounds/sq. ft. floor load of regular bookstacks. These hold up to fifty books per square foot.

This area can be used to store back issues of periodicals, holding books and other in frequently used materials can also be the shelved here.

- Floor pressure device immobilizing stacks when pressure is applied.
- Obstruction pressure sensors on shelf edge and bottom shelf.
- Motion detectors at stack access points.
- Closing resistance clutch slippage device.

Compact High Density Stack Performance Considerations

(a) Track structural rigidity for floor unevenness.

(b) Stack bracing across the top.

(c) Rail shape and steel quality for resistance to deformation.

(d) Ease of starting and stopping.

(e) Force necessary to continue motion.

(f) Maintenance—location, response time, track record and back-up.

(g) Lighting—Pantograph suspension system and automatic switch off.

(h) Flanged wheels or other device to present derailling.

(i) Interfaces—Fire prevention (halon gas), security, building security.

(j) Mannual operation if power fails—Convenience required.

(k) Track height and floor system.

SOLAR ENERGY

Active solar building use the sun's energy to heat or cool a space. A variety of methods of generating electricity, from solar panels to photovoltaic cells, have been proposed for active solar buildings. As fuel costs increase and technology changes, active solar technology may move effective.

Passive solar design is very useful. In house building that emphasize passive solar design which are concentrated on:

— Siting in a house to take advantage of sheltering trees as windbreaks and sun shade.

— Locating windows so that they are exposed to winter sun but shaded in the summer•when the leaves are out.

— Making windows so that they are sealed where necessary.

— Organizing a careful balance and proper locations for insulation and ventilation.

— Locating the front door so that northern winds cannot blow directly into the library and there is a lobby weather baffle, or offset double doors.

Many of these principles are applicable to the design of libraries, however, in larger buildings there are other considerations. Material's may itself provide useful insulating mass. Reader and lighting supply considerable heat and lighting may be significant energy consumer and require additional cooling power.

HVAC: Heating, Ventilating, Air Conditioning

Heating, ventilating and air conditioning is too important to leave to the experts plans for this area which will not only affect the comfort of library users but staff productivity and ultimately, the economic viability of library services. Air conditioning in the summer often costs more than winter heating and also benefits from insulation. Several improvements in air conditioning have been made. Economizer controls permit increased use of outside air for cooling in the spring and simultaneously fall temperature. Heat pumps provide lower cost and more versatility where electrical rates are low. Variable air volume control systems provide increase control in large areas and often reduce the size of the air conditioning units required. Four pipe systems provide the flexibility to heat and cool different areas at the same time. Hybrid air conditioning systems using through-wall perimeter

Fig. 22.2: Natural light entering into reading room

Fig. 22.3: Reading room

units and a smaller central unit offer increased flexibility and the possibility of some coding when the central system breaks down. There may also reduce installation and operating costs in medium sized system.

A few questions to ask and things to look for in discussing HVAC or heating, ventilating and air conditioning with architect and mechanical engineer:

(a) Where are the thermostats? They should be located where reader are sitting and working and never where the sun can strike them directly?

Fig. 22.4: East Entrance

(b) Where is the entrance? Does it face north? Is there a wind and temperature baffle?

(c) Where are the air conditioning units and fans? Is there room to reach their for maintenance?

(d) How thick is the insulation? 12 inches on celling, 4 inches on walls is required.

(e) Where are the windows in relation to north? How will seating areas near windows be heated and cooled? Direct sunlight should never fall on long-term seating areas.

(f) What will it take to heat, cool and light this building? Light intensity should not require more than two watts per square foot.

Energy conservation features to be considered:

1. To offset entry locks reduce the amount of heat or cool air lost at the entry of the building.

2. To passive insulation — large masses surrounding the building such as term building, underground buildings, or building with thick earth coverings on the roof which provide stabilized temperature.
3. To only outside wall building which middle vacant portion is provided water circulator system. It will continue only from April to September which has economic viability. Another method is doubling wall system.
4. To window wells — instead of the windows looking directly out on an area where air could blow into the window, the windows are let down into the earth in light wells bellow ground level so that the air is more controlled and does not blow directly to the window.
5. To economizer controls in air conditioning use large percentages of outside air in spring and fall. In summer, cool night air is brought into the building in quantities to cool it down in the evenings.
6. To building orientation with windows pointed south and blank walls north.
7. To hygrometer and thermometer are necessary for all office and small room spaces, with exception of storage areas and closets.
8. To in winter, cold outdoor air is brought into the building only through ducts that are solar heated so that fresh air enters only after it is heated.
9. To lighting can be used to assist in heading outside air as well as being designed in a task mole, so that instead of general lighting, which could consume as much as 2 watts per square foot, task lighting can be used, which would bring that consumption down to one half watt per square foot.

10. To variable volume air conditioning should be considered as it offers useful flexibility and good economy.
11. To area controls for program, children's technical, and administration areas will be necessary.
12. To area controls should be used for heating and air conditioning on day, night and holiday cycles.

LIGHTING

Lighting has most important part to play not only in the design but also in the function of libraries with a view to preservation. The way in which readers use the library and their feelings about the building are often determined by making the proper choice in lighting design. Lighting will not only make the building easy to use but will affect behavior and give readers a comfortable feeling about the library.

Natural light is by far the best way to light a library but natural light in this sense does not mean direct light from the sun. Ultraviolet ray of the sunlight damages the library resources. Design the library so that direct sunlight never strikes a book or a place where a reader might be sitting. Direct sunlight will present any possibility of cooling that location, and the light will be so bright that it will be almost impossible to see anything. It is important that the building overhangs and that the way in which the building is sited prevent direct sunlight from ever striking a reader location. Indirect sunlight coming through windows, skylights or clerestories will provide the most pleasing and easy-to-see light. The natural lighting locations may create problems for heating in the winter time and cooling in the summer, so heating and ventilating systems must be carefully articulated to window design. Windows and even clerestories cannot properly illuminate all parts of the building:

since libraries operate for almost a third of the working day after sundown in the late fall and winter, it is important not to depend too much on natural light for any building location.

Bright Light: Natural light from the sun, not exactly overhead but coming through a sky-light or through a window, can be as bright as 1,000 foot candles. Readers who are partially sighted find that they can read much more easily with this intense natural light as long as it is indirect. The reason is a Phenomena called **"inter reflection"**. That is, if the light strikes the reading surface from a variety of angles, the effect is to eliminate glare and to provide the best possible lighting. This corresponds to indirect lighting from a dome ceiling.

Fluorescent lights work by an electrical current exciting gas in a long thin glass tube. The coating of the tube determines the colour of the light which can vary from cool white with a colour rating of 42000 degrees Kelvin to warm white fluorescent light with a rating of 3000 degrees Kelvin.

Incandescent light producing 2805 degree Kelvin colour give in return is what most of us are useful. It is a point sources of light and are relatively inefficient, compared to **fluorescent** or high-intensity discharge lamps. The average incandescent lamp with 100 watts rating will deliver about 800 illumination of light. While a fluorescent lamp burning fourty watts may produce as high as 3000 illumination of light. The rated life of most incandescent lamps is less than 1,000 hours while the rated life of a fluorescent lamp can be more than 10,000 hours. The incandescent lamp has to be changed more than often and the bulb is almost as expensive as the fluorescent lamp which lasts ten times as long. Library function the selection of lighting for the stack is an bookstack areas since their long length is much more effective than the point source lighting produced by high intensity discharge or incandescent fixtures. Weather the fluorescent light are perpendicular or parallel to the way the stack runs is an important decision. There is no one correct method. The perpendicular type of placement will result in less costly installation and greater flexibility. However, the parallel placement will result in more comfort for the user and improved lighting intensity in the stack.

Carrel lighting or reading table lighting is an important consideration since carrels or desks will be occupied for a much longer time than will bookstacks and lighting is important for the long term comfort of the reader. Supplemental lighting mounted to the side instead of infront of the user substantially reduces vailing reflections. Carrels should be designed with the lighting mounted on the sides rather than in the rare. Of-course this is a difficult design problem and a costly one since it requires two lighting fixtures instead of one and since the light fixture has to be strong enough to throw light over the full width of the carrel.

It would be interesting to set up fluorescent lights mounted on the sides of the table or carrel with reflectors that would bounce the light full distance across the reading surface.

The following list of illuminating considerations includes:

(a) To limit light intensity variation in small rooms.

(b) To avoid intensity of illumination and reflection by careful selection of diffusers louvers and light locations.

(c) To use electronic fluorescent ballasts.

(d) To select lenses or louvers that diffuse light and prevent intensity of illumination.

(e) To use fluorescent lights for high heat in cool country.

(f) To use low intensity light in non-reading areas.

(g) The bat wing reflector spreads limit over a wide area which provides inexpensive.

(h) To parawedge louvers minimize ceiling brightness and veiling reflections, but provide directional lighting and do not eliminate direct dazzling light.

(i) To locate fixtures to minimize ceiling intensity light and veiling reflections caused by light striking the viewing surface at a 45- degree angle.

(j) While ceilings and white walls will increase illumination especially in small rooms.

(k) Electricity and maintenance involve costilier, so install fixtures and lenses that burn cool and are simple to clean and replace.

(l) Let readers control lighting misuse will stop.

(m) Visibility in a room is affected by size of room colour and contrast with in the room, and illumination of lamps.

(n) To use sodium or tungsten halogen lamp for outdoor parking lights.

(o) To use CAPSYLITE for spotlights.

(p) To avoid direct sunlight which is damaged book and difficult to control.

Ultraviolet light damages paper and bindings.

(q) Warm white fluorescent lamps provide better rendition of skin tones than cool white lamps. Cool white deluxe lamps like sunlight.

THE ARCHITECT'S VIEW

The most successful features of the library and archival building are:

The library must be in a location where it can be constantly visible to all of these users. A good location is:

(i) On a high road used by most people.

(ii) Near a shopping centre post office that is open nights and saturday when the library will open.

(iii) Near parking and mass conveyance.

(iv) Easy for padestrians and children on bicycle to find and safe for them to come to safe traffic control.

(v) Convenient for the elderly and handicapped no curbs, or at least curb cuts, no hills from the parking lot to the library.

Locations to Avoid

1. To parks which are dangerous at night.
2. To schools, close in mid-afternoon and are noisy. Most town residents do not attend school.
3. To offices, are closed at night, crowded and noisy in daytime.
4. To Town Halls or Civic Centres are often closed at night.
5. To proper sized and located with an identification sign at the corner of the site which is readily seen by automobile traffic.
6. To entrance area that is clearly identified by architectural from with steps and flanking curbed walls that direct attention to the entrance in an inviting and welcoming manner.
7. To one way traffic entrance to the site which provides safe and easy access.
8. To disconnect of service traffic to a visually shielded receiving and dumpster area. There is concern for safety of users crossing through traffic which passes between the entrance and the general parking lot. This could be relieved by closing the end of the enterance driveway between the binding entrance and the service way and creating a pedestrian remain is land to the parking

lot. Through traffic would be directed to turn rights into the parking lot prior reaching the building enterance.

External Architecture

1. To preservation and conservation of handsome modern styled library.
2. To building and sensitive integration of new with old.
3. To excellent match of new pink colored brick with old building brick, while repeating flemish bond pattern.
4. To repeat of existing details in new building including brick corner wooden shutters, traditional shutter hardware, and roof edge details.
5. To sheltered cover approach entrance, with weather protected bookdrop.
6. To sign at entry with hours and date of operation and notices.
7. To automatic doors for easy access for the handicapped and users with full load of books.

Internal Architecture

1. The floorwise organizational chart at entry: View to circulation desk, entrance to meeting rooms, toilets, telephone and xerox, e-journal.
2. That engaging view from entry into circulation desk, lending, information desk and stack.
3. That soft warm and pleasant colour choices for carpet, walls and furnishings ornamental chair and table.
4. That exciting central skylighted area with bright sunlight and exposure of brownstone walls, slate roof, dormers and window of the original building.

5. That level changes between new and old building nicely arranged by rampant stairs.
6. That preservation of library materials detailed original library rooms with their fire places, paneling and wood shelving.
7. That detailed organization of bookstacks in one integrated aisle system with well distributed fluorescent light on all shelving levels.
8. That peasant variety collection building and arrangement of furnishings readers desk.
9. That nicely detailed, traditionally styled study carrels with buildings lighting arrangement between shelve student and teacher.
10. That area centrally located to give important recognition to this age group, but in a shut off alcove with direct visual observation from the reference desk.
11. That busy functional and efficient staff area that is located at the center of the building adjacent to the circulation desk.
12. That children's library that is interestingly subdivided and with an upper level entrance lobby that provides architectural entrance features to specialize this area. Materials are interestingly displayed for young users.
13. That use of undivided glazing to separate staff offices at circulation desk and children's readers area provide for easy viewing and sense of openness.
14. That utility of many handsome repaired antique chairs.
15. That nicely scaled, traditional wall light fixtures with glass shades over built in metal shelving in old reading rooms.
16. That dual height railing for stair to children's area.

These features can be corrected as the environmental circumstances allow:

Interior Architecture

1. That reduce excessive illumination from the skylight by adding shading film to the glass and hanging vertical blind panels. This would prevent slanting sun rays from penetrating the space below. Also change white wall surfaces to a tan tone to reduce reflectance.
2. That shining to the children's area access stair more attractive and exciting by the use of a banner. Also, decorate this stair's walls with banners or artwork, painting pictures. The access seems dull compared with exciting area for which set up aquariam.

   Lighting system is elaborately discuss previously.

Mechanical

1. The return air grilie in the book stack area on the lower level transmits a lot noise from the nearby air handling unit. If the noise level reduction is desired, relocate the grilie further from the unit and provide acoustics lined ductwork and bends.
2. That air handling equipment rooms on the lower and upper levels are not totally insulated and might contribute to unnecessary heat losses in winter.

   These features are not considered specifically:

   - That the view of the exterior end of the skylight looks industrial and would have been more consistant in design if it was brick gable end.
   - That the handicapped access ramp is long.
   - That the blast unit heater over the inner vestibule door is bulky and unsightly and might have been replaced by units built into side walls.

- That the main meeting hall seems undersized for this size library.
- That the custom made study carrels are designed with desk heights to allow antique arm chairs to fit under. But this feature provides writing surfaces at 30.75 inches, which is 1.75 inches higher than normal. The children's area carrels are the same height, but perhaps manufacturer of these units would be feasible using armless chairs.
- That many tables are 30 inches high, one inch higher than normal.
- That the building is not expandable due to site limitations. Acquisition of adjacent property is highly recommended.

MODERN DOUBLE WALL LIBRARY

A few salient points on modern double wall stack building is considered from the experience of librarian and as well as conservator.

(a) Centurian's old building needs deplastering and replastering inside and outside the building.

(b) Pre-and post-constructional anti-termite treatment is required of library building.

(c) Post-constructional anti-termite soil treatment with aldrine, heptachlor, diclorine each 0.5% one inch diameter bore is diduged one feet away from the wall. The bore is 10 inches distance each other and 2 feet deep 3 feet deep and 2 feet wide stench is diduged out side the wall of the building. Simultaneously, pore the above one chemical in the bore inside wall until filled in the bores and out side wall pit and strench's chemical is required to gray at the bottom.

(d) Dead tree should be uprooted before new construction.

(e) Outside the building at least 10 ft. vacant space needs to keep clean to prevent the insect attack.

(f) Bath, toilet and urinal should be installed outside the stack area with a view to control of relative humidity and temperature.

(g) Germans in the construction of the Archive building in 1971 and Bundesruchiv in Coblence tried to solve the problem by the best possible thermionic insulation of the storage areas. The walls are double more than a meter thick obviously without window.

(h) By insulating the walls thoroughly, the most, common choice nowadays in franch is a double walls, exterior facing, a vacuum, thermic insulation then a concrete wall.

(i) In case of medium size library stack area, where fund does not permit air conditioning due to cost affair basement floor height will be 12 feet out of which 6 feet is underground and then small air tight windows will be set up. Thickness of the double wall will be 35 inches faning the stack area during duty hours, windows will remain air tight during April to September in every year and pedestal fan will run properly.

(j) Ground and first floor walls will be double layer vacuum metered insulated wall (wall thickness is about 35 inches). At the outside 10 inches brick and then 4 inches concrete wall next vaccum 12 inches (gap). Next 4 inches concrete wall and vaccume side thermionic insulation, last inside wall is 5 inches brick work last of all thermionic insulation. The vacuum 10 inches in the middle will be filled up by Silver Sand or any Non-conducting material in order to maintain ideal temperature and relative humidity. The insides of 10 inchs gap net cement work is done. Other inside and outside wall thermionic insulation.

(k) 2nd floor will be exclusively used as reading room and toilet outside the library bath which will be adjacent in building.

(l) Direct sun light should not allow inside stack area even in winter season.

(m) Doors will be air tight system.

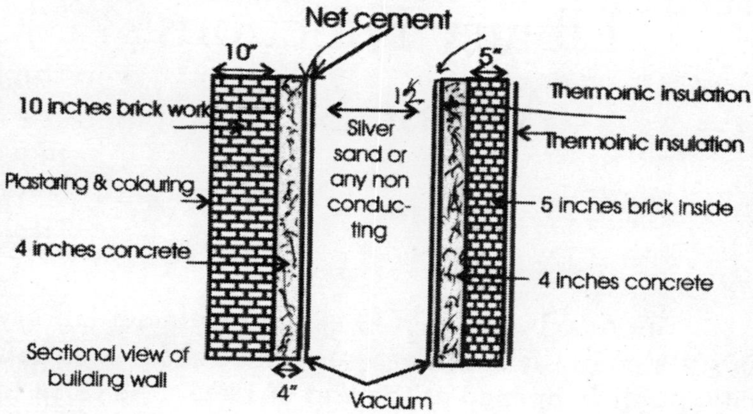

Fig. 22.5

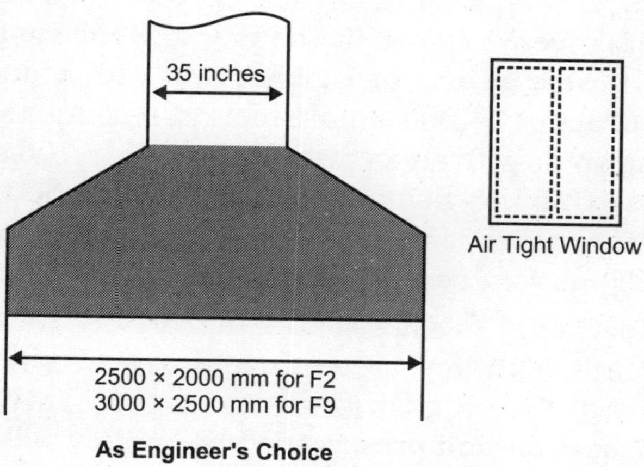

Fig. 22.6

23

Design Requirement of Library Functions: A Case Study

The new building of Zhejiang Provincial Library is situated in the south of Shuguand Road, Hangzhou city, publicly opened at the end of 1998. It is close to the beautiful West Lake and is surrounded by the districts of the government administration, education, culture, sports, scientific research, historical site and beautiful scenic sports in the city of Hangzhou. This library covers an area of 4.19 hectares with a total floor space of about 34,000 square meters. It contains many reading areas with altogether 1,670 seats, a 700 square meters exhibition hall and lecture hall with 500 seats. The future collection of the library is estimated to reach 4.5 millions volumes. Building plan is given in detailed.

In China, the librarian summarised the library work into four key areas purchasing or collection building, cataloguing, accessing or retrieving modernisation and preservation when they will desire the China to design a successful library building. There have full understanding of these functions in order to provide everything and satisfy anything for professional functions. China has to investigate every department of the library, understand every step of the work for creating good conditions of lighting, ventilating, floor planning, and easy use by readers and librarians.

LIGHTING

China designed the entrance lobby with floor space of 600 square meters, and a lighting belt of glass roof with 2 × 73.8 meters through to the bibliography access area and circulation counter. In this way, the area has natural light and creates an atmosphere to welcome their readers.

The reading area is on the roof. They designed eight sloped glass roofs which made in the natural lighting come directly into this area each of the sloped glass root is 14.4 meters long and 3 meters wide. They also designed different spaces of courtyards of 300, 200 and 100 square meters. These courtyards can also provide the natural light entering reading room areas. They also designed sculpture and miniature landscape in the courtyard for readers to enjoy the natural atmosphere.

On the roof of the lecture hall corridor, they set up "Five Bright Peals" of one square meter each. As a result; the natural light comes through these "Five Bright Peals" to the corridor without using any electric light in the daytime.

A small glass pyramid was designed in which the reception chamber provides a comfortable atmosphere for distinguished guests.

The large area of the new building is for reading room. They put this area in the east south and southern part of the building. China designed these walls of glass from the ceiling to the floor. In this way, not only did they make the natural light come directly into the reading areas, but also they created the wall of the east and southeast side of the building separately.

VENTILATION

The library is the place for readers to assemble and depart. Ventilation in the reading areas, in the lecture hall, in the exhibition hall, etc. is of vital importance. Although they installed a large the air conditioner. China only considered the reading area, lecture hall, exhibition hall, AV area, technical service and the administration area. In the closed stack rooms, they installed an air circulation system, with the exception of the closed stack room for rare books, manuscripts and precious materials in this building. In the main building for the entrance lobby, the bibliographic access area, and the circulation counter, China allowed floor space of about 1,200 sq. m. area with a long lighting belt of glass root.

Smoking is not allowed in the building; when spring and autumn come, air conditioning is not necessary, so they can just circulate air through out the large reading area if it is necessary, the staff member can open windows and let the fresh air circulate in the reading area.

FLOOR PLANNING

Librarian and other members investigate different function of the library service and library building.

Divided these services into Reading Areas, Circulation and Bibliography Retrieval Area, Lecture Hall, Exhibition, Audiovisual and Multimedia Areas, Technical Service and Administration Area.

The Floor Planning of the Stack-Rooms

Organizing, preserving and readers service are

the main task in the library. To create at atmosphere of "Books for Readers, Readers Among the Books", they separated the new library's stack room into two parts, the open stack and the closed stack. The floor space of these two parts are almost the same. The open stack is located in the reading area, and the floor space designed for 1.5 million volumes, serves the readers directly. The closed stack is located in the basement and in the upper floor of the building because these library materials are seldom used.

"Three Same" Rule

With a view to start designing of the new building, they adapted six words as their guiding principles. Use fullness, flexibility, efficiency, economy, safety and artistic view. To carry out these principle. They applied the "three same" rule in designing the new building.

Same Loading: They designed 500 kg per square meter for the builder's floor loading to create safety and flexibility in future use.

Same Floor Level: On every floor of the new building, they avoided all small slopes or steps for the safety and convenience of the readers, especially for the aged and the handicapped readers. It is also beneficial to the librarian in transporting book, journals and other materials to different areas for readers to use.

Same Distance between Column: A lot of library personnel could not understand the importance of the distance between column when designing a library building. It is not only the relationship with the investment, but also for designing the library facilities. For example, normally, the specification of a bookshelf is 900 × 450 × 2250 mm. Therefore, they can design the distance between the column by 6600 × 6600 mm;

7200 mm × 7200 mm × 7500 mm × 7500 mm or 7800 mm × 7800 mm, etc. In their new library building, they used distance between column by 7200 mm × 7200 mm.

IMPLEMENTATION OF THE PREMISES DISTRIBUTION SYSTEMS

Modern library building require an effective telecommunications information to support the wide variety of services that depend on the electronic transport of information. The infrastructure can be treated as the collection of those components. (telecommunication spaces, cable pathways, grounding, wiring and termination hardware, etc.) that provide the basic support for the distribution of all information within the library building. Telecommunication refers to all forms of information conveyed electronically within and out of the library building (e.g. voice data, video, alarms, environmental control, security, audio, etc.)

The Structure of the Premises of Distribution System

Through investigation and long-term research, China decided to use the distribution system in the new building to create well conditions of library modernisation. They made distribution system in six subsystem: outlet subsystem, equipment subsystem, backbone subsystem, management subsystems, horizontal subsystems and working area subsystem.

Distribution of the Information Access Points

Only librarian or owner of the library has the duty to increase the requirements for the distribution of the information access points and not the architect or engineer who is not familiar with the library's function.

For designing a modern library building, they took the following eight points for the decision of distribution of the information access points.

The equipment of the computer and network center should be located at the center of the building. It contains the computer network center room for CD-ROM, VCD, CD and other electronic publications, rooms for UPS and also a training room. They installed 50 information access points, which included the training room.

The bibliographics database access area in a library will exit for a long time, but how many access points shall they install? They had considered the following factors:

- That readers can get their materials in the open stacks of the reading area.
- That readers using the catalogue access terminal will be reduced.
- That they have already installed some terminals in the reading room, so the readers will not have to squeeze into the bibliographic database area.
- That readers can get information of the library's bibliographic database through MAN (Metropolitan Area Network) at home and therefore, they do not need to set too many information access points in this area. They only installed 25 of those are here. The technical service department is so important that nobody could avoid it. Therefore, they provided one information access point for each librarians and set 55 points here altogether.

In recent years, electronic publications has been popular in China's libraries, but they consider, this only a temporary use. Several years, the collection of electronic publication will increase to hundreds of thousands and none of the present equipment can handle this. They can use this room as the electronic tool books room for training readers to use the network, and for the searching for the information in WAN (Wide Area Network) or the Internet, etc. They set 50 access points in reading room.

In the reading and reference working area are the most reader, and it is also the busiest area for librarians. Although they decided to display all the new books of the recent decade is open stacks. They have to solve the problem of using the large number of electronic publications and help the readers use them. They set one access point in each of the columns in the reading area and also set 10–15 access points near the reference service desk to fulfil the reference required and help readers use computers and the network.

In the audiovisual and multimedia area, there are two functions, one for entertainment and the other for checking the information through the network from the multimedia materials. They installed 75 access points for the requirement of this area.

There are two or three information access points for each office management. A new library is a permanent building. When China decided anything, they had to take special care of the long-term point of view. During discussion on setting information access points, they would rather consider altogether factors than only the professional function field. Therefore, China installed 750 access points including professional access, security control point, fire fighting control access points, etc.

Many librarians understand that electronic transmission is easily destroyed, so they took special care of electronic wire. Cable of pathways for electricity and electron materials should run parallel, and never overlap. China also paid special attention to avoid crossing the generator for the copying machine elevators, and other machine. Another thing they want to point out is the turning of the electronic wire's pathways. It should never be turned by more than 90 degrees, because that will affect the quality of the electronic transmission. To avoid thunder's damaged cause, that must not be forgotten when designing any new building. The ground wires to the electronic computer equipment must never be neglected.

THE COMPUTER NETWORK SYSTEM

The infrastructure of premises distribution system provides advantages for building the library's computer network system. They decided to use the software INNOPAC, which integrates the public and technical services of the library through nine working stations in the whole building. The network server of the library enables our readers both in and out of the premises to access digitalized resources on the web, including the bibliographic database of the library's collections, daily news and other information. The computer management system is of advance level, highly reliable, unrestrictive safe and expandable. This system has an online catalogue at its center, combining acquisition, cataloguing and circulation and 10 other functions in one unit. It can satisfy the needs of both readers and librarians at the same time, and demonstrates the great advantage of modern equipments and facilities for the various cultural and educational services for their users. There is close coordination among the librarian, conservator, architects engineers and the building construction company. Librarian takes a very important role during the construction period.

The public library is under the control of the government administration. 'Failure is the piller of success. They visited many new modern libraries buildings. Not only they have learnt from their experiences but also they studied and analysed the other's failure. Therefore, their success has been built on other's experiences and shortcomings. The successful plan is given here as a reference.

NEW BUILDING OF ZHEJIANG PROVINCIAL LIBRARY CHINA

The Floor Planning of the Basement

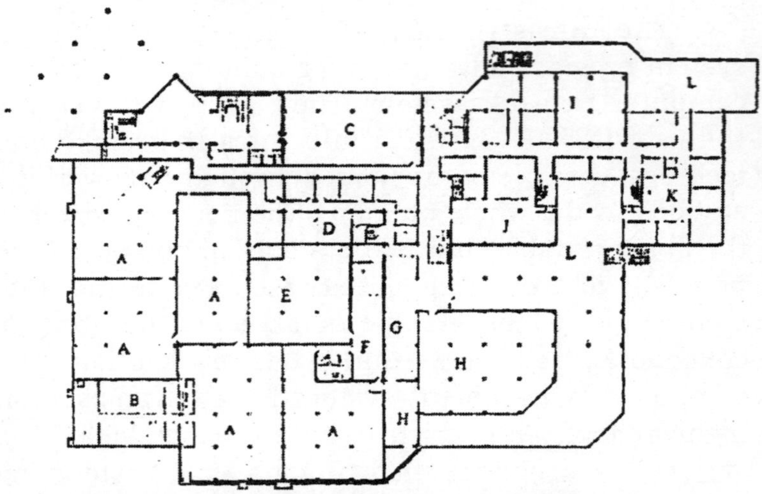

Fig. 23.1: The Floor Planning of the Basement

A	Close Stacks for the Back Issues of Newspaper and Periodical
B	Rooms for Transmit Electricity
C	Area for Service the Readers
D	Rooms for Library Computer Equipment Centre
E	Close Stack for Rare Books
F	Close Stack for Micro Materials
G	Reading Rooms for Rare Books and Micro Materials
H	Reading Area for the Back Issues of Newspaper and Periodicals

I Area for the Library Staff Leisure Time.

J Department for Staff Training and the Work of the Provincial Society of Library Science

K Area for the Library Materials Digitalized

L The Sunken Courtyard

First Floor Planning

A The Exhibition Hall

B The Administration Office

C The Lobby of the Lecture Hall

D Snack Counter

E Xerox Center

F Courtyard

G Entrance Lobby

H Handbag Room

I Retrieval Center

J Circulation Counter

K Close Slack Rooms

L Open Stack of Chinese Fiction for Lending and Reading

M Current Newspaper and Periodical for Reading

N Self-study Room for Readers Using Their Own Books

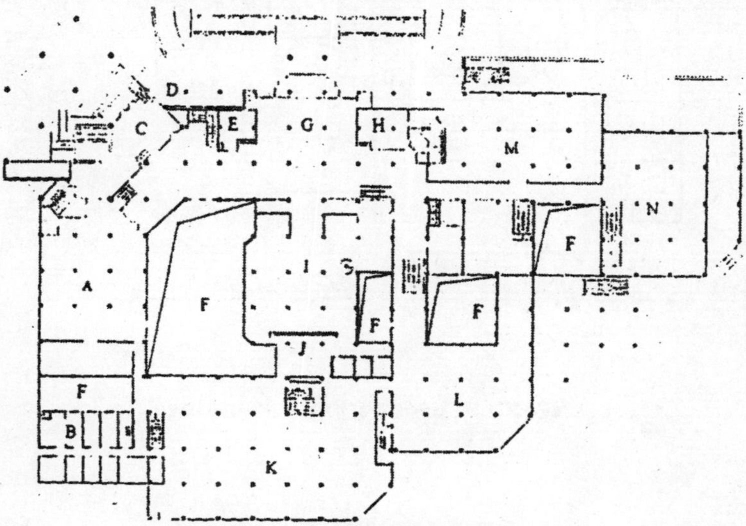

Fig. 23.2: First Floor Planning

Second Floor Planning

A	Lecture Hall
B	VIP Reception Room
C	Area for AV and Multimedia
D	Courtyard
E	Area for Administration Office
F	Library Directors' Office
G	Department of Technical Services
H	Area for Social Science Lending and Reading
I	Area for Natural Science Lending and Reading
J	Area for Reading the Electronic Publications
K	Area for Applied Science Lending and Reading
L	Area for the Library Materials of Arts and Crafts

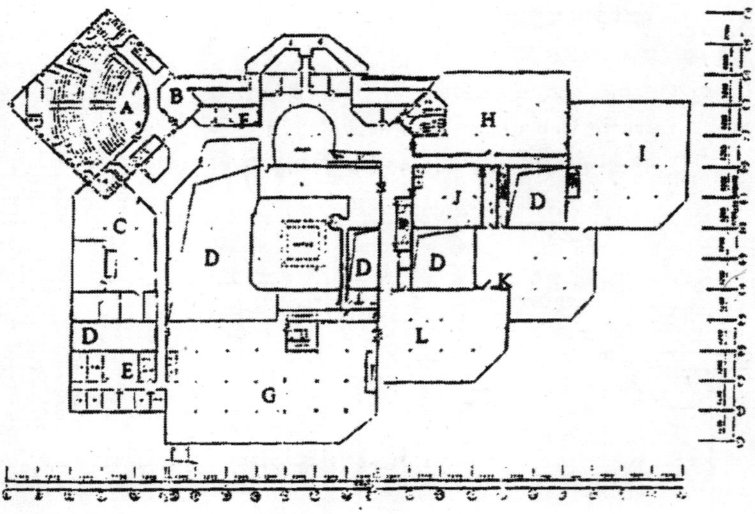

Fig. 23.3: Second Floor Planning

Third Floor Planning

A Roof of the Lecture Hall

B The Bright Pearls of Glass Roof Above the Corridor of the Lecture Hall

C A Glass Pyramid on the Roof of the VIP Reception Room

D Long Lighting Belt on the Roof of the Building

E Courtyard

F Close Stack

G Area of Japanese and Russian Languages Books for Lending and Reading

H Area of Western Languages Books for Lending and Reading

I Area for Tool Books

J Close Stack Reading Room (Only for the Sample Books)

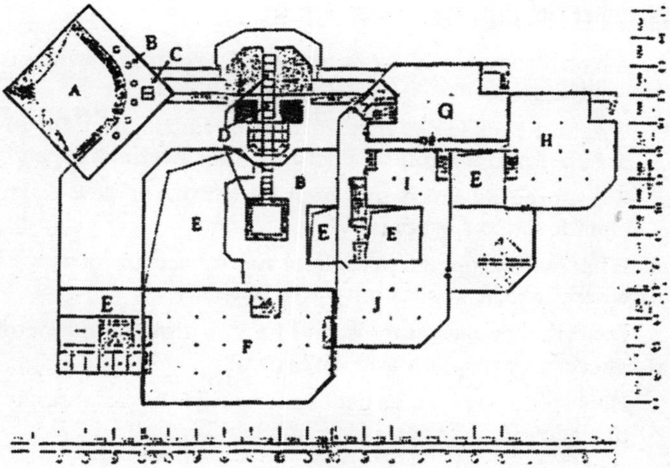

Fig. 23.4: Third Floor Planning

Fourth Floor Planning

A Roof of the Building

B Courtyard

C Close Stack Room

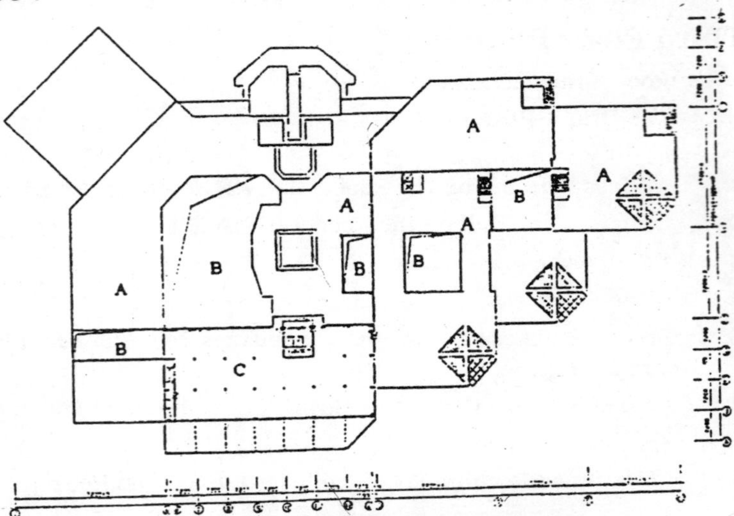

Fig. 23.5: Fourth Floor Planning

QUESTIONS FOR DISCUSSION

1. Why library building is growing organism even at the electronic age?
2. What are the ideal temperature and relative humidity in case of paper and microfilm, microfiche restoration respectively?
3. What process can be adapted for control of slow down bio-chemical deterioration?
4. What will happend periodical non-check up of stack area where insect, infestation takes places?
5. Describe, causes of mold and fungus growth and metabolic successive reaction and its control.
6. How solar-powered assist conservation the non-supply area of electric?
7. Define dewey break labels.
8. The size projections of book-stack need to include a few salient points.
9. Enunciate the lighting system in an ideal library. What ray causes of damages the library resources?
10. Describe compact stack-area-high density.
11. Describe architect concept of large (*i.e.*, 6th and 5th category) library and author's views of medium (*i.e.*, 4th to 2nd category) library building.

24

Function of Library Building for the Close of 20th Century

Libraries throughout the history have been extra ordinarily successful social spaces. There are the location for encounters of several kinds. A library may good be regarded as a rare collection of documents. The building that houses the collection, though, is the most obvious physical manifestation to the population as a whole, many of those may never actually enter the library. The popular image of the National Library, was, at least until very recent, of the new building being constructed in Kolkata. The new building has acclaimed a great success. Readers certainly have seen to like it.

Foreign scholar, researcher and Indian scholar are more interested to work in the new reading room where reader's hostel are also available. They find the new reading rooms comfortable, and that working condition are good. Library personnel deliver books to readers more quickly, reliably and predictably.

But there is more to a library than simply the

comfort of the readers and up keep the books. Additional consideration, since the conservation is part and parcel of the library functioning. So conservator is required to involved alongwith the librarian and architects when planning a new library building.

A useful way of considering libraries is to examine the relationship that characterize with those. An obvious one is the relationship between the library building and the readers other key relationship are those between readers and the library's collection, between readers and libraries, between librarians and collection and between the collection and the building.

Let us look first at library building and its relationship with collection. After all, the buildings are intended to house the collection. But how can these cope? Will these ever be large enough, and how can these provide for storage of electronic publication. In the information age, huge quantities of information are being produced. One ancedotal measure of the quantity being produced is that the amount of knowledge and information being created in the world, at present, doubles every five years. More books are being published their over before in history. The National Library received about 30,000 new items including maps. All the rare and frazile documents, palm leaves Tibatian xylograph, etc. are kept in twelve alcoves at ground floor of the Annexe building which are fully air conditioning. Eighty-six thousands conditional gift of Sir Ashutosh Mukhapadhya are kept in extensive air conditioning system where temperature and humidity and cleanliness of the air can best be controlled. About 10 lakhs books are shifted from main historic building (Viceroy residence) to new constructed building Bhasha Bhawan. Recently, main building opened as an exhibition hall, Director's and Administrative office. The need to accommodable the incoming collection and improved the conservation condition for the old collection was one of the chief reason for commissioning the Bhasha Bhawan. This building is splendors of the National Library building is all very well. The environment for our books and manuscripts is *appalling*. The books which are not all use on duplicate, are stored in a separate building. All old news papers are stored in reading room Explanade East, where huge number of readers attend per day for information and 42 readers seats are available. Important frazile news papers are microfilmed by Reprography Division at the National Library.

The physical storage of that kind of item is technically these relative and by easy. A much greater challenge for libraries is how to ensure long-term access or to retain in any real way. The information which is now produced as an online, that issue has little directly to do with buildings.

The electronic data can be stored anywhere as a result we need not sit next to the books and manuscripts. So, do we still need buildings to store library materials now that we can digitalize those? The answer is yes, because the author is certainly not intending to make digital copies of the English translation of Euclid's geometry publish from London in 1570, manuscript of Thibant collection in Sanskrit language about Indian philosophy, religion, history, astronomy, etc. and then throw away the originals. One of our responsibilities is to care for a substantial historic collection of the books and manuscripts and not simply copies of these, electronic and otherwise. However, reader's test of original format is more valuable than information in electronic media.

The relationship between a library building and the library's collections is changing. We do not necessarily need a building to house a collection. It is also the case, that the building is needed for reasons other than simply to store a collection of manuscripts and printed books. Readers still crowed to library buildings. They come to consult books and catalogues and so on, but there is more to a visit than just that the libraries have always been successful social spaces. Libraries are regarded as ideal locations for intellectual encountered of many kinds. The intellectual encounter is not exclusively with the books and manuscripts consulted in reading rooms. The library building should recognize the desirability of those other kinds of encounter, and provide opportunities for them. It is essential that a library has a decent restaurant, reader's hostel, post office and other locations to let the readers meet and exchange ideas. The library can impart much more than just research materials. There are other kinds of stimulus in a library for scholarly and creative attempt. There is quite clearly a benefit from simply working in a reading room among fellow scholars. To make more of the relationships between readers, or scholars, the British Library has set up, at the request of scholars, a regional in which they may note their research subject, in order to make contact with other readers, researching on identical subjects.

There are other ways of consulting a library than browsing in the catalogue hall or along the book stacks. New technology has given a new meaning to library research.

The use of library material has its alternative. There are other ways of consulting a library than browsing in the catalogue hall or along the books stacks. Libraries have to cater for expectations among the users that they should be able to access the catalogues and collections in an increasing number of ways. Readers want to exercise choice in how they visit library. Most large library catalogues can now be consulted on the Internet. 20,000 readers consult the British Library's web version catalogue every day without coming near the building. The wide availability of their catalogue and its case of access gives massing advertisement to their holdings. Computerised searching is so efficient that researchers turn up many more references that would have been possible in the old card catalogue days. The result is that because of the new technology heading rooms are in even greater demand.

The nature of the library's content is changing, the catalogue is now invariably electronic. The relationship between reader and collection is changing. Similarly, the relationship between collection and library building is changing. Less of the collection will be under the library's roof. The collection can be housed actually anywhere. More radically, the library may not contain anything like what today we consider as a "collection". The librarian may not be responsible for looking after a collection of publications, but instead of expected merely to arrange access to electronic publications stored in servers which might be located on several other continents. In that sense, the librarian operates in the mode of what is now widely described as the guide through this information jungle.

This marks yet another change in a fundamental relationship between reader and librarian. Librarians are custodian of what readers need to consult, and are sometimes said to be regarded by readers as protective to the point of obsession. On the other hand, readers are frequently said by librarians to be disrespectful of the library's book and to be the major cause of their deterioration.

The author has observed at the National Library India that a group of sincere library professionals, who have a deep knowledge about the collection for which they are responsible and a keen understanding of the scholarly research process. Both those areas of expertise are at the disposal of our readers. The nature of scholar's question is changed. Generally, readers asking the librarian whether a particular book is available. The librarian is now just as likely to be asked what is published in an area of particular interest, who the leading authors are and what are the main issues under discussion.

Electronic technology is inexorably changing the relationship between readers and librarians and between both of those groups and the collection. All people realise these changes as for the better, reading new technology as the major means for improving the nature of the service to readers. In any case, impact of new technology is inevitable, we cannot just ignore it.

Readers of the British Library using everything is electronic. They particularly disapproved of the online catalogue. The readers feared that it just would not work, it would constantly crash, data. Would be lost, the massive keyboarding exercise in converting the old paper catalogue into machine—readable form would introduce hosts of errors. Readers made a lot of valid points—librarian sought to answer them all and to reassure them. The librarian of China provincial library understood that electronic transmission is easily distorted, so they took special care of electric wire. Cable of pathways for electricity and electronic material should run parallel, and never overlap. They made arrangement to avoid crossing the generator for the copying machines, elevators and other machine with motors. It should never be turned by more than 90 degree because that will affect the quality of the electronic transmission and so on. Librarian admires the technology of course, on the other hand he loves the smell and feel of the cards—but because the paper, printed catalogue is important information in its own right which is a source for various kinds of bibliographic research.

The machine—readable catalogue are more efficient research tools. Entry to the British Library's Collection in the reading rooms is now, possible only through a computer. They feared that this would intimidate some readers, events did not bear this out. The library provided training and seminars on how to use the **new-style catalogue**, but it is good to see **octogenarians** sitting at catalogue terminals, their fingers flying over the keyboard. They had no problems with the new technology. They do not believe it has stood in an undesirable way between the readers and the collection, or between the readers and the staff. It has definitely made the readers less reliant on the staff.

The book is a bound volumes of print on paper, which has a firm future. But much of what is presently being produced as books will give way to electronic publishing. How has the telephones directory survived for so long? Here is a book which no one reads. Consult it, yes, but never read it, because 99.9% of the content is of no interest. Surely a CD-ROM some online service must be more efficient.

In case of peotry, novels, drama, guidebooks and traditional textbook this is an ideal format for these. The defining characteristic of the book has become its self-contained mature. To open a book and read requires no electric power, no software protocol, no password. Take it to bed or anywhere or beach. Read it by torch under the covers. Throw sand in it and it makes no complaint. The **unsurpassed feature** of the book is its immediacy. Nothing stands between the printed page and librarians. The book has a flourishing career ahead of it. As long as books are produced we will need library building to house those. That direct relationship with information is a precious gift which has been the very basis of learning and progress for thousands of years. We must not take that for granted or treat it lightly. Information technology is only a means to an enlighting end. We must beware any temptation to develop the technology for its own sake, rather than for what it can help us to achieve.

We can still pursue, though, the best use of the new digital technologies, these are already providing exciting services and possibilities of new services. Librarians are making substantial use of digital technology to offer their readers infinitely better services. New technology offers escape from the constrictions of the printed page. But new technology does not threaten the library.

Beowulf is a 1,000 year old manuscripts. It is an understanding of which is essential for any knowledge in which the English language has spread and developed. This manuscript has been in the case of the British Library and its predecessors for many countries, but was unfortunately badly damaged by fire 250 years ago. However, the manuscript has been digitally scanned. It is now possible to read substantial parts of the manuscripts which were damaged by fire, and decipher passages in which the scribe changed his mind and deleted some words and substituted other. Beowulf is now on the world wide web.

Therefore, contempt the impact of new technology. The basic mission of libraries is left infact. In Author's view, is to catalogue published information and acquire it if that is appropriate. If acquired, it should be properly stored. The librarians should be responsible for arranging access to any of that information or published material to readers require it. The material may be in library reading room or elsewhere.

The electronic library is well on this way, but author is sure that building will still have a role to play. Traditional and electronic media will continue to sit side by side. So users, in consultation with librarians, will decide which is the more appropriate for a particular purpose. No new technology has ever totally driven out an earlier one. Libraries will involve library building, some of the time, for some purpose.

The Government of India, Ministry of Culture which funds the National Library and is responsible for national policy on libraries, has put libraries higher up. Proper money and just as important, Political backing, has been put behind libraries. India Government observes libraries as a key resource for education. The central building Bhasha Bhawan's Fundation Stone of this complex was laid down by Late Rajiv Gandhi. The Prime Minister of India on 7th April, 1989 and completed in the year 2002 (photo). Education is the **backsbone** of the Nation.

Author realises that libraries are the most important institutions ever created virtually every new invention and every new concept, builds on existing knowledge. The book is the most potent artefact ever invented by humankind. Libraries deserve great modern building.

Fig. 24.1: North east view Bhasha Bhawan

**Fig. 24.2: Reading room (East)
Natural light entiring through glass**

Fig. 24.3: Bhasha Bhawan (Front View)

QUESTIONS FOR DISCUSSION

1. What are the three same rule?
2. Describe the distribution of information access points in China.
3. Conventional method of readers service is needed simultaneously in spite of electronic publication justify.
4. What are the criteria to be a good library and librarian?
5. Librarian is a media for exchange of thought among the Foreign and India scholars who are studying identical subject.
6. Define depository library.
7. "Reader's test and need of original format are more valuable than electronic media". Discuss.
8. "The catalogue is now electronic as a result relation between reader and collection is changing." Explain.
9. How Beowulf is now possible to read in spite of substantial parts damaged by fire 250 years ago?

Consulted Bibliography

1. *Cunha, C.D.M.* Conservation of Library Materials, Metuchen N.J. Scarecrow Press 1967.
2. *Barrow, W.J.* Procedure and Equipment in the Barrow Method of Restoring Manuscript and Documents, University of Virginia Press, 1955, USA.
3. *King, H.A.* Adhesive Age 5,2,22 (1972)
4. *Jackson, L.* Adhesives Age 6.9.34 (1963)
5. *Shields, John,* Adhesive hand book/J.Shields.-3rd, ed-London, Buther Worth, 1984.
6. *Nolan Lushington,* Games M. Kusack. The Design and Evaluation of Public Library Buildings.
7. *Charles. V. CAGLE*: Hand book of Adhesives binding.
8. US Government Printing Office, Washington: Theory and Practice of Book Binding (Apprentice and Training Series) Washington, 1950.
9. Cheng Xiaolan, Xing Changxing. LIN ZUZAO to Create and Atmosphere of "Books for Readers and Readers Among the Books" on the New Building of Zhejiang Provincial Library, China.
10. Plenderleith, Harold James. The Prevention of Leather, Book Binding, London, British Museum 1953.

11. *Brian Lang,* Library Building for the New Millennium. Chief Executives the British Library, London, United Kingdom.
12. *Melean Runri*: Victorian Publications, Book binding in cloth and leather London, Gordon, Fraseer, 1974.
13. *Pearce Willam Bonner*: Practical Book Binding.
14. *Lyden Berg. Henry Millon*: The Care and Repair of Books, 4th Rev. ed by John Aleen, New York, R.R. Bowrer company, 1960.
15. *Cockerell D.* Book Binding and the Care of Books. Sri Isaac Pitman Sons, London.
16. *Vanghan, Alexander J.* Modern Book Binding a Treatise Covering Both Letter Press and Stationary Branches of the Trade with a Section of Training and Design, new addition London Charles Shilton 1960.
17. *Cockerell S.M.*: The Repairing of Books, Shappered Press 18. Claments Jeff Book Binding, London.
19. Library Building—Congress IFLA, section on Library, building and equipment, seminar 11th, 1999 (Shanghai) preceding edited by Maire Francoise bisbronck — Munchen K.G. Saur, 2001
20. Library Building by Hushington - Nolan 1929.
21. International Seminar on Research in Preservation and Conservation K.G. Saur. Munchea 1993.

Index